peas love & carrots

danielle renov

ARIELLA GOLDWICHT
art and graphic designer

MOSHE WULLIGER
photographer

FRANCES BOSWELL
food stylist

AYESHA PATEL
prop stylist

Published by **ARTSCROLL / SHAAR PRESS**
313 Regina Avenue / Rahway, NJ / 07065
(718) 921-9000 / www.artscroll.com

Distributed in Israel by **SIFRIATI / A. GITLER**
POB 2351 / Bnei Brak 51122 / Israel / 03-579-8187

Distributed in Europe by **LEHMANNS**
Unit E, Viking Business Park, Rolling Mill Road Jarrow,
Tyne and Wear, NE32 3DP / England

Distributed in Australia and New Zealand by
GOLDS WORLD OF JUDAICA
3-13 William Street / Balaclava, Melbourne 3183, Victoria / Australia

Distributed in South Africa by **KOLLEL BOOKSHOP**
Northfield Centre / 17 Northfield Avenue
Glenhazel 2192 / Johannesburg, South Africa

ISBN-10: 1-4226-2578-8 / ISBN-13: 978-1-4226-2578-1

Printed in PRC

dedication

To *HaKadosh Baruch Hu*, Master of the world, King of kings and Creator of all. This book is dedicated to the One Who has made all of this possible. May the words on these pages and the dishes cooked from its recipes illuminate Your glory in the homes of all who have it.

To my husband Eli,
my children in this world, Yechezkel Meir, Yisroel Dov,
Leah Baila, Shifra Batya, Margalit Bracha, and Elisheva Tova,
and my son in the next world, Yaakov Rafael *z"l*.

All I am, all I do, and all I have is for you.

May we all be blessed to greet *Mashiach Tzidkeinu* speedily and in our days so that we can be whole again.

May all the *berachos* (blessings) said over the food cooked from these pages be a *zechus* for the incredible people who are not here in this world but are in my heart forever and helped shape who I am today, thus making this book what it is.

Yaakov Rafael Renov *z"l* ben Eliyahu Yerachmiel *n"y*

Leah Gleitman bas Pinchas HaKohen *z"l*

Aron Gleitman ben Avraham Moshe *z"l*

Mesoda Corcos bas Samuel *z"l*

Meir Corcos ben Shimon *z"l*

acknowledgments

Please note: Anyone listed here has been thanked, personally, effusively, and privately. The "thank you's" here serve to recognize them publicly and give credit to them because this book wouldn't be in your hands today were it not for them and their contributions.

HaKadosh Baruch Hu: On the days when it was impossible for me to go on, when my feet were incapable of movement, my voice incapable of sound, my heart incapable of beating, it was You Who carried me. Moved my feet, put words to my feelings, and blew breath into my lungs. Not a single word of this book could have happened without You by my side. I am eternally grateful for the blessings You continuously bestow upon me and hope that my presence in this world can spread the light You so brightly emanate.

Eli: To put a label on what you are to me would undermine the value I place on our relationship. Nothing I do in this world, let alone write this book, could be done without you by my side! You have given me the confidence, courage, and love I needed to make it happen. Your advice, help, and guidance made my dream a reality. I continue to learn from, and be inspired by, your *emunah*, *bitachon*, and *ahavas Yisrael*. Thank you for your unconditional love, endless support, and unwavering optimism.

My children: The very best taste testers, Instagram cameo contributors, dance partners, garlic peelers, shuk shoppers, travel buddies, puzzle builders, Chinese food consumers, and children I know! You not only put up with my crazy antics, but you stand right beside me and are always ready to join in on the fun. The past few months of getting this book together left our house cluttered and our dinners eclectic, sent me to New York twice, and you all stepped up and rose to the occasion. You're my biggest cheerleaders and there is no one in the world I would rather cook for than all of you. Sitting around the dinner table, talking about school, watching you eat the food I make is the best part of my day. Thank you for being you! I love you all!

My parents, Marc + Nicole Gleitman: I don't even know where to start, so I guess I'll start at the very beginning. Without the two of you, I wouldn't be here, and without me, no book ... so thanks for, well, my entire life! From day 1 (fine, at least day 1,825, because I can definitely remember that), you have been my biggest cheerleaders and my best role models. Your endless love, support, friendship, and advice have helped shape me into who I am today. I have the two of you to thank for my love of good food. It is not easy living 6,000 miles apart (still not moving back though, sorry) and yet not a day goes by that I don't feel like you are right by my side. Thank you for stepping in the last few months (and always) to help babysit, food shop, chauffeur me, and everything else while I got this book together! You're the best!

My brothers, Eric + Benjamin Gleitman: I'm older, wiser, and know more than both of you about everything. And now that's in print, so it's a fact. Also, I'm the Taboo champion. Just kidding. Only about the Taboo. You guys rock. But everything else is a fact now. For real though, you are the best brothers, brothers-in-law, and uncles in the world to Eli, the kids, and me. You have been there for me to celebrate the good times and stood by my side at the hard times. Thank you for always supporting me, listening to me ramble, tasting my food, and being my best friends. I love you both!

My in-laws, Ruki + Kal Renov: Not to sound repetitive or anything, but if I wouldn't be here without my parents well, then, you know, Eli wouldn't be here without his. Thank you for raising the kindest, smartest, most humble, and wonderful man I have the privilege to be married to! The children, Eli, and I are so lucky to have both of you! Thank you for showing us all unending love and encouragement always!

To the extended Renov and Davis families: Thank you so much for all your positive encouragement over the years! We cherish the time we get to spend together even though we live so far away, and I am so grateful for the playdates and sleepovers the kids got to have that covered for my "I'm too busy with the book and need help" frantic days spent in New York!

My mother, Nicole Gleitman; my maternal grandmother, Marcelle Corcos; my paternal grandmother, Lila Gleitman; my aunts, Janey Glodny, Linda Enbar, and Claire Kamhi z"l; and my cousins, Melissa Benzel and Rebecca Richmond: Thank you to the women in my life who helped shape the cook I am today by passing down their best family recipes, dishes, and techniques to me so that I can share them with all of you!

Rifka Ganz: If there is one person who knows how much I put into this book, and life in general, it is you. Thank you for helping me to find a way to live with both pain and happiness, for helping me to recognize my own capabilities, for teaching me how to push past my own insecurities, recognize my strengths, and actualize my potential. There were days I did not think I could get this book done and your support and encouragement guided me time and time again. Thank you.

Udeni Karunanayaka, Rachel Dimmerman, Sandra Batres: They say it takes a village and although I don't know exactly who "they" are, I'm almost positive it was a woman somewhere with a bunch of small kids who was trying to write a cookbook. I feel so lucky to have each of you in the children's lives and in my life! You treat all of us with so much love and care and we are eternally grateful for all you do for us. Each one of you is now and forever a part of our family!

Rabbi Gedaliah Zlotowitz/ArtScroll: Thank you for believing in all of us here in Peaslovencarrots land! Your support and guidance throughout this process have meant so much to me and I feel honored to be a part of the ArtScroll family!

Mrs. Eisner: Once upon a time a girl sent her editor a book written in entirely lowercase letters, without one bit of punctuation and zero regard for spelling. Her editor painstakingly reinserted every capital letter, comma, hyphen, and period and spellchecked each and every sentence. Then spent many hours negotiating the necessity of each and every bit of punctuation, for their absence in the original document was extremely intentional. After hours and hours of negotiating, girl and editor came up with a plan. A wonderfully modern, updated, and still grammatically correct plan within the confines of our very fluid system of rules of the English language with which to edit the book. #truestory. If it sounds like lots of work, it was. So, thank you, Mrs. Eisner, for all your help, guidance, and patience!

Devorah Cohen: I am so incredibly grateful for your attention to detail, the speed at which you work, the level of patience you possess, and the time you spent working on the layout of this book with me. Thank you so much, Devorah, for your crash course on how to effectively use my computer (not joking, I'm tech challenged), working with me on laying out every recipe, and being so open to my crazy ideas!

Ariella Goldwicht: Who knew when we lived next to each other 13 years ago, we would end up working together on my cookbook! It's been 4½ years since you designed the first (and only!) peaslovencarrots logo that I love so much. Your passion and devotion to this book are so deeply appreciated. Thank you for the hours and hours of hard work you spent creating the magnificent artwork and beautiful graphics for this book. Your talent and creativity are unmatched and I am truly grateful you were a part of this!

Frances Laurd: Food stylist extraordinaire. Thank you. Thank you for the hours every day you spent on your feet, food shopping, sourcing, and recreating every recipe in this book. Thank you for your attention to detail to make sure the food looked as beautiful as could be in each and every photo. I am so grateful that we were able to make the times work out because I can't imagine having to spend 4 weeks in the studio with any other food stylist! I have learned so much from you and Elisheva, and I will miss spending endless days in the kitchen together with you!

Ayesha Patel: The first time we spoke, you asked me what I liked and I said, "Well, I like modern clean props that are also Moroccan and vintage-y, and I like neutral tones and sometimes color, especially purple, and oh, I love linens that are wrinkly, but not too wrinkly, ya know?" All you said was, "I got you," and yes, you got me. You managed to encapsulate my style in every photo in the most effortless and sophisticated way. I have learned so much from working with both you and Frances (and Elisheva) and I truly cherish the time we spent in the studio! Thanks for being a part of my team and making the book as beautiful as it is!

Moishe Wulliger: It's not easy shooting in natural light, since no matter how hard we try (and boy, did we try) we cannot control the clouds moving or the sun setting! You made it happen for every photo and I am grateful. Thank you so much for all your hard work.

Leila Clifford: Wow. The hardest-working woman I know. On your feet all day long, it doesn't matter how many times you have to run to the market, how many chickens you need to butcher, the smile on your face never leaves! Having you in the studio with us was a tremendous help and an absolute pleasure, especially for Elisheva, who misses you terribly! Thank you for all your hard work!

Yisroel Cohen: We are so lucky to live in Israel and be so close to you. You are a part of our family and we love you! Thank you for everything you do for us.

Rachel Shapiro: Being my editor from day 1, you know how hard of a job it is to edit someone who finds the rules of grammar to be a nuisance. And yet, you did not hesitate one bit to help me proofread the entire book. Really, though, your job began 13 years ago, when we first met on a park bench and discovered our shared love of talking about food. You are one of my most trusted taste testers, idea receptacles, and closest friends. Thank you so much for sticking by me in the hard times, the fun times, and the grueling work times.

Elise Aguilar: The first step of writing any book is getting your thoughts in order. That means the 250+ recipes you see here in this book were narrowed down and edited from the endless number of recipes swirling in my mind. Getting my thoughts organized and down on paper was no easy task and I could not have done it without you and Rachel! Thank you so much for all the hours you spent around my table helping me!

Abby Isaacs, Dena Katz, Elise Aguilar, Karen Grobman, Michal Kestenbaum, Rachel Shapiro, Ruksi Mauskopf, Shana Wirzberger, and Stacey Shapiro: No one ever should have to put their friends to the test to see what kind of friends they are. Lucky for me, I knew what kind of friends I had before we were tested, but I could have never imagined needing you the way I did. Each one of you took care of us when we needed it most and has been there for my family in ways I can never repay in this world. From taking care of my kids, to hosting us for Shabbos meals, sending over dinners, and arranging playdates, you all have done so much. I feel so blessed every day to live in the most amazing community (shout out to all the beautiful people in Rechavia!) and have all of you as friends! Thank you for sticking by me always!

My Bris-kit Ladies, Aliza Kalton, Gitty Roth, Lily Weichholz, Lisa Kuflik, Rikki Hirmes: There is nothing like old friends! The people you who have known since you were little girls and have gone through this crazy life journey together. You cannot ever know how much *menuchas hanefesh* you have brought and continue to bring to Eli and me for all you do for the Bris Gemach. Many days, when it was difficult to write or cook, a small message on our WhatsApp was exactly what I needed to get my creative juices flowing. Thank you all for stepping up and being such incredible friends and *baalas chesed*. May Hashem bless you all with energy to always bring *menuchas hanefesh* into people's lives!

My fellow bloggers, cookbook authors, and instafriends: I feel humbled and honored to be a part of a community filled with so many creative, smart, kind, and charitable people. You accepted me into your ranks with open arms and have helped in ways you cannot imagine. You rallied together by my side when I needed it most and have been there through every professional and personal milestone since I started peaslovencarrots. Thank you for your endless love and support. May we all be blessed to see the best in our community and to continue to use the resources we were given to bring light and kindness into this world.

Adeena Sussman, Chanie Apfelbaum, Chaya Suri Leitner, Dani Klein, Leah Schapira, Melinda Strauss, Miriam Pascal, Naomi Elberg, Naomi Nachman, Rivky Kleiman, Shloime and Shifra Klein, Suzanne Sasson, and lastly (but only alphabetically), Teri Turner: We met on Instagram and became friends quickly, and our relationships have moved from direct messages, to WhatsApps, to sleepovers, coffee dates, and food crawls. Thank you for all your help and advice in getting this book together! You all believed in me from the very beginning and your guidance and friendship mean a lot to me. Thank you all so much!

Mishpacha Family/Chanie Nayman/Michal Frischman: To say I love being part of the Mishpacha Family is an understatement. The "Family Table WhatsApp chat" is the best group to be in. Filled with the best banter, most creative ideas, and delicious recipes, it truly feels like one big happy family and I am honored to be among all of you amazing women. Chanie and Michal: Thank you so much for believing in me from the very beginning, and for all of your extremely valued advice, feedback, and late night (well, late for me) phone calls throughout the cookbook process.

Kosher.com/Kayco, Mordy Herzog, Chaim Herzog, Chanie Nayman, Kim Cassar, Jenna Grunfeld, Leah Gottheim, and the whole team: Your support over the years has meant so much to me. Thank you for taking a chance on me and bringing me into the kosher.com family! I love being part of the team that is at the forefront of kosher food! Oh, and the tomato sauce. You know how I feel about the Tuscanini tomato sauce ... the best!

Gourmet Glatt/ Rabbi Yehoshua: Thank you for all your support through this process, your generous sponsorship, and, of course, for being the place I get to spend quality time with my father on Friday mornings! Oh, and we can't forget Rabbi Yehoshua, who is always helping us out here in peaslovencarrots land to get the most delicious and beautiful meat that is proudly featured on these pages! Thanks for being the best supermarket with the best yellow bags!

Nissan's spice shop (AKA Oshrat and Lital), Benny's Meat, David Dagim, Yaakov and Uri Binyamini: To my favorite Israeli vendors whose beautiful and delicious ingredients have ignited my creativity time and again and allowed me to develop the most delicious recipes for my family for the past 13 years and, more recently, for this book!

To all the companies that have taken a chance on peaslovencarrots and sponsored content to help make this book possible: Anette & Dov Dahan (@esteezonline), Tamara Wagner (@tamara.skincare), Jack (@jacksgourmet), @lulukidsclothing, Tuscanini Foods, Gefen Foods: You have all believed in me and peaslovencarrots from the very beginning and for that I will always be grateful. Thank you for your support, encouragement, and love!

David Herskovitz and Splash Creative for being the best Web developers out there!

contents

meat

sides

dairy

sweets

contents

introduction

I have stopped and started writing this introduction multiple times a week since November. Sentences have been written and deleted. Thoughts were composed into lists, then formed into beautifully flowing paragraphs and were promptly erased. Nothing felt right. I have one page to introduce myself and this book to anyone reading it. Some of us may already know each other, others may know me although I haven't had the privilege yet to meet them, and many of you will have never heard my name before holding this book. What an overwhelming task it is to sum up who I've become in the 33 years I've been blessed to live in this world in a way that those who know and don't know who I am can fully connect to. Couple all that with introducing the book that I've poured my heart and soul into and you can see why this page has been the most daunting page to compose thus far.

After much contemplation about the importance of "an introduction," it occurred to me that nothing matters more than our health, our family and friends, and our faith. As I sit here today, writing under the pressure of a deadline, it occurred to me that the book is a manifestation of those 3 values that I live by.

For me food is so much more than sustenance. It is what ties our future to our past. It is what brought me to the table growing up in my parents' home and what brings my own children to the table today. The strong French Moroccan heritage my mother infused into my parents' home, through food, was sprinkled with the Eastern European / American fare my father grew up with. It was a marriage of cultures whose traditions and customs were lovingly passed down to us around the dinner table. Once I married my husband, Eli, I too was blessed with the task of harmonizing the traditions I grew up with, together with his. Today and every day, the symphony of flavors, customs, and traditions that we are continuously fine tuning are influenced by our devotion to Hashem (God), the family we've been privileged to raise in Israel for 13 years, our weekly shopping excursions to the Machane Yehuda Shuk in Jerusalem, the journey we have taken together through this world, our various travels, and of course, our life experiences.

This book is a reflection of all that. Its recipes are timeless. They are meant to bring you and your loved ones to the table. Some contain only 4 ingredients and take no time to prepare, others are multi stepped and require 2 days of preparation. Most are budget friendly and a handful are splurge worthy. A large portion are for the everyday dinner, since there are more of those kinds of days than any others; however, there are plenty for Shabbos and holidays. There are vegan and gluten-free recipes. Chicken off and on the bone. There are recipes classically defined as Moroccan and just as many that are Ashkenaz in origin.

Hidden in each recipe are gems of information that will not only make the dish you are creating better but help you master cooking techniques and concepts to make you a better cook. The chapters were divided very thoughtfully so that any time you want to find a recipe, you will know exactly where to look for it. Any recipe at all that is dairy will be found in the dairy chapter and within that chapter, the order of the recipes will follow the order of the book. Meaning that the dairy salads are first, followed by the dairy soups, and ending with dairy sweets! The rest of the chapters are equally thought out, starting with the least expensive dishes (think weeknight dinner ideas) and ending with the most pricey recipes (think holiday) and of course Shabbos falling in between! The book is meant to be inclusive of everyone and a companion to join you and, hopefully, future generations in the kitchen as you pass down your own heritage.

Since the beginning of Peas Love & Carrots, I have been open with my community about who I am, where I come from, and what I stand for. In return, I have been humbled by the way you have opened your homes and hearts to me. We have formed relationships through which I have grown and been inspired time and time again. Peppered throughout the book are anecdotes, little stories, notes, and tips + tricks. Those little bits of my mind, weaving their way in and out of the pages of the book, are me continuing to connect to you and extending our conversations from the virtual space they exist in onto the pages of this book. They are a way for me to acknowledge that the creation of this book is a means for me to glorify God, Who has bestowed this platform upon me and to give thanks for this kind, strong, beautiful, and powerful community we've created on (and off) Instagram. It is in the kitchen, preparing food for my family, that I express my love for Hashem. Providing the nourishment and sustenance they need to enable their own personal journeys of learning and growth that will then enable them to illuminate His presence in this world through Torah and mitzvos is how I serve Him.

My hope is that my words and recipes here bring us together around the table and open the lines of communication with our friends and family. That they can elicit and facilitate the kind of dialogue and discourse that help form the deepest and most meaningful relationships we have in this world. The kind of bonds that inspire us to grow to be better people every day.

May we all be blessed with long, healthy, happy, and fulfilling lives filled with people we love and of course, good food!

Happy cooking,

Danielle

how to follow a recipe

There are three types of cooks out there: those who create recipes, those who follow recipes, and those who cook but don't create or follow recipes. Each category consists of people who are excellent cooks or soon to be excellent cooks, and they are all uniquely different.

Recipe developers are people who can taste food in their minds. They see an ingredient not as a sole item but as a component to a dish that they can already taste in their thoughts and that they will create around it. All they have to do is go home, play around with the flavors swimming in their heads, adjust amounts to perfect their "vision," and voila, a brand new dish!

Recipe followers are true foodies, although they may not necessarily admit it. This category of cooks can be divided into a few types. There are those who want delicious food on their tables and in their mouths as quickly and efficiently as possible without having to put too much thought into it. They are the "tell me exactly what I need to do and I will do it" type. Next, there are others who know precisely what they want to eat and they rely on Google and WhatsApp chats to help them execute it. They are the "who has the best meat sauce recipe out there?" type. Finally, there's the category that we all fall into at some point (like me, for instance, when I need to make something Ashkenazi and I am at a total loss!). It's the category of people who need a recipe now and again and want that dish to be as perfect as possible. They want it to look like the photograph, taste like it was made in a Michelin star restaurant, and make the diners feel that they have been given a warm hug.

The last category of cooks we mentioned, the "I don't follow or create recipes, and if you ask me for one it will include a lot of pinches, dashes, arounds, and undisclosed cooking times" is mostly comprised of mothers, aunts, grandmothers, and the occasional very busy, always running, but somehow pulls off the best meals friend. They are most likely not going to be reading this, for the purpose of this page is where we part ways with our recipe handicapped but somehow always the best cooks, friends.

Now, let's get down to business.

HOW DO YOU ACTUALLY FOLLOW A RECIPE?

Well, first things first, it is always advantageous to follow recipes from consistent people. That is not to say that trying a new recipe won't be good; it may very well be the best thing you eat all year. However, if you're new to the world of following recipes, getting to know a recipe developer's "style" in terms of how he or she relates relevant information to you can only be to your advantage. Basically, the more you cook from this book (or any book but you're here, so for now, this book...), the better you will become at creating its recipes.

That said, whether you are the creator or the follower, there are certain unwritten rules that should be followed by the creator and adhered to by the follower to produce the most accurate representation of the dish.

THERE ARE 6 BASIC RULES TO FOLLOWING A RECIPE:

1. Read the recipe through in its entirety. That includes any notes or tips the author (me, hi!) includes.

2. Be sure you have all ingredients required and note any changes or swaps to the recipe you would like to include (which is highly encouraged, because these recipes were created according to my palate; yours will likely vary to some extent, so customize, adapt, and swap to suit YOUR likes!).

3. Notice nuances in the wording: 1 cup strawberries, chopped vs. 1 cup chopped strawberries. Follow the order of the ingredients. 1 cup strawberries, chopped means first you measure the strawberries, and then you chop. 1 cup chopped strawberries means first you chop the strawberries and then you measure 1 cup.

4. Prepare all your ingredients. Yes, like on a cooking show. No, this will not take extra time. Whether you are prepping the ingredients before you start or throughout the process, it will need to get done. Prepping in advance will afford you the luxury of being organized and precise and you will feel less rushed throughout the cooking process, which WILL ultimately save you even more time and mess!

5. Get to know your kitchen. Being familiar with your stove and your oven will only make your food better. You will only find out that when your oven says 350°F it actually means 340°F by serving a slightly underbaked cake once or twice. Do not get discouraged. Just keep trying. Every single cook on the planet has overcooked, undercooked, mixed too much, whipped too little, and swapped salt for sugar!

6. Cut yourself some slack. If you are new to cooking or cooking in a new kitchen and all of this feels unfamiliar to you, go easy on yourself. Cooking is a skill that anyone can learn, it just takes practice. The more you do it, the more confidence you will build and the better you will get.

Whether you are the recipe follower, developer, or neither, my final bit of advice is to just get yourself into the kitchen. Try every recipe that appeals to you, recreate dishes you've tasted before, and just get cooking. The more you do it, the easier it will become. Eventually, you will feel so confident in the kitchen, recipes will become suggestions. A spark to ignite your imagination and get you in the kitchen cooking the food exactly the way YOU want to eat it!

86 things

I want you to know about this book + cooking in general

1. Before you start cooking, wash your hands. TIA.

2. Recipes are not laws. They are meant to inspire. If you don't like something in a recipe, leave it out. If you want more of something, add in more. Use the recipe as a suggestion to create the dish YOU want to eat!

3. Color and write all over this book. Add your own notes and tips to make it uniquely yours!

4. Peel your celery. No one likes to chew strings that get stuck in their throats.

5. Paprika in oil is sometimes called "Moroccan paprika" and is in my opinion more delicious than regular paprika. However, they are interchangeable in a recipe!

6. Acid is usually what's needed when you think something is not salty enough. First add citrus, vinegar, or wine. Taste. Then adjust seasonings.

7. Iceberg > romaine

8. It is much easier to go on a cooking marathon when you are comfortable. Put on your most comfortable shoes and clothes, make a cup of tea, and then dive in!

9. Arugula is extremely underrated. So are endives and radicchio.

10. Children are guaranteed to be more open to tasting new foods and dishes when they are in some way involved in how it ended up in front of them.

11. Tomato paste is the unsung hero of the kitchen. A little goes a long way and it is shelf stable, which means you can always have it on hand.

12. Take the time to sear your chicken and meat when noted. And once you're searing, don't jump the gun. Give it the time it needs to actually become deeply golden. The extra 2 minutes are worth it.

13. Meat is delicious and has its own natural flavor. Which is, you guessed it, delicious. Respect your meat.

14. Cinnamon and ginger are not just for baking. Expand your horizons.

15. For the love of pasta, once it is finished cooking, do not rinse it under cold water. If you don't want to eat the pasta right away, drizzle a little olive oil over it and give it a quick stir to keep it from sticking together.

16. Table manners exist for a reason. Chew with your mouth closed, hold the fork and knife properly, and place your napkin on your lap. If this sounds foreign to you, google table manners.

17. Salt and especially pepper are extremely important when it comes to the overall flavor of a dish. Which means you need to season the protein itself AND very often the actual dish.

18. In my humble opinion, blasting music, or listening to a really good podcast, makes cooking way more pleasurable.

19. Anytime you sauté greens like spinach or kale, wait until the leaves have cooked down before salting them.

20. If you don't understand the definition of a cooking term, or anything for that matter, google it. It's 2020. Welcome.

21. Base your cooking times according to the weight of YOUR protein. Usually a few ounces here or there won't affect anything. A pound up or down may mean less or more cooking time. Adjust time, keep ingredient measurements the same.

22. Food made with love tastes better. Guaranteed.

23. Most slow cooked meat recipes can be replaced with dark meat bone-in chicken or turkey.

24. ½ tablespoon is NOT a real measurement.

25. Raisins are the unfulfilled potential of grapes. They could have been wine. Now they are ruining noodle kugel for children everywhere.

26. My kitchen is small. I get it done. Mostly by doing all the prep work for a recipe before I actually start the cooking.

27. Set a timer. Always.

28. Paprika in oil > regular paprika (however, the two can be used interchangeably if you only have one!)

29. If (and this is a big if) I had to narrow my spice cabinet down to 10 spices (not including salt and pepper), this is what it would include- Paprika in oil (sometimes called Moroccan paprika), granulated garlic, mustard powder, sumac, turmeric, ground coriander, cumin, smoked paprika, cinnamon, and cardamom!

30. Also, onion soup mix forever. So 11 "spices"!!!

31. Most soups benefit from the addition of wine.

32. There is no good place for "cooking wine". Buy a less expensive but decent bottle (something you wouldn't mind drinking) and use that.

33. Whenever you make a batch of cookies or slice a cake, take a few of those cookies and a few slices of cake, wrap them individually in plastic wrap and pop them in your freezer so you always have something to serve an unexpected guest. Nothing says "welcome" like a homemade treat!

34. Any braised protein must cool down IN the liquid it was cooked in or the protein WILL dry out! Once cooled, you can then remove from the sauce.

35. Always char your tortillas and wraps to remove the plastic-y taste they get from being in the bags!

36. Every oven is different. Learn yours.

37. Cloth napkins > paper napkins.

38. Kosher salt and table salt are not the same. Kosher salt has more surface area; therefore 1 teaspoon of kosher salt is not be equal to 1 teaspoon of table salt. Do not use them interchangeably. If you're in a pinch (as in bind, not a measurement) and only have table salt, use half the amount the recipe calls for, then taste and add only a small amount at a time.

39. Any recipe that calls for garlic is always referring to peeled garlic unless it specifies that it is unpeeled!

40. Become friends with your butcher. And your fishmonger. And your produce seller. Ask them what is the freshest that day and use that. Also, they usually have the best cooking tips, so chat them up!

41. Before juicing any citrus, place it on the counter. Use the palm of your hand to apply slight pressure and roll citrus back and forth a few times to get the juices flowing before you cut it open!

42. Invest in a good sharp knife. Or have your knives sharpened. That's right. You are less likely to get hurt using a sharp knife than you are using a dull one!

43. Don't overcrowd your pan.

44. Clean as you go. Well, as much as you can. It will make the cooking process a lot less overwhelming if you know there won't be a mountain of dishes awaiting you.

45. If you live in a country where you can only get limes for 2 months of the year, make sure to juice them and freeze them in ice cube trays. Wait till the limes are at their peak (usually a few weeks into the season) then juice away!

46. Pesach is only 7 or 8 days long (depending where you live!). Keep that in mind when doing your food shopping. Pesach leftovers, after Pesach, are an even harder sell at the dinner table than Shabbos leftovers!

47. The only way to guarantee that your food will turn out delicious is to actually taste it! Take small tastes throughout the process so you can adjust the dish to your liking!

48. Do not spray your nonstick pots and pans with nonstick spray. The spray will actually ruin the coating and cause it to leech into your food (yuck!). Better to just add a small drizzle of oil!

49. Always make a double batch of rice, quinoa, bulgur .... You can repurpose these leftover cold grains into a stir fry, patties, grain bowls, etc.

50. Say goodbye to frozen garlic! Also your garlic press. Toss 'em both! Every week peel 4 bulbs of garlic. Add them to the bowl of your food processor and pulse just a few times to finely mince garlic. Stir in 1 tablespoon neutral oil. Add to a jar and top off with 1 additional tablespoon of oil. Seal the jar and keep in the fridge all week to use for all your garlic needs.

51. Residual heat is a thing. Account for it.

52. Buy tomato paste in tube form. It makes things so much easier.

53. A quick pickle can solve almost any cooking pickle. Hahaha, see what I did there? Seriously though, combine salt, sugar, white vinegar, and a bit of hot water. Pour over thinly sliced vegetables and allow to sit for at least 30 minutes. Top any dish with this goodness!

54. Always deglaze your pan. That means adding a little bit of liquid to a hot pan that has bits and pieces of whatever you are cooking in it stuck to the bottom and using a wooden spoon to scrape them up. Those bits are flavor and you want those in your dish!

55. Ground spices do not have a long shelf life. Stop buying spices in bulk and buy smaller amounts more often to maximize the flavor they bring to your dishes.

56. Stop cooking in foil pans and expecting the same results that are achieved when cooking in actual cookware. Aluminum does not conduct heat well. Also, the environment is suffering. Save the planet.

57. Scrambled eggs start off in a cold nonstick pan with a pat of butter and a pinch of salt and pepper. Use a rubber or silicone spatula to continuously stir the eggs as the pan is heating up. Pull the pan off the fire 30 seconds before they are finished cooking. They will finish cooking from the heat of the pan.

58. When cheap cuts of meat go on sale, make sure to pick up a few packages and store them in the freezer for a rainy day. Use them to make a beef stock or stew!

59. "Neutral oils" are oils that don't impart flavor to your food and are can mostly be used for anything cooking related (think baking, frying, sautéing etc.) and are interchangeable. The most common ones are canola, avocado, peanut, safflower, grapeseed and vegetable. My personal favorite is avocado!

60. Change your sponge often. Besides being more sanitary it will also make the job of doing the dishes less, well, less gross.

61. The only time you bring something to a boil with the lid on is when you are boiling plain water. Anything else should be brought to a boil uncovered. Then reduce heat and cover if necessary.

62. Turmeric will stain your hands. And nail polish. Wear gloves.

63. Dry your greens. Herbs and salad. Watery salads are not delicious.

64. Wash and cut your radishes and keep in ice cold water to maximize their crunchiness.

65. The vessel you are preparing your food in should be significantly larger than the contents within it. That will make your job easier and cleaner!

66. Bread that is properly wrapped in plastic wrap, meaning each slice of bread or individual roll, bagel or challah is wrapped tightly, will freeze and defrost really nicely.

67. Write the date on anything that goes in your freezer.

68. If your cutting board is slipping and sliding beneath you, lightly dampen a tea towel and stick it between the counter and board!

69. Never put something hot in the fridge or freezer. Allow it to come to room temperature first!

70. Place fried food on a cooling rack once it comes out of the oil, not a paper towel. The food will just sit on the oil soaked towel and reabsorb what dripped out and become soggy!

71. Use liquid measuring cups for water, oil, juice, wine, vinegars, coffee, melted butters and milks. Use dry measuring cups for everything else.

72. Salt your eggplant after cutting it and let it sit for at least 30 minutes before cooking it.

73. Buy a salt cellar (preferably one with a lid that doesn't screw on so it is easy to remove and replace) and keep it next to your stove.

74. When baking, set your timer for 3-5 minutes less time than the recipe says to account for every oven being a little different!

75. Don't use a wet towel to take hot things out of the oven. I speak from experience.

76. If your hands are no longer heat sensitive, do not trust yourself when it comes to filling a bath for a child. Again, I speak from experience.

77. If you accidentally drop your cell phone on something you are cooking, say because you are trying to Instagram the process, throw it out and start again. Phones are not clean.

78. If a recipe says room temp butter, that means butter that has naturally softened. Not melted butter.

79. If you want to cook or bake with your kids, remember to have everything all set up like a cooking show. Don't start pulling ingredients out as you go. It's when you turn your back to take out new ingredients that all will go awry and someone will spill the open bottle of oil all over the floor!

80. Do not attempt to cook or bake (or do anything at all for that matter) with hungry children.

81. Keep a sharpie and roll of masking tape or some easy peel labels in your kitchen.

82. Have a pump bottle of hand moisturizer by your kitchen sink. All hands can thank me now.

83. The only way to improve your cooking is to keep cooking. Same goes for baking and chopping.

84. Did you roast a whole chicken? Don't throw out the bones. Stick them in a pot with some carrots, celery, onion and herbs, add water, bring to a boil, reduce heat and simmer for 4-5 hours for a delicious chicken stock.

85. Invest in heavy duty kitchen scissors.

86. This is a banana, raisin, and marinara free book. Just so you know.

all

you

knead

is

love

foundations

challah recipe

MY CHALLAH RECIPE IS 14 YEARS IN THE MAKING. I STARTED WITH ONE RECIPE WHEN I WAS 18 AND TWEAKED IT AND TWEAKED IT UNTIL I ACHIEVED A DOUGH THAT WAS LIGHT AND FLUFFY AND, MOST IMPORTANTLY, ADAPTABLE. ADD IN A LITTLE MORE HONEY, NO PROBLEM. WANT TO GO WITH SAVORY TOPPINGS, SURE. MAYBE SOMETHING INDULGENT LIKE STUFFING IT WITH CHOCOLATE CHIPS AND A SWEET CRUMB TOPPING, GO FOR IT! THE DOUGH IS VERSATILE AND EASY TO WORK WITH. AND THAT, MY FRIENDS, IS WHY I CHOSE TO BEGIN THIS BOOK, PROBABLY THE MOST IMPORTANT PROFESSIONAL TASK I'VE TAKEN ON THUS FAR, WITH THIS RECIPE. CHALLAH, ONE OF THE THREE MITZVOS GRANTED SPECIFICALLY TO WOMEN, IS AN EXTREMELY HOLY AND BEAUTIFUL COMMANDMENT. IT CAN EASILY FEEL DAUNTING AND INTIMIDATING. I GET IT. SO I CREATED THIS RECIPE TO OVERCOME THAT: TO HELP MAKE IT APPROACHABLE, DOABLE, AND, MOST OF ALL, TO MAKE IT A MITZVAH THAT WE ARE BLESSED TO BE ABLE TO DO JUST A LITTLE BIT MORE ACCESSIBLE!

MAKES 6 MEDIUM OR 4 LARGE CHALLAHS

3 heaping Tbsp dry yeast
¾ cup sugar
4 cups warm water

1 cup oil
2 eggs
¾-1 cup sugar (depending on how sweet you want your challah to be)
2 Tbsp honey (optional)
1 Tbsp vanilla (trust me)
1 (5 lb) bag flour (or **2 (1 kg) bags +
¾ cup** flour)
2 Tbsp kosher salt

1 egg + **2** yolks, lightly beaten

In a very large bowl, combine yeast, sugar, and warm water.
Set aside to allow yeast to bloom for 8 minutes.

Meanwhile, in a second bowl, combine oil, eggs, sugar, honey (if using), and vanilla.
Mix well.

When yeast mixture is very bubbly, pour in oil mixture; stir to combine.
Add a little less than half the flour to the bowl.
Using a spoon, mix the flour into the liquid very well.
Mix for 2-3 minutes to help the gluten start to develop.
Add salt; mix till incorporated.

Reserve 1 cup flour in case the dough will be too sticky; add the remaining flour.
(Remember, you can always add flour but you can't take it out!)
Mix with a spoon until it becomes too difficult to stir.

Pour dough out onto your work surface. No need to flour the surface.
Knead for 10 minutes, working in more flour as needed.

Once dough is smooth and elastic, place back into the bowl.
Pour a little bit of oil into your hand and rub all over the dough.
Place a piece of plastic wrap directly on dough; cover the bowl with a towel.

Allow to rise until it has at least doubled in size.
Remove plastic wrap and punch down the dough.
Replace plastic wrap and let dough rise again.
(You can repeat this step as many times as you need until you are ready to braid the dough.)

Divide dough into 4-6 sections, depending on how many and what size challahs you would like to make.
Cut each section into 4-6 parts; roll each into a strand. Alternatively, wind each section around itself to form round challahs.
Braid the strands, place onto a baking sheet or into baking pans, and cover with a towel.
Let challahs rise for 45 minutes to an hour. (Don't skip this step.)

NOTE
Rising can take anywhere from 90 minutes in the summer or when using white spelt, to 2-3 hours on a cold day. (Spelt flour rises faster!)

Recipe continues on next page.

Use a 4 cup measuring cup that is also marked with a ¾ cup measurement. After you pour in the water, measure your oil and add the rest of your ingredients to the cup. No need to dirty another utensil!

The more you knead the dough, the smoother and more elastic it will become. Be patient. If, after 7 or 8 minutes of kneading, the dough feels very dry or too sticky, add a bit more water or flour.

To prevent dough from drying out, make sure it is completely covered with the plastic wrap.

I like to let my dough rise a few times, which results in a fluffier challah. Let it rise completely, punch it down, and then let it rise again. Do this at least once, and up to three or four times!

Preheat oven to 350°F / 180°C. (For round challahs, heat oven temperature to 340°F / 175°C.)

Brush each challah with beaten egg; add toppings as you like.
Bake for 25-45 minutes until challahs are deeply golden and baked through.
Remove pans from the oven; allow challahs to cool for 5 minutes.
Transfer challahs to a cooling rack; cool completely.

I like to wrap my challahs individually in foil.

If I make them on Friday, I leave out what I need for Shabbos, but if I make them on another day, even Thursday, I freeze them.

TO THAW

Remove from freezer a few hours before serving.

Place wrapped challah on the plata (hot plate) or in the oven to reheat with the rest of your food.

Serve warm and enjoy!

TOPPING IDEAS

Egg wash and a sprinkle of sugar.

Egg wash and minced garlic, parsley, and chili flakes.

Egg wash and everything spice.

Roasted garlic, or garlic confit on the bottom. (Place roasted garlic cloves into a greased challah pan, top with formed challah; brush with egg wash and sprinkle with salt and paprika. Bake as usual. The garlic bakes into the bottom of the dough and it is heavenly!)

Egg wash followed by crumb topping: In a bowl, combine 2 cups flour, 1½ cups sugar, ¼ tsp kosher salt, ⅛ tsp cinnamon, and scant ½ cup canola oil to form crumbs. If it's too dry, add oil, little by little, until desired texture is reached.

For my favorite challah ever, place 1 cup golden sautéed onions (page 22) and 1 cup lightly golden sautéed garlic into a greased and parchment lined challah pan (don't drain off the oil; add that into the pan also!). Place braided uncooked challah onto onions and garlic. Rise, egg, and bake as usual. Serve hot and enjoy!

moroccan seudat shlishit challah

WHAT I LOVE ABOUT THIS VERY TRADITIONAL SEUDAT SHLISHIT (THIRD SHABBOS MEAL) CHALLAH IS THAT YOU MAKE A BATCH OF THE REGULAR CHALLAH DOUGH, SHAPE 5 OUT OF 6 CHALLAHS, AND USE THE REMAINING 1/6 OF DOUGH TO MAKE THIS, AND ALL OF A SUDDEN SEUDAT SHLISHIT IS TAKEN CARE OF! (WHICH IS EXTRA AWESOME ON THOSE LONG SUMMER SHABBOSIM WHEN EVERYONE IS ACTUALLY HUNGRY AT THAT TIME!)   MAKES 1 CHALLAH

⅙ batch of challah, risen but not yet braided

1 cup salade cuite (page 34)

2 (5-oz) cans tuna in oil, drained, roughly chopped

1 egg, lightly beaten

⅛ tsp paprika

⅛ tsp Maldon salt

Preheat oven to 350°F / 180°C. Line a baking sheet with parchment paper.

Roll challah dough into a large rectangle (about 12" x 8").
Spread the salad cuite directly down the center third of the rectangle.
Top salad cuite with tuna.

Fold left half of the dough over the top of the tuna; fold right half of the dough over that to form a log.
Pinch closed the ends of the log. Transfer to prepared baking sheet.

Brush log with beaten egg; sprinkle with paprika and salt.
Bake for 35-40 minutes until the top is golden brown.

Remove from oven; place on a cooling rack.
Once cooled, completely wrap in foil and freeze.

To thaw, remove from fridge the night before or 5-6 hours before serving.

To serve, heat gently, still wrapped in foil, for 45 minutes. Remove foil; heat for 15 minutes.

Serve with large dollops of garlic mayo and some preserved lemon puree and enjoy!

NOTE

Traditionally, a hard boiled egg is sliced right on top of the tuna before rolling up the dough. I, however, am not a fan, so I choose to leave it out. If you are an egg lover, like, say, everyone else in the world, definitely give it a try!

TIPS + TRICKS

If you don't want to make homemade salade cuite (even though I highly recommend you do, but this is a judgment free zone!), you can use any good store bought matbucha or even Turkish salad.

rabbanit toledano challah

RABBANIT MARGALIT TOLEDANO ZICHRONAH LIVRACHAH WAS MY MOTHER'S BEST FRIEND AND ONE OF THE MOST INFLUENTIAL PEOPLE IN MY YOUNG ADULT LIFE. A GRANDDAUGHTER OF THE BABA SALI AND DAUGHTER TO BABA MEIR, SHE WAS INFUSED WITH HOLINESS, PIETY, WISDOM, HUMILITY, AND GRACE. EVERY WORD THAT I EVER HEARD COME OUT OF HER MOUTH WAS UTTERED WITH INTENTION AND PURPOSE. AND YET, ALL OF THOSE TRAITS DID NOT NEGATE THE MOST WONDERFUL SENSE OF HUMOR. SHE WAS A WOMAN WHO FOUND A WAY TO BALANCE THE INTENSITY OF ALL THOSE TRAITS AND LIVE WITH THEM SIMULTANEOUSLY. IN ADDITION TO ALL THAT, SHE WAS, OF COURSE, A FABULOUS COOK. THE RABBANIT FED SO MANY PEOPLE OUT OF HER PERFECTLY CLEAN AT ALL TIMES (STILL UNCLEAR HOW SHE PULLED THAT OFF), SMALL, BUT WILDLY EFFICIENT KITCHEN. THIS CHALLAH, ONE OF OUR FAVORITE TREATS, IS HER RECIPE. MAKE IT, SHARE IT, ENJOY IT. AND THINK OF HER. HARABBANIT MARGALIT BAS RABBI MEIR ABUCHATZEIRA. MAY HER NESHAMAH HAVE AN ALIYAH.

MAKES 6–8 CHALLAHS

4.4 lb (2 kg) white flour
4½ Tbsp yeast
5 Tbsp sugar
5 cups warm water
2 Tbsp kosher salt
½ cup oil
1 egg, lightly beaten

Add all the flour to a large bowl.
Make a deep well in the center of the flour.
Add yeast and sugar.
Pour water into the well; allow mixture to sit for 3-4 minutes.

Add remaining ingredients.
Mix for 6-8 minutes until the dough comes together.
The dough will be sticky.

Place a piece of lightly greased plastic wrap tightly over the bowl.
Allow dough to rise to the top of the plastic wrap.

At this point the dough is ready to shape.

Preheat the oven to 350°F / 180°C. Line 3 baking sheets with parchment paper; coat with nonstick cooking spray.

Divide dough into 6 portions (or 8 smaller ones).

Using lightly greased hands, take 1 portion of dough and form into a smooth ball by folding the top of the dough under the bottom.
Place smooth ball of dough on one side of the baking sheet.
Repeat this process until you have 2 challahs per baking sheet.
The dough will settle and become wider and flatter as it rests for 35-40 minutes.

Bake for 40 minutes until golden brown.
Remove from oven and place onto a cooling rack.

Serve hot (preferably with Moroccan fish and plenty of dips) and enjoy!

NOTE

Rabbanit Toledano very often used 1 portion of dough to make pizza on Friday afternoons! Prepare the dough and allow to rise, then roll out one portion into a large circle, par bake at 350°F / 180°C for 15 minutes, then remove from oven, top with sauce, cheese, and any toppings you like. Return to oven to finish baking for about 12 minutes!

big batch sauteed onions

HAVING A HEAP OF SWEET, DEEPLY GOLDEN, MELT–IN–YOUR–MOUTH ONIONS IN YOUR FRIDGE IS ALMOST LIKE HAVING A PERSONAL CHEF. ALMOST. FINE, NOT A PERSONAL CHEF IN TERM OF THE ACTUAL COOKING PREPARATIONS, BUT IT ABSOLUTELY IS IN TERMS OF HAVING AN INSTANT FLAVOR BOOSTER AT YOUR FINGERTIPS. ALSO, NOT TO MENTION THE TIME IT SAVES, PEELING AND CHOPPING ONIONS FOR BASICALLY EVERY SINGLE RECIPE IN THIS BOOK!

40 large yellow onions peeled, halved, thinly sliced

1 Tbsp canola oil

2 tsp kosher salt

Add oil to a large, heavy bottomed pot set over low heat. Dump in onions and salt. Stir to combine.

Place lid on the pot, to get the onions to begin softening for just 10-15 minutes, lifting the lid and stirring every 5 minutes.

After that initial period, remove pot cover.

Allow onions to cook for 6 hours (uncovered), stirring every 20-30 minutes.

After 6 hours the onions should be golden and very, very soft.

Raise heat to medium (not high), and cook the onions for 30-40 minutes, stirring every 5 minutes to ensure they don't burn.

At this point the onions should be a deep golden brown and very, very soft.

Transfer onions to a bowl. Allow to cool.

Once cool, divide onions into ¼ cup portions in either small ziptop bags or small containers with tightly fitted lids.

Store in the freezer to have on hand all the time!

VARIATIONS

You can do this in the crockpot. Add all ingredients to the pot, set on low, and cover. Cook for 4-5 hours. Lots of liquid will accumulate at this point. Raise temperature to medium, remove lid, and cook for 3-4 hours, stirring every 30 minutes or so until all the liquid evaporates and the onions are deeply golden. Store the same way.

TIPS + TRICKS

You can easily slice your onions by putting the slicing blade into your food process (hint: it looks like a sideways peeler), and processing the onions!

preserved lemon & limes

EVERYTHING ABOUT PRESERVED CITRUS MAKES ME HAPPY. GOING TO THE MARKET TO BUY BRIGHT COLORFUL CITRUS. RUNNING THE COARSE GRAINS OF SALT THROUGH MY HAND AS I STUFF THE FRAGRANT FRUIT. AND WATCHING HOW I SIMPLE INGREDIENT, LIKE SALT, GIVEN TO US BY HASHEM (GOD), HARVESTED BY MAN, CAN TAKE FRUIT, ANOTHER MAGICAL GIFT FROM OUR MASTER, AND TURN SOMETHING TART AND SLIGHTLY CRUNCHY INTO THE SWEETEST BUT STILL ACIDIC, LUXURIOUS, AND MOST SILKY FOOD THERE IS. ALL YOU NEED TO MAKE THIS HAPPEN IS CITRUS, SALT, AND TIME — ALL COMPONENTS THAT ARE ONLY GRANTED TO US BY HASHEM — AND A LITTLE BIT OF PATIENCE. THE PROCESS WILL FEEL DAUNTING BUT IT TAKES A MERE 30 MINUTES OF ACTIVE PREP TIME AND THEN YOU ARE SET FOR THE YEAR! SO PLEASE, IF YOU TAKE A LEAP OF FAITH ON ANY RECIPE IN THIS BOOK, LET IT BE THIS ONE!

2 large (1-2 liter) glass jars (I use various brands; just make sure there is a tight fitting lid!)

2.2 lb (1 kg) kosher salt (you may have some left over, but it's salt. You'll find a use for it!)

citrus (lemons, Meyer lemons, limes, kumquats), enough to fill the jar PLUS 8 additional ones for squishing in during the following days

NOTE
Please note, there are NO real amounts here. I will do the best I can to explain what you need and to give you enough direction to make sure you don't have to run back to the store!

NOTE
For easy access, I like to wash and clean a few preserved lemons at the same time and puree the soft rinds in the food processor to make a preserved lemon puree to use in marinades, dressings, dips, and spreads!

Wash and dry jars well. I like to do this the night before.
Wash citrus with warm soapy water. Rinse with clear water.
Wipe citrus and place on a towel to dry for at least 1 hour.

Pour 2 cups salt into a bowl to begin with. (You may need more but you can always add more.)

Hold the citrus upright, with the stem end on the cutting board.
Use a sharp knife to cut down ONLY ¾ of the way through the citrus.
Rotate the citrus 90 degrees and make another cut ONLY ¾ of the way through.
You should now have 4 citrus wedges that are still attached at the bottom, almost like it's blossoming like a flower.

Now it's time to fill the jars.
Hold one fruit over the bowl of salt.
Gently pry open the citrus wedges slightly and pour in salt, making sure to get some into all four segments.

Gently place the fruit into the jar.
Repeat this process until your jar is full.
You can use a little effort to push the citrus down and squeeze in 1-2 more fruits, even if they are sideways.

Once you can no longer fit in any more, simply close the jar.
Place jar in a cool, dark, or shady cabinet.

A few hours later, check the jar.
You should be able to squeeze in 1 more of the salt packed citrus.
Place jar into cabinet.
For the next 6 days, add 1 or 2 more salt packed fruits to the jar.

Every day, the level of natural juices released by the citrus will rise.
Once the juices reach the top of the jar and the citrus is fully submerged in the juice, your job is done.

Set the jar back in the cabinet and forget about it for 3 weeks.
At the end of the 3 weeks your preserved citrus is ready to be refrigerated!

To use, simply open the jar, remove 1 fruit, gently give it a quick rinse under room temp water and scrape out the inside flesh and seeds.
What you are left with is the most tender, syrupy, and delicious citrus rind. At this point it is ready to use.

Store jar in the fridge for up to a year.

sumac pickled onions

I KEEP THESE IN MY FRIDGE AT ALL TIMES. NOT ONLY BECAUSE I LOVE THE GORGEOUS PURPLE HUED ONIONS SITTING SO PRETTILY ON MY FRIDGE SHELF, BUT ALSO BECAUSE I PUT THEM ON EVERYTHING! CHEESE SANDWICHES, EGGS, SALADS, TACOS, BURGERS, AND RIGHT ON TOP OF A PERFECTLY ROASTED PIECE OF CHICKEN!

2 purple onions, halved, thinly sliced

2 tsp kosher salt

3 Tbsp sugar

2 tsp sumac

½ **cup** apple cider vinegar

very hot water, to cover

Place onions into a jar; add salt, sugar, sumac, and vinegar.
Add hot water to cover.
Cover jar tightly; shake well and place into the fridge.

These are best after 24 hours and actually get better and better by the day.
They stay fresh in the fridge for 1 month!

mayos

NO SHABBOS MEAL IN MY HOUSE IS COMPLETE WITHOUT HOMEMADE MAYO. THE GARLIC MAYO IS A STAPLE, BUT EVERY ONCE IN A WHILE I LIKE TO ADD IN SOME SPECIAL MAYOS. TRY IT ONCE, TASTE IT, DIP YOUR CHALLAH INTO IT, SHMEAR SOME ON YOUR SANDWICH, PILE IT HIGH ON EGGPLANT, AND YOU'LL SEE, THERE IS NO COMPARISON TO STORE BOUGHT MAYO.

assorted mayo

garlic mayo

1 cup canola oil
1 egg
1 Tbsp Dijon mustard
2 cloves garlic, chopped
1 tsp kosher salt
1 tsp coarsely ground black pepper
juice of ½ lemon

curry lime mayo

2 eggs
2 large cloves garlic
2 tsp kosher salt
2 tsp coarsely ground black pepper
2 tsp curry powder
zest of 1½ limes (1½ tsp)
juice of 2 limes (about ⅓ cup)
2 cups canola oil

horseradish mayo

2 eggs
1 large clove garlic
2½ tsp kosher salt
1 tsp coarsely ground black pepper
juice of 2 lemons (about ¼ cup)
⅓ cup prepared white horseradish
2 cups canola oil

truffle mayo

2 eggs
1 large clove garlic
2½ tsp kosher salt
2 tsp coarsely ground black pepper
juice of 2 lemons (about ¼ cup)
2 cups canola oil
3-4 tsp truffle oil (depending how truffle-y you want it)

USING AN IMMERSION BLENDER

Place all the ingredients into the tall container that comes with your immersion blender.

Gently place the immersion blender down to the bottom of the container. Once it gets to the bottom, immediately turn it on. Continue juzzing until it looks like the oil is no longer streaming down. Carefully lift up one side of the blender to allow more oil to stream in. Continue lifting alternate sides of the blender until you reach the top of the mixture. Give the final thick mayo one or two buzzes and that's it!

USING A FOOD PROCESSOR

Add an additional ½ cup oil and use 2 egg yolks instead of 1 whole egg.

Place all the ingredients besides the oil into a food processor fitted with the "S" blade.

Pulse on low speed (speed 3 out of 10), until mixture becomes pale yellow. Slowly start streaming in oil, drop by drop, till you have used all the oil.

Place the mayo into an airtight container and use within 5-7 days.

penina's jalapeño mayo

I LOVE THIS MAYO AS MUCH AS THE LITTLE GIRL, WHO'S NOT SO LITTLE ANYMORE, WHO MADE IT UP! OF ALL THESE MAYOS, THIS ONE IS THE ONLY ONE THAT USES STORE BOUGHT MAYO AS THE BASE. YOU CAN MAKE WITH HOMEMADE IF YOU LIKE, BUT I FIND THAT THE EXTRA WORK IS NOT NECESSARY HERE!

3 cloves garlic
10 pickled jalapeño peppers (think the canned variety)
1 cup mayonnaise
⅛ tsp kosher salt

Place garlic cloves and peppers into the bowl of a food processor fitted with the "S" blade.
Process till finely minced. Add mayo and salt.
Process for 1 minute to combine.

Since peppers vary in size and heat level, make sure you taste and adjust to your liking.
If it's too spicy, add more mayo, 1 tablespoon at a time.
If you can handle the heat (you're my people!), add additional peppers, 1 at a time.

Store in an airtight container.

NOTE

Since the mayo contains raw egg, I take out only what I need and put the jar right back in the fridge so that it doesn't spoil. If there's any left after it's been sitting out for a while, I do not return it to the jar.

PHOTO ORDER
FROM TOP TO BOTTOM
Garlic Mayo
Jalapeño Mayo
Curry Lime Mayo
Horseradish Mayo
Truffle Mayo

spicy dips

I COLLECT VERY FEW THINGS. TWO OF THE THINGS I DO COLLECT, THOUGH, ARE GLASS JARS, OF ALL SHAPES AND SIZES, OF COURSE, AND MUSTARDS, HOT SAUCES, AND DIPS. HOMEMADE, STORE BOUGHT, FACTORY PRODUCED, YOU NAME IT. IF IT'S SPICY, YOU CAN FIND IT IN MY HOUSE. WHAT I LOVE MOST ABOUT THESE SPICY DIPS IS THAT MOST OF THEM LAST FOR A REALLY LONG TIME. SO MAKE A BATCH (EVEN DOUBLE IT IF YOU REALLY TRUST ME), AND KEEP THEM IN YOUR FRIDGE. I GUARANTEE THEY WILL ELEVATE EVERY EGG, PIECE OF CHICKEN, BOWL OF RICE, AND SALAD YOU HAVE FOR AS LONG AS THEY LAST!

lemon jalapeño gremolata

Peel the lemons with a knife as thinly as possible, then mince the peels (or zest them, using a zester or microplane).

Segment the lemons over a bowl to catch the liquid. Add minced lemon peel to segments.

Add remaining ingredients; stir to combine.

Serve cold over cooked chicken, fish, or meat!

Store in an airtight container in the refrigerator for up to 3 weeks.

2 lemons, washed and dried

½ purple onion, finely diced

2 cloves garlic, finely chopped

1-2 Thai chilies, finely chopped (depending how spicy you want it)

1 cup cilantro leaves, chopped

½ cup parsley leaves, chopped

1 tsp kosher salt

1 tsp coarsely ground black pepper

1 Tbsp olive oil

harissa

5 oz assorted dried spicy red peppers (see Note)

1 cup fresh cilantro

¼ cup fresh parsley

4 cloves garlic

½ tsp ground cumin

¼ tsp kosher salt

2 tsp white vinegar

extra virgin olive oil, to cover

Wash dried peppers very well.
Add peppers to a bowl.
Pour boiling water over peppers; rehydrate for 10 minutes.

Remove rehydrated peppers from water and just give them a simple shake to remove excess water.

Remove and discard stems, then add peppers to the bowl of a food processor fitted with the "S" blade. Add herbs, garlic, cumin, and salt.

Process for about 3 minutes, scraping down the sides of the bowl every 30 seconds or so, until mixture is evenly pureed.

Add vinegar; stir to combine.

Transfer harissa to a large glass jar; smooth the top.
Add a thin layer of olive oil; cover tightly to help preserve the harissa.

Store in the fridge for up to 6 months.

TIPS + TRICKS

A good rule of thumb is that the smaller the pepper, the spicier it is. Also, the heat exists in the ribs and seeds. If you want your food to be less spicy, remove them first.

NOTE

Everyone will ultimately come up with their own blend and amounts of dried spicy red peppers; this is mine: about 4 very long ones, 4 of the second largest size, 4 of the second smallest.

TIPS + TRICKS

While your food processor is out and filled with harissa anyway, now is a perfect time to make the preserved lemon harissa puree (page 32). Simply leave ¼ cup harissa in the food processor and continue with the recipe.

PHOTO ORDER
LEFT ROW
Moroccan Schug, Harissa, Lemon Jalapeño Gremolata

MIDDLE ROW
Garlic Confit, Simply Schug, Preserved Lemon Harissa

RIGHT ROW
Roasted Jalapeño Garlic, Chimmi-Schug-Pesto

chimmi-schug-pesto

1-3 jalapeño peppers (depending how spicy you like it)

7 cloves garlic

1 cup cilantro leaves

1½ cups parsley leaves

juice of ½ lemon

½ tsp kosher salt

¼ cup + 2 Tbsp extra virgin olive oil

Place jalapeños and garlic into the bowl of a food processor fitted with the "S" blade. Blend till finely minced.

Add herbs, lemon juice, and salt.

With food processor running, drizzle in oil.

Taste to adjust seasoning.

Transfer to an airtight container; store in the fridge for up to 10 days!

preserved lemon harissa

Add harissa and preserved lemon peels to the bowl of a food processor fitted with the "S" blade.

Process for 4 minutes, scraping down sides often until mixture is smooth.

Transfer to a jar; cover with a thin layer of olive oil to preserve.

Store in the fridge for up to 6 months (although I'd be shocked if it lasted 6 days!).

¼ cup harissa (store bought or homemade, page 30)

2 cups preserved lemon peels (page 24) (remove seeds and flesh before measuring)

extra virgin olive oil, to cover

NOTE

If you are using store bought versions of either or both of these ingredients (which is a completely acceptable shortcut!) you may have to adjust the amounts by adding a little bit more harissa if it is too lemony or a bit more lemon if it is not strong enough.

This is by far in my top five condiments to have in my fridge. I slather it on everything from cheese sandwiches to hot off the grill pan chicken cutlets to burgers, even going as far as mixing it into my techina and using that as a dip for crudité. It's tangy but not sour, hot but not spicy, and adds instantaneous brightness to whatever you eat it with!

simply schug

FOR ISRAEL

10 cloves garlic, roughly chopped

15 long spicy green peppers, roughly chopped

½ tsp kosher salt

2 tsp fresh lemon juice

FOR EVERYWHERE ELSE IN THE WORLD, WHERE JALAPEÑOS ARE SHORT & STUBBY

8 cloves garlic, roughly chopped

18 jalapeño peppers, roughly chopped

½ green bell pepper, roughly chopped

½ tsp kosher salt

2 tsp lemon juice

Place garlic into the bowl of a food processor fitted with the "S" blade; use a few pulses to mince.

Add roughly chopped jalapeños and bell pepper (if using). Process for 1 minute, pausing to scrape down the sides a few times.

Add salt and lemon juice, pulsing once or twice to incorporate.

Store in an airtight container for up to 2 weeks and eat with every single thing you consume!

garlic lemon + chili confit

45 cloves garlic

1 lemon, washed, thinly sliced, each slice cut in half

1 red chili, thinly sliced

1 cup extra virgin olive oil

1 tsp kosher salt

¼ **tsp** coarsely ground black pepper

1 sprig fresh rosemary

½ **tsp** paprika

Preheat oven to 350°F/180°C.

Put all ingredients into an ovenproof baking dish.
(Pyrex is ideal because you can see through it to check on progress.)

Cover tightly with foil.

Bake for 1 hour-1 hour 20 minutes until golden, soft, smushy, and delish!

roasted jalapeño garlic

Set oven to broil. Line a baking sheet with parchment paper.

Place peppers on prepared baking sheet.
Broil on all sides until peppers have blackened and charred all the way around, turning peppers when each side is charred.

Remove from oven; place peppers into a bowl. Cover bowl tightly with plastic wrap and cover with a towel.
Allow peppers to steam in the bowl for 15 minutes.

Wearing gloves, uncover the bowl and peel the peppers.
If you'd like the mixture to be little less spicy (although it will still be spicy), remove and discard the seeds.

Cut peppers into long thin strips.

Place a pan over medium low heat. Add oil, garlic, and salt.
Cook for 2-3 minutes until the garlic starts to brown. Add peppers.
Cook for 12-15 minutes, until fragrant.

Remove from heat; set aside to cool.

Serve hot or cold and enjoy!

12 long spicy green peppers, washed and dried

4 Tbsp extra virgin olive oil

12 cloves garlic, minced

¼ **tsp** kosher salt

NOTE

This is very spicy and not for the fainthearted. If you use only a little at a time, I suggest storing it in small condiment containers in the freezer and pulling one out a few hours before you plan to eat it!

moroccan schug

1 long spicy green pepper

4 cloves garlic

1½ **cups** cilantro leaves

¾ **cup** parsley leaves

2 mint leaves

2 tsp paprika in oil

½ **tsp** kosher salt

1 Tbsp vinegar

1 Tbsp fresh lemon juice

3 Tbsp extra virgin olive oil

Place green pepper and garlic into the bowl of a food processor fitted with the "S" blade; process until minced.

Add cilantro, parsley, mint, paprika in oil, and salt.
Pulse until very finely minced. You may have to scrape down the sides of the bowl a few times.

With the processor running, drizzle in vinegar and lemon juice.

Turn off food processor; use a spoon to mix in the oil.

Transfer schug to an airtight jar; store in the fridge for up to 3 weeks.

Serve hot and enjoy!

salade cuite (salada taybe)

THIS GETS ITS OWN PAGE BECAUSE IT IS MY FAVORITE OF ALL THE DIPS. MY GRANDMOTHER ALWAYS HAD AN ABUNDANCE OF IT, AND SERVED IT AS A DIP, SPREAD ONTO SANDWICHES, MIXED INTO OMELETTES, AND ALONGSIDE WHATEVER WAS FOR DINNER. NOTHING MAKES ME FEEL MORE CONNECTED TO HER, AND LIKE A TRUE MOROCCAN WOMAN, THAN HAVING A HUGE BATCH OF THIS IN MY FRIDGE!

4 Tbsp extra virgin olive oil

4 heads garlic, peeled, minced

10.5 lb (4.8 kg) canned whole peeled tomatoes

5 red bell peppers, washed and dried

3 green bell peppers, washed and dried

6-10 long green spicy peppers washed and dried

1 tsp kosher salt

½ tsp paprika

FREEZER TIP

This recipe makes a huge amount because it is so time consuming to make. Make it once, allow the mixture to cool, then freeze it in pints to have ready every Shabbos. Remove from the freezer a few hours before you want to serve. Bonus points if you put the thawed salad cuite into a small ovenproof bowl and heat it up before you serve it.

TIPS + TRICKS

Every shakshuka benefits from the addition of salad cuite to its sauce.

Set a large, heavy bottomed pot over very low heat.
Add oil and garlic; stir to combine.

Place a large piece of foil on your work surface with a plastic cutting board on top.

Working near the pot so that you can stir the garlic every 5 minutes or so, open tomato cans.
Remove 1 tomato from a can; trim off and discard the stem end.
Roughly chop the tomato; add to a bowl.
Repeat with remaining tomatoes.

Throughout this process, juices will accumulate on the cutting board.
Reserve 1 cup of the juice (you may not need it, but in case you do); set aside.

Once the garlic has slightly browned, add in the chopped tomatoes.
If you're only a little bit into the chopping, just add what you've accumulated so far and then add tomatoes as you chop them.
Once all the tomatoes have been added to the pot, bring heat to medium; stir to combine.

As soon as you see some bubbles emerging from the tomato garlic mixture, return heat to low.
Cover the pot most of the way, so that a part of the pot is still uncovered.
Cook for 6-7 hours, stirring every 30 minutes or so, until the mixture is a deep, dark red and smells heavenly.
(If the mixture starts to look too dry too soon, add in 1 tablespoon reserved tomato juice.)

About 1 hour before tomatoes are ready, set oven to broil; line a baking sheet with parchment paper. Prepare 2 bowls: 1 large, 1 small.

Place all the peppers on prepared baking sheet.
Place in the oven. (This step can be done over an open flame as well.)

Broil peppers on all sides until each side has really blackened and charred.
The spicy peppers will be done before the bell peppers, so remove them from the oven when they are done.

As the peppers char, place them into the bowls (spicy in the medium and bell in the large), cover bowls tightly with plastic wrap, and cover with a towel.
Let peppers steam for 15-20 minutes.

Wearing gloves, peel the peppers, discarding the peels and the seeds.
(Keep the seeds of only the spicy peppers, unless you want to minimize the heat, then discard those too.)

Cut peeled peppers into long ⅛-inch wide strips.
Add peppers to the pot of tomatoes; add salt and paprika.

Allow mixture to simmer for 1 hour, stirring every 20 minutes.

Serve hot and enjoy!

dips

ARE YOU REALLY MOROCCAN, SCRATCH THAT, SEPHARDI IN GENERAL, IF YOU HAVE A SHABBOS MEAL THAT DOESN'T START OFF WITH A SELECTION OF DIPS? NO. NO, YOU ARE NOT. JUST KIDDING. YOU CAN BE STILL SEPHARDI AND DO ANYTHING. ALSO, ASHKENAZI AND DO ANYTHING. YOU KNOW WHAT, BE WHOEVER YOU WANT TO BE. JUST BE SURE TO STOCK YOUR FREEZER WITH A BUNCH OF YUMMY DIPS FOR PEOPLE TO EAT THEIR CHALLAH WITH, DIP THEIR SHNITSEL INTO, OR ELEVATE A PLAIN OLD DISH THAT NEEDS ELEVATING, BECAUSE LAST MINUTE COMPANY IS A THING.

techina

3 cloves garlic

juice of **1** lemon OR **2 small** limes

½ cup tahini paste

2 tsp kosher salt

1 tsp coarsely ground black pepper

1¼ cups very cold water as needed

In a blender or food processor fitted with the "S" blade, blend garlic with lemon juice. Add tahini, salt, and pepper. Blend again until combined.

Depending on how thick or thin you want your techina to be, while blender is on, slowly drizzle in water until you reach the desired consistency. (You may need to adjust the seasoning, so taste!)

Refrigerate until serving.

TIPS + TRICKS

For the creamiest techina, shake the tahini paste bottle very well before pouring and make sure to use very cold water!

almond "techina" (sesame free)

In a food processor fitted with the "S" blade, pulse together almonds, lemon juice, garlic, salt, and pepper, scraping down the sides as necessary.

Once almonds start to resemble a paste, add water, ½ cup at a time.

The techina is done when the mixture is loose and runny.

Turn the food processor to high and process for 1 minute to smooth out the techina as much as possible.

Add parsley; blend once more to incorporate.

Taste and adjust seasoning.

2 cups whole raw peeled almonds (blanched almonds)

juice of **3** lemons

3 cloves garlic

1½ tsp kosher salt

1 tsp coarsely ground black pepper

2-4 cups water

1 cup fresh parsley leaves

chimichurri

2 cloves garlic

½ cup parsley leaves

½ cup cilantro leaves

¼ tsp crushed red pepper flakes (optional but recommended)

¾ tsp kosher salt

½ tsp coarsely ground black pepper

2 tsp red wine vinegar

2 tsp extra virgin olive oil

Place all ingredients except oil into a food processor fitted with the "S" blade. Process for a few seconds, then start streaming in oil. Stop to scrape down sides a few times.

I like my chimichurri a bit chunky, meaning not finely blended, but you can pulse until desired consistency is reached.

PHOTO ORDER

LEFT ROW
Babaganoush, Chimmichurri, Chermoula, Techina, Pesto

RIGHT ROW
Olive + Pistachio Gremolata, Nondairy Ranch, Tomato Dip, Almond Techina

olive & pistachio dip

1 cup pitted Kalamata olives, roughly chopped

¼ cup salted pistachios, roughly chopped

½ cup parsley, chopped

1 Tbsp mint, chopped

zest of **1** lemon

juice of **1** lemon

2 small shallots, finely diced

1 tsp extra virgin olive oil

¼ tsp cracked black pepper

kosher salt, to taste

Place all ingredients into a large bowl; stir well to combine. Because olives are already on the salty side, taste the mixture and then add salt as needed.

Refrigerate until serving. This dip stays fresh in your fridge for up to a week, and it gets better as it sits!

fire roasted babaganoush

Turn the largest stovetop element to the highest heat. Place eggplant directly on the grate.

Allow to roast until the entire surface of the eggplant is charred. This should take about 3 minutes per side.

You may have to move the eggplant around if the eggplant is longer than the circumference of the grate because you want the eggplant to char all over.

Place charred eggplant into a bowl; cover the bowl immediately with plastic wrap. Allow eggplant to steam in the bowl for 20 minutes.

Wearing gloves, take the eggplant out of the bowl, discarding any accumulated juices (they are bitter!). Remove and discard the charred peel.

Place peeled eggplant into a food processor fitted with the "S" blade. Add remaining ingredients. Blend until smooth.

Taste and adjust flavors to your liking!

1 large eggplant, pierced with a fork in a few places

3 Tbsp tahini paste

juice of **1** lemon

¾ tsp kosher salt

½ tsp coarsely ground black pepper

abby's pesto

5 packed cups basil leaves (4 oz)

20 cloves garlic

1½ tsp sugar

5 tsp kosher salt

2½ tsp coarsely ground black pepper

1¾ cups olive oil

2 cups canola oil

Using a blender or a food processor fitted with the "S" blade, process all ingredients until smooth.

Refrigerate until serving.

This recipe is huge. It makes a little over a quart of pesto. Use what you need for whatever you are making and freeze the rest in small containers.

My friend Abby makes the best pesto ever. It's nut free, a kid favorite, and makes a ton. Be sure to freeze the leftovers in small containers so that you have some readily available at all times!

nondairy ranch dip

1½ cups vegan sour cream

1 cup mayonnaise

1 cup fresh parsley leaves, finely chopped

⅓ cup finely minced scallions (from **3-4 large** scallions)

1 tsp dried parsley

2 cloves garlic, minced

¾ tsp granulated garlic

1¼ tsp granulated onion

1 tsp kosher salt

¾ tsp coarsely ground black pepper

2 tsp lemon juice

Place all ingredients into a bowl or large jar.
Mix or shake well until combined.

Store in the refrigerator in an airtight container for up to 2 weeks.

NOTE

Serve the ranch dip alongside tiny shnitsel poppers. You're welcome.

chermoula

Place all ingredients into a jar or airtight container. Stir or shake to combine. Allow flavors to combine for at least 30 minutes before using.

The longer this sits, the better it gets! (If using) for a marinade, I suggest making it 1-2 days in advance!

It will stay fresh in the refrigerator in an airtight container for up to 10 days.

NOTE

Stuff the mixture inside fish or chicken or rub it on top of a roast. Yum!

2 cups cilantro leaves, finely chopped

4 cloves garlic, minced

1 Tbsp paprika in oil

1 Tbsp spicy paprika (or just use **2 Tbsp** paprika in oil)

2 tsp cumin

1 tsp kosher salt

½ tsp ground ginger

½ tsp turmeric

3 Tbsp fresh lemon juice (from about **1** large lemon)

3 Tbsp extra virgin olive oil

tomato dip

3 cloves garlic

½ purple onion

1-2 jalapeño peppers (if you want it less spicy, remove the ribs and seeds)

4 tomatoes, halved

1 tsp kosher salt

½ tsp coarsely ground black pepper

3 Tbsp olive oil

In the bowl of a food processor fitted with the "S" blade, pulse together garlic, onion, and jalapeño.

Add tomatoes, salt, and pepper; process till smooth.

With food processor running, drizzle in olive oil.

Taste and adjust seasoning.

NOTE

I double this recipe so that I have enough left over on Sunday morning to use as the base of the best shakshuka ever! Bonus: If you have a little salade cuite left over also, throw it in.

savory jams 3 ways

THESE JAMS ARE MY ANSWER TO PLAIN CHICKEN. HAVING LOTS OF GUESTS AND DON'T KNOW WHAT THEY LIKE? MAKE SIMPLE GRILLED CHICKEN, ROASTED MEATS, OR KABOBS AND FANCY THEM UP WITH AN ASSORTMENT OF SAVORY JAMS! ALSO, LET'S NOT IGNORE THE ELEPHANT IN THE ROOM … PESACH!

fennel and onion jam

2 Tbsp olive oil

2 fennel bulbs and fronds, thinly sliced

½ tsp kosher salt

¼ tsp coarsely ground black pepper

3 cloves garlic, minced

½ cup sautéed onions (page 22)

¼ cup dry white wine

Heat a large pot over medium high heat. Add oil, fennel, salt, and pepper. Cook for 15 minutes stirring often, so that fennel doesn't burn.

Once fennel is soft and very tender, add garlic. Cook for 1 minute until garlic is fragrant. Add onions.

Add wine; cook until all the liquid has evaporated. Remove from heat and allow to cool; transfer to an airtight container.

This will stay fresh in the fridge for up to two weeks.

Serve hot or cold!

jalapeño and onion jam

Heat a large pot over medium heat. Add oil, jalapeños, and salt. Cook for 15 minutes, stirring often, until peppers have softened.

Raise heat to medium high; add garlic and paprika. Stir to combine. Cook for 2 minutes until garlic is fragrant.

Stir in onions. Once onions have heated through, add wine. Cook until liquid has evaporated.

Remove from heat; allow to cool. Transfer jam to an airtight container.

Refrigerate for up to 2 weeks.

Serve hot or cold!

2 tsp olive oil

3 jalapeño peppers, thinly sliced on an angle

¼ tsp kosher salt

4 cloves garlic, minced

2 tsp paprika

¾ cup sautéed onions (page 22)

¼ cup dry white wine

melted pepper and onion jam

3 Tbsp olive oil

1 red bell pepper, thinly sliced

1 green bell pepper, thinly sliced

2 yellow bell peppers, thinly sliced

1 tsp kosher salt

2 tsp cayenne pepper OR 1-2 jalapeño peppers

4 cloves garlic, minced

¾ cup sautéed onions (page 22)

⅓ cup dry white wine

Heat a large pot over medium high heat. Add oil, peppers (including jalapeño, if using) and salt. Cook for 5 minutes, stirring constantly to prevent burning.

After 5 minutes reduce heat to low; cook peppers for 25 minutes, stirring every so often to prevent them from sticking to the bottom of the pot.

Once peppers are soft, add cayenne pepper (if using), and garlic. Cook until garlic is just heated through (about 2 minutes).

Add onions to the pot; raise heat to high. Add wine. Cook until all the liquid has evaporated (about 1 minute). Remove from heat.

Serve hot or cold! Store in an airtight container in the fridge for up to 2 weeks.

lettuce

turnip

the

beet

salads

dressings

IT IS ACTUALLY MY DREAM TO HAVE MY REFRIGERATOR STOCKED AT ALL TIMES WITH 5–6 DIFFERENT SALAD DRESSINGS. USUALLY I CAN ONLY PULL OFF 1 OR 2 (MAAAAAYBE 3 IF I'M FEELING SUPER SUPERWOMAN-Y THAT WEEK), AND NOTHING ON THE PLANET MAKES ME HAPPIER THAN OPENING MY FRIDGE AND SEEING BEAUTIFUL GLASS JARS FILLED WITH DRESSINGS. THEY ARE SO VERSATILE AND CAN REALLY MAKE OR BREAK A MEAL! USE THEM AS MARINADES, DIPS, SALAD DRESSINGS, SANDWICH SPREADS, OR JUST FILL YOUR FRIDGE WITH THEM AND STARE AT YOUR WORK TO BRING YOU THE UTMOST SATISFACTION! JUST KIDDING — YOU WORKED SO HARD, YOU MIGHT AS WELL EAT THEM! I'VE BROUGHT YOU A VARIETY IN THE SENSE THAT A FEW ARE MAYO-BASED, A FEW ARE VINAIGRETTES, A FEW ARE SWEET, A FEW ARE SAVORY, AND ALL ARE DELICIOUS! NOW THAT YOU HAVE A PANTRY OF DRESSING RECIPES, A GOOD SALAD (OR SANDWICH, OR MARINADE, OR SPREAD) IS NEVER THAT FAR AWAY. PLAY WITH MIXING TOGETHER VEGETABLES WITH DIFFERENT COLORS AND TEXTURES, ADDING IN HERBS, CRUNCHY TOPPINGS, AND DIFFERENT PROTEINS. I'M PRETTY SURE THAT IF YOU DO THE MATH (WHICH I CANNOT), THERE ARE PROBABLY ENOUGH VARIATIONS TO MAKE YOURSELF A DIFFERENT SALAD EACH DAY OF THE YEAR!

NOTES

Taste and adjust flavors to your liking.

Too lemony: add olive oil

Too salty: add a little more lemon

Not enough salt: add more

Don't have kosher salt: use a smaller amount of table salt, then go to the grocery store and stock up!

Don't have a pepper grinder: see kosher salt note!

PHOTO ORDER

LEFT ROW
Memes Big Batch Lemon,
Raspberry Vinaigrette,
Old School Balsamic,
Diner Style Vinaigrette

MIDDLE ROW
Creamy Greeny,
Turmeric Vinaigrette,
Cilantro Lime, Caesar Dressing

RIGHT ROW
Creamy Sesame,
Spicy Tahini Dressing,
Roasted Garlic and Herb,
Carrot Ginger Dressing

best caesar dressing ever

- **2 tsp** kosher salt
- **2 tsp** coarsely ground black pepper
- juice of **1** lemon
- **12 cloves** garlic
- **4 tsp** red wine vinegar
- **4 tsp** Worcestershire sauce (OR imitation OR soy sauce)
- **¼ cup** Dijon mustard
- **¾ cup** mayo
- **1⅓ cups** oil

Place all ingredients except oil into a food processor fitted with the "S" blade.

Process until the garlic is well blended into the rest of the ingredients.

While processor is running, slowly drizzle in oil.

Dressing will stay fresh in an airtight container, refrigerated, for up to 2 weeks.

carrot ginger dressing

- **2 large** carrots, peeled and chopped
- **1** shallot, peeled and halved
- **2 Tbsp** roughly chopped ginger
- **¼ cup** white miso paste
- **¼ cup** rice vinegar
- **3 Tbsp** toasted sesame oil
- **3 Tbsp** water
- **¼ cup** canola oil

Place carrots, shallot, and ginger into a food processor fitted with the "S" blade.

Pulse until finely grated. Add remaining ingredients except oil.

Purée, scraping down the sides as needed.

While processor is running, slowly drizzle in oil.
Process for 1 minute.

Transfer to a container with an airtight lid.

Dressing will stay fresh, refrigerated, for up to 5 days.

roasted garlic and herb dressing

3 Tbsp finely chopped herbs (I like parsley and cilantro)

1 head roasted garlic (see below)

1 Tbsp Dijon mustard

½ cup mayo

juice of **½** large lemon

½ tsp kosher salt

¼ tsp coarsely ground black pepper

Squeeze roasted cloves out of the garlic skin.

Place all ingredients into a food processor fitted with the "S" blade or into the cup of an immersion blender.

"Juzz" until smooth and creamy. Transfer to a container with an airtight lid. Dressing will stay fresh, refrigerated, for up to 1 week.

ROASTED GARLIC

Heat oven to 375°F / 180°C

Cut off the top of the garlic head to expose the cloves.

Drizzle 1 tablespoon olive oil over the top.

Sprinkle a small pinch of salt and pepper over the exposed cloves.

Wrap entire bulb in a foil packet.

Bake for 40-45 minutes.

diner style vinaigrette

3 cloves garlic, minced

1 tsp granulated garlic

½ tsp coarsely ground black pepper

1 tsp granulated onion

1 tsp kosher salt

1 tsp dried parsley

3 tsp cider vinegar

3 tsp red wine vinegar

1 tsp fresh squeezed lemon juice

1 tsp Dijon mustard

14 Tbsp olive oil

Place all ingredients into a bowl or a jar with a tight-fitting lid.

Whisk or shake well to combine. Transfer to a container with an airtight lid.

Dressing will stay fresh in the refrigerator in an airtight container for up to 3 weeks.

Remove from refrigerator 10 minutes before using and shake well before pouring.

turmeric vinaigrette

1 inch fresh turmeric, peeled

1 garlic clove

1 Tbsp preserved lime or lemon purée, store bought or homemade (p. 24) (alternatively, you can use **2 Tbsp** fresh lemon or lime juice)

1 Tbsp honey

2 Tbsp water at room temperature

3 Tbsp oil

kosher salt, to taste

coarsely ground black pepper, to taste

Place all ingredients except oil into a blender or a food processor fitted with the "S" blade.

Pulse until everything is finely minced.
Slowly drizzle in oil.

Depending on how salty your preserved limes/lemons are, you may not need to add salt, so taste to adjust seasoning!

Transfer to a container with an airtight lid.

Dressing will stay fresh, refrigerated, for 10 days.

creamy sesame dressing

3 Tbsp mayo

4 Tbsp tahini

2 Tbsp + 2 tsp rice vinegar

2 tsp sesame oil

2 cloves garlic, minced

¼ inch ginger, minced

2 Tbsp soy sauce

¼ tsp kosher salt

½ tsp coarsely ground black pepper

2 Tbsp honey

¼ cup canola oil

Place all ingredients except oil into a jar with a tight-fitting lid.

Shake it up.

Add oil; shake again for 1 minute until combined!

Transfer to a container with an airtight lid and refrigerate for up to 2 weeks.

meme's big batch lemon vinaigrette

2 Tbsp minced garlic

2 cups extra virgin olive oil

2¼ cup fresh squeezed lemon juice (from about **10** lemons)

2 Tbsp Dijon mustard

2¼ tsp kosher salt

1 tsp freshly cracked black pepper

Place all ingredients into a jar with a tight-fitting lid.

Shake well till combined.

Remove from refrigerator 10 minutes before using and shake well before pouring.

This dressing will stay fresh in the fridge for 3-4 weeks! No joke!!!

old school balsamic vinaigrette

2 cloves garlic, minced

2 tsp Dijon mustard

6 Tbsp balsamic vinegar

4 Tbsp cider vinegar

½ tsp kosher salt

½ tsp coarsely ground black pepper

2 tsp honey

1 cup + 2 Tbsp avocado oil

Place all ingredients into a bowl or a jar with a tight-fitting lid.

Whisk or shake well to combine. Transfer to a container with an airtight lid.

Remove from refrigerator 10 minutes before using and shake well before pouring.

Dressing will stay fresh in the refrigerator in an airtight container for up to 3 weeks.

creamy greeny dressing

8 cloves garlic

1 cup chopped scallions

1 cup fresh parsley leaves

1 Tbsp Dijon mustard

zest of **1** lemon

⅓ cup lemon juice

⅔ cup oil (I use half olive, half canola)

1 tsp kosher salt

½ tsp coarsely ground black pepper

Place all ingredients except oil into a food processor fitted with the "S" blade.

Pulse until well blended. With processor running, slowly drizzle in oil.

Transfer to a container with an airtight lid.

Serve any way you'd like!

Dressing will stay fresh, refrigerated, for up to 2 weeks.

spicy tahini dressing

1 cup prepared tehina

2 Tbsp fresh lemon or lime juice

2 Tbsp seasoned rice vinegar

1 garlic clove, minced

1 shallot, finely diced

2 Tbsp harissa

¼ tsp kosher salt

3 Tbsp olive oil

Place all ingredients into a bowl or a jar with a tight fitting lid.

Stir vigorously with a whisk or shake well till combined. Transfer to a container with an airtight lid.

Dressing will stay fresh in the refrigerator in an airtight container for up to 3 weeks.

cilantro lime dressing

1 Tbsp minced garlic

juice of **8** limes (about **½ cup**)

2 Tbsp honey

⅓ cup avocado oil

¼ tsp kosher salt

½ cup cilantro leaves

Place all ingredients except cilantro into a blender or a food processor fitted with the "S" blade.

Pulse to combine.

Add cilantro leaves. Process until leaves are finely chopped.

Store in an airtight container and serve with everything or drink from a spoon.

Dressing will stay fresh, refrigerated, for up to 7 days.

raspberry vinaigrette

½ cup seedless raspberry jam

1 Tbsp Dijon mustard

1 Tbsp finely diced shallots

2 Tbsp fresh lime juice

2 Tbsp balsamic vinegar

¾ tsp kosher salt

¼ cup extra virgin olive oil

Place all ingredients into a bowl or jar with a tight fitting lid.

Whisk or shake well until everything is combined. Transfer to a container with an airtight lid.

Dressing will stay fresh, refrigerated, for up to 2 weeks.

salatim

WHEN I HEAR THE WORD "SALATIM," I AM TRANSPORTED TO MY SHABBOS TABLE. OR YOUR SHABBOS TABLE. OR MY MOTHER'S. REALLY, ANY SHABBOS TABLE. SET NICELY, WITH CHALLAH ON THE BOARD, A KIDDUSH CUP, FULL CHAIRS, AND AN ASSORTMENT OF LITTLE BOWLS FILLED WITH CRUNCHY, BRIGHT, FRESH SALADS READY TO BE PILED ON PEOPLE'S PLATES AND DEVOURED OVER LAUGHS, TORAH (PROBABLY A FEW SQUABBLES AND SPILLS FROM THE LITTLE ONES), AND MOSTLY, LOTS OF LOVE. NO SHABBOS MEAL CAN BEGIN IN OUR HOME WITHOUT AN ASSORTMENT OF THESE SALATIM.

moroccan carrots

4 carrots peeled, cut with a ridged carrot slicer into ¼ inch rounds

2 tsp kosher salt

2 Tbsp extra virgin olive oil

1 lemon, halved, juiced

¼ tsp cumin

1 tsp spicy paprika

½ tsp coarsely ground black pepper

¼ tsp kosher salt

1 cup cilantro leaves

Add carrots and salt to a small pot; cover with water.

Place pot over high heat; bring to a boil.

Allow carrots to boil for 4 minutes until carrots are easily pierced with a skewer but not mushy.
(MUSHY CARROTS ARE A HUGE NO-NO HERE!)

Drain carrots; return to the pot while the pot is still hot.

Add remaining ingredients except cilantro; stir gently to combine.

Add cilantro leaves if serving immediately; otherwise, store carrots in an airtight container in the fridge for up to 5 days, adding the cilantro before serving!

israeli salad

8 small cucumbers, cut into ¼ inch dice

2 plum tomatoes, cut into ¼ inch dice

½ purple onion, minced

1½ tsp kosher salt

1 tsp coarsely ground black pepper

2 lemons, juiced

2 Tbsp extra virgin olive oil

Place all ingredients into a bowl.

Toss to combine.

OPTIONAL ADD-INS

1 jalapeño pepper, minced

½ cup parsley leaves, chopped

1 green bell pepper, cut into ¼ inch dice

dovi's pickle salad

1 (19-oz/560 gram) can pickles, diced

½ small yellow onion, minced (that's **8 Tbsp**)

4 tsp white vinegar

½ tsp granulated garlic

⅛ tsp kosher salt

scant **¼ tsp** coarsely ground black pepper

Place all ingredients into a large bowl.

Toss to combine.

> **PHOTO ORDER**
> **CLOCKWISE FROM TOP LEFT CORNER**
> Beet Salad, Red Pepper Carpaccio, Zucchini Carpaccio, Moroccan Carrots, Israeli Salad, Morrocan-Sih Carrot Slaw, Fennel + Avocado Salad, Dovi's Pickle Salad (in small bowl on plate), Kohlrabi Salad, Fire Roasted Eggplant, Spicy Cucumber Salad

kohlrabi salad

2 kohlrabi, trimmed, peeled

¾ tsp kosher salt, or more to taste

¼ tsp freshly ground black pepper, or more to taste

juice of **1** lemon (about **2 Tbsp**)

2-3 Tbsp olive oil

½ cup chopped fresh parsley

Cut kohlrabi in half, then slice into thin, flat panels (approximately ⅛"x½"x3").

Place kohlrabi into a large bowl.

Add salt, pepper, lemon juice, oil, and parsley.
Toss to coat and blend.

Season to taste with additional salt and pepper, as needed.

rachel's spicy cucumber

14 very small cucumbers, sliced on mandoline (**3 cups**)

1-2 red Thai chilis, sliced on mandoline

1 clove garlic, minced

1¼ tsp kosher salt

3 Tbsp lemon juice

Place all ingredients into a bowl.

Stir to combine.

Store in an airtight container until serving.

> **NOTE**
> This salad gets better as it sits!

roasted red pepper carpaccio

3 bell peppers

8 tsp olive oil, divided

zest of **1** lemon, then cut lemon in half

1 cup niçoise olives, chopped

½ cup capers, chopped

½ cup fresh parsley, chopped

1 shallot, finely chopped

⅛ tsp kosher salt for each layer

¼ tsp coarsely ground black pepper for each layer

Roast peppers over an open flame.

Once charred, place in a bowl and seal tightly with plastic wrap.
Cover bowl with a towel.
Allow to steam for at least 15 minutes.
Peel off and discard charred skin.

Cut peppers into 3 large pieces, discarding any seeds.

Place 2 teaspoons olive oil into a serving dish.
Add a layer of peppers.

Marinade layer: Add 2 teaspoons oil, ⅓ of the zest, a small squeeze of lemon juice, ⅓ each olives, capers, parsley, shallots, salt and pepper.

Repeat twice more for a total of 3 pepper layers and 3 marinade layers.

Place plastic wrap directly on top final layer; seal dish.

Refrigerate at least 1 day before serving!!!

moroccan-ish carrot slaw

14 oz (400 g) grated carrots

1 jalapeño pepper, very thinly sliced (optional)

1 tsp kosher salt

1 tsp coarsely ground black pepper

1 Tbsp paprika

¼ cup cider vinegar

¼ cup honey

1 Tbsp extra virgin olive oil

1 Tbsp Dijon mustard

¼ cup pomegranate arils

Place all ingredients into a large bowl.
Mix thoroughly.

Allow to sit for at least 5 minutes, then mix again.

Taste to adjust seasoning.

Will remain fresh in the fridge for up to 5 days. It will soften as it sits.

roasted beet salad

4-5 small or **3-4 large** red beets, trimmed and scrubbed

1½ tsp kosher salt, divided

4 Tbsp olive oil, divided

¼ tsp freshly ground black pepper, or more to taste

juice of **1** lemon (about **2 Tbsp**)

1 tsp ground cumin

3-4 Tbsp chopped fresh cilantro

Preheat oven to 350°F / 180°C.
Cut a few large pieces of foil.

Place beets on a few layers of foil. Sprinkle beets with about ½ teaspoon salt; drizzle with 2-3 teaspoons oil.
Wrap foil tightly around beets to create a tight packet.

Roast for 1-2 hours (depending on size) or until very tender (a fork should be able to slide in and out easily).

When beets are done, remove from oven and allow beets to cool and rest in the foil.

Peel beets when cool; skins should slide off effortlessly.
Cut beets into ½ inch cubes and place into a large bowl.

Add remaining 1 teaspoon salt, oil, pepper, lemon juice, cumin, and cilantro.
Toss to coat and blend.
Season to taste with additional salt and pepper, as needed.

shaved fennel & avocado salad

2 large or **3 small** fennel bulbs

2 ripe avocados, peeled, pitted, and diced into ¼-inch cubes

2 cups assorted cherry tomatoes, halved

juice of **1½** lemons (about **3 Tbsp**)

¼ cup olive oil

1½ tsp kosher salt

½ tsp freshly ground black pepper

Trim fennel bulb root ends and cut off woody stalks from the top of the bulbs, reserving 1 tablespoon feathery fronds for garnish.

Cut fennel bulbs in half. Using a mandoline or Asian slicer, carefully shave fennel into paper-thin slices (should yield about 8 cups).

Place shaved fennel into a large bowl.

Add avocados, tomatoes, lemon juice, olive oil, salt, and pepper.
Toss to coat and blend.
Season to taste with additional salt and pepper, as needed.

Serve garnished with reserved fronds.

zucchini carpaccio

ZUCCHINI

3 zucchini, sliced on a mandoline on the thinnest option

FOR EACH LAYER OF ZUCCHINI YOU'LL NEED

⅛ tsp kosher salt

⅛ tsp coarsely ground black pepper

½ tsp balsamic vinegar

⅓ tsp extra virgin olive oil

GREMOLATA

1¼ cups sliced blanched almonds

1 small shallot, minced

1 cup pitted Kalamata olives, roughly chopped

¼ tsp coarsely ground black pepper

1 Tbsp olive oil

Layer zucchini slices in a single layer in a serving dish so they slightly overlap, covering the surface of the dish.

Top the layer of zucchini with salt, pepper, balsamic, and oil.

Add another slightly overlapping layer of zucchini.

Repeat the seasoning process.

Keep going until all the zucchini is used.

Top zucchini with one last layer of salt, pepper, balsamic, and oil.

Place plastic wrap directly over zucchini. Cover dish tightly and refrigerate till ready to serve with gremolata, below. (Carpaccio will stay fresh in the fridge for up to 10 days!).

GREMOLATA

Set a small pan over medium high heat.
Add sliced almonds.

Cook for about 3 minutes, stirring constantly, until almonds are slightly toasted and just becoming fragrant.
Immediately transfer to a bowl to stop the cooking.

Once almonds have cooled, roughly chop them.

Combine with remaining gremolata ingredients in a bowl.

TO SERVE ZUCCHINI CARPACCIO

Lay zucchini slices flat on a platter.

Top with a few teaspoons gremolata.

fire roasted eggplant

1 eggplant, washed and dried

¼ tsp kosher salt

¼ tsp coarsely ground black pepper

1 lemon, halved

2 Tbsp olive oil

OPTIONS FOR SERVING

techina

Israeli style ground meat

chummus

herb salad

Place a small piece of foil over the stem of the eggplant (this will keep it pretty for presentation).

Place whole eggplant directly over a high flame on a gas burner.

Roast for 2-3 minutes until you start to smell an amazing barbecue aroma. At this point the side touching the fire should be mostly charred.

Using a pair of tongs (not your hands!), rotate the eggplant so that the next side can char.

Keep doing this and slightly adjusting the eggplant so that all of it has come into direct contact with the fire at some point until the whole eggplant is charred.

Remove eggplant from fire; place into a bowl.
Seal bowl tightly with plastic wrap.
Cover with a kitchen towel.
Allow eggplant to steam for 35-45 minutes.

Remove the towel and plastic wrap. At this point there should be some juice accumulated in the bowl; discard that liquid.

Wearing gloves, peel off and discard the charred skin of the eggplant.

Wet your hands just a little, remove any remaining eggplant skin, and then gently pat the eggplant dry with a paper towel.

Place in a serving dish or a Pyrex bowl. Using a knife, make ¼ inch cuts vertically through the eggplant, starting just below the stem until the bottom.

Turn the eggplant on its side to create a "fan" of eggplant. Sprinkle with salt and pepper. Squeeze lemon over the top and drizzle with oil.

Serve hot or cold!

NOTES

Sometimes I like to sauté 1 lb ground beef in 1 tsp canola oil together with ½ tsp each of salt, pepper, and cumin, and 1 clove minced garlic until cooked, and then pile it on top of the eggplant and drizzle the whole thing with techina!

shuk salad

WALK THROUGH THE SHUK AND STOP AT ANY CAFE OR SIDEWALK RESTAURANT OF ANY TYPE, AND ANY DISH YOU ORDER WILL MOSTLY LIKELY COME WITH SALAD ON THE SIDE. USUALLY IT IS SERVED IN A LITTLE BOWL, MADE OF WHATEVER VEGETABLES ARE ABUNDANT AND CRUNCHY IN THE MARKET THAT DAY. IT'S ALWAYS BRIGHT AND FRESH, ALWAYS HAS CUCUMBERS, ONIONS, AND TOMATOES, AND IS ALWAYS DELICIOUS. EACH PLACE WILL CUSTOMIZE THEIRS AND THIS IS MY FAVORITE VERSION.

4 Persian cucumbers, halved, deseeded, cut into half moons

1 purple onion, diced

10 heirloom cherry tomatoes, quartered

2 carrots, peeled, diced

1 red pepper, diced

1 orange pepper, diced

1 long green spicy pepper, minced

5 radishes, thinly sliced

½ cup freshly squeezed lime juice (from **6-8** limes)

3 Tbsp extra virgin olive oil

1½ tsp kosher salt

1 tsp coarsely ground black pepper

½ cup spiced nuts (page 82)

1 tsp sumac

Place all the vegetables into a large bowl.
Add lime juice, oil, salt, and pepper to the vegetables; stir to combine.

Mix in spiced nuts.
Sprinkle sumac over the top.

Serve and enjoy.

burnt cauliflower and herb salad

YOU'VE SEEN ENOUGH SHABBOS ROUNDUPS BY NOW (OR MAYBE FAST-FORWARD 50 YEARS, INSTAGRAM IS A THING OF THE PAST, YOU HAVE NO IDEA WHAT SHABBOS ROUND-UPS ARE AND YOU'RE USING THIS BOOK ON A DIFFERENT PLANET THAT YOU FLEW TO VIA THE NEW INTERGALACTIC HIGHWAY?), WHICH IS WHERE I SHOW YOU WHAT I'VE PREPARED FOR SHABBOS EACH WEEK, TO KNOW THAT BURNT, LEMONY CAULIFLOWER IS A STAPLE IN MY HOUSE. WHAT YOU DON'T KNOW IS WHAT I DO WITH IT THE NEXT DAY!

YIELD: 2+ QUARTS

CAULIFLOWER

2 (24 oz) bags frozen cauliflower florets

3 Tbsp olive oil, divided

4 cloves garlic, minced (about **1½ Tbsp**)

1½ tsp kosher salt

½ tsp freshly ground black pepper

2 tsp turmeric

1½ tsp sumac

½ tsp paprika

1 lemon, halved

HERB SALAD

½ cup chopped parsley

½ cup chopped cilantro

½ cup chopped scallions (from about 4 scallions)

2 Tbsp chopped mint, optional

1 small purple onion, finely diced (about **1 cup**)

1-1½ Tbsp white vinegar

kosher salt, to taste

freshly ground black pepper, to taste

CAULIFLOWER

Preheat oven to 350°F / 180°C. Line a baking sheet with heavy duty foil; coat with 1 tablespoon olive oil.

Toss frozen cauliflower with 2 tablespoons oil, garlic, salt, pepper, turmeric, sumac, and paprika.
Spread out on baking sheet in a single layer.
Roast undisturbed for about 45 minutes (DO NOT OPEN OVEN DOOR DURING THAT TIME!).

After 45 minutes, cauliflower should begin to get crispy and charred.
Open oven door, remove baking sheet, and squeeze both halves of the lemon over the cauliflower. DO NOT MIX OR STIR. Just squeeze over the top, return to oven and cook for 5-6 minutes.

Serve and enjoy.

HERB SALAD

While cauliflower is roasting, combine parsley, cilantro, scallions, mint, and onion in a large bowl.

When cauliflower is done, add to the herb mixture, tossing to combine.
Add vinegar; toss to combine.
Season to taste with salt and pepper.

Serve warm or cold.

NOTE

If not serving the same day, combine herbs with cauliflower before serving time.

spiralized beet, radish, and carrot salad

I LOVE A SALAD THAT'S AS BEAUTIFUL AS IT IS DELICIOUS. THE JEWEL TONES OF THIS BOWL ARE SO EYE APPEALING THAT EVEN IF YOU'RE NOT THE HUGEST FAN OF ONE OF THE COMPONENTS, I GUARANTEE YOU WON'T BE ABLE TO STAY AWAY!

2 beets, peeled, spiralized or julienned

4 large carrots, peeled, spiralized or julienned

1 watermelon radish, peeled, spiralized or julienned

1 cup chopped scallions

2 Tbsp seasoned rice vinegar

2 Tbsp fresh lime juice

2 Tbsp soy sauce

1 tsp sambal oelek

1 Tbsp honey

1 Tbsp avocado oil

½ cup cilantro, for garnish

In a large bowl, combine beets, carrots, radish, and scallions.
Toss together to tangle the spiralized vegetables into each other.

Add remaining ingredients to a small bowl; whisk to combine.
Pour over salad 10 minutes before serving to allow vegetables to marinate.

Garnish with cilantro and enjoy!

artichoke and arugula salad

THIS SALAD COMES FROM ONE OF MY CLOSE FRIENDS, SHANA W. SHE IS ONE OF THE BEST SALAD MAKERS I KNOW AND THIS IS MY VERSION OF A SALAD THAT SHE JUST "THROWS TOGETHER." I ABSOLUTELY LOVE ARTICHOKES (AS YOU'LL SEE THROUGHOUT THE BOOK, AND I URGE YOU, IF YOU'VE NEVER HAD THEM BEFORE, TO SEEK THEM OUT!) THEY HAVE THE MOST UNIQUE, CREAMY TEXTURE AND A TASTE THAT IS JUST IRREPLACEABLE.

2 (14 oz) packages frozen artichokes hearts/bottoms (about **15-18**), thawed

3 Tbsp olive oil

1-2 cloves garlic, minced (about **1 tsp**)

juice from **1½** lemons (about **3 Tbsp** fresh lemon juice)

1 tsp kosher salt

½ tsp freshly ground black pepper

1 small shallot, minced (about **¼ cup**)

2 cups baby arugula

Inspect thawed artichoke hearts, trimming away any leftover choke hairs, if necessary.
Halve hearts (or quarter, if very large).

Heat oil in a large skillet over medium heat.
Add artichokes and garlic, sautéing briefly.

Cover the pan; allow artichokes to soften for 12 minutes, stirring every few minutes.
Remove cover; sauté until artichokes brown slightly, 3-4 minutes.

While still on the heat, add lemon juice, salt, and pepper.
Remove from heat.
Add shallot; stir to blend.

Toss with baby arugula before serving.

farro and cherry tomato salad

I CALL THIS MY SHEMITTAH SALAD. SHEMITTAH, AKA THE "SABBATICAL YEAR," COMES ALONG EVERY SEVENTH YEAR. DURING THAT YEAR, JEWISH FARMERS IN ISRAEL TAKE A COMPLETE BREAK FROM HARVESTING OR PLANTING THEIR FIELDS (THERE ARE DIFFERENT CUSTOMS REGARDING HOW THIS IS DONE. I JUST BUY THE PRODUCE, SO YOU'LL HAVE TO ASK A FARMER. OR A RABBI.). WELL, THAT LEADS TO A VERY UNFORTUNATE YEAR OF REDUCED FRUIT AND VEGETABLE CONSUMPTION. AND IF YOU LIVE IN ISRAEL, I WILL VALIDATE YOU RIGHT NOW ... REALLY A YEAR AND A HALF UNTIL WE'RE FULLY RESTORED! OF COURSE, WE MOVED HERE DURING A SHEMITTAH YEAR. SO NOT ONLY DID I HAVE TO FIGURE OUT HOW TO SHOP IN FOREIGN SUPERMARKETS, WHERE I HAD NO IDEA HOW TO SAY TOMATO PASTE OR TOOTHPICK (TRUE STORY), BUT I HAD TO LEARN HOW TO SHOP AND COOK DURING SHEMITTAH. GRAIN SALADS BECAME MY BEST FRIEND, BECAUSE SOMEHOW WE NEVER RUN OUT OF GRAINS (OR TOMATOES), AND THIS IS MY FAVORITE ONE. SO MUCH SO THAT I MAKE IT ALL 6 YEARS BETWEEN SHEMITTAHS!

FARRO

1 Tbsp olive oil

2 cups farro (or barley)

3½ cups water

1 tsp kosher salt

SALAD

cooked farro

1½ cups quartered cherry tomatoes

¼ cup cilantro (or parsley), chopped

2 Tbsp extra virgin olive oil

¼ cup red wine vinegar

1 Tbsp honey

½ tsp kosher salt

¼ tsp coarsely ground black pepper

Put oil and farro into a small pot over low heat.
Stir for 1-2 minutes until farro is slightly toasted.
Add water and salt.

Bring to a boil.
Cover, reduce heat to low, and simmer for 20-25 minutes until farro is tender and water is absorbed.

Cool farro for 10 minutes before making salad.

Add all salad ingredients to a large bowl. Stir to combine.

If you want to prepare in advance, you can combine everything WITHOUT the tomatoes. Add tomatoes before serving.

quinoa, sweet potato, cranberry & almond salad

IT'S UP FOR DEBATE WHETHER THIS IS, IN FACT, A SALAD AT ALL. HOWEVER, QUINOA IS TECHNICALLY A SEED (NOT A GRAIN), IT'S HEALTHY, COLORFUL, HAS FRUITS AND VEGETABLES IN IT, AND I SERVE IT ALONGSIDE A PROTEIN. SO NOW IT'S A SALAD.

1 cup red quinoa, rinsed well

¼ cup + 1 tsp extra virgin olive oil, divided

¾ tsp kosher salt, divided

1¾ cups water

3 Tbsp apple cider vinegar

2 Tbsp honey

½ tsp coarsely ground black pepper

1 large sweet potato (or **2 small**), peeled, cut into ¼ inch cubes

¼ tsp paprika

¼ tsp sumac

½ tsp granulated garlic

½ cup slivered almonds

1 cup dried cranberries

4 scallions, chopped

1 cup parsley leaves, chopped

Place 1 teaspoon oil, quinoa, and ½ teaspoon salt in a small pot (that comes with a lid) over medium high heat.
Stir for about 1 minute to ever so slightly toast the seeds.
Add water. Bring mixture to a boil.

Reduce heat to low, cover the pot, and allow quinoa to simmer for about 15 minutes, until it is tender.

Pour cooked quinoa into a fine mesh strainer and allow any excess liquid to strain out. (Quinoa retains lots of liquid, so, although this step is not absolutely necessary, it is highly recommended.)

Add vinegar, honey, and pepper to the drained quinoa. Mix to distribute evenly.

While quinoa is simmering, preheat oven to 350°F / 180°C. Line 2 baking sheets with parchment paper.

Place sweet potato, 2 tablespoons oil, paprika, sumac, garlic, and ¼ teaspoon salt onto 1 prepared baking sheet.

Bake for 35 minutes, until the edges of the sweet potato begin to char ever so slightly.
Remove from oven; with a spatula, gently move sweet potatoes around so they don't stick.

Meanwhile, place almonds on second prepared baking sheet.
Bake for 10-12 minutes, stirring every few minutes, until almonds are fragrant and lightly golden.

Allow each element to cool separately.

Once cooled, combine quinoa, sweet potato, almonds, cranberries, scallions, and parsley in a large bowl.

Serve cold and enjoy!

TIPS + TRICKS

Rinsing quinoa is an essential step. The quinoa seed has a bitter exterior and rinsing the quinoa very well actually removes that outer layer and yields a more palatable flavor!

layered grain salad
with orange juice dressing

THIS SALAD DEFINITELY TAKES ME BACK IN TIME. YES, BECAUSE IT'S LAYERED, WHICH LENDS ITSELF TO A TRIFLE BOWL — AND WHO EVEN HAS A TRIFLE BOWL ANYMORE? BUT ALSO, BECAUSE THIS WAS PROBABLY THE FIRST SALAD THAT I CAME UP WITH ON MY OWN AND SERVED ON REPEAT WHENEVER I HAD COMPANY FOR LIKE THE FIRST 5 YEARS OF MY MARRIAGE. AS I SIT AND WRITE THIS, I WONDER HOW IT FELL OUT OF THE ROTATION, BECAUSE MY MOUTH IS LITERALLY WATERING THINKING BACK TO HOW GOOD AND FRESH AND BRIGHT THIS SALAD IS. FEEL FREE TO CUSTOMIZE IT BY ADDING OR SUBTRACTING ANY VEGGIES YOU LIKE.

SALAD

1 cup quinoa, uncooked

1 cup wheat berries, barley, cracked wheat, or wheat, uncooked (see instructions below)

1 tsp salt, divided

2 Tbsp umami plum vinegar, for wheat berries

1 cup frozen edamame beans, partially defrosted

1 clove garlic, minced

2 Tbsp soy sauce

1 cup shredded carrots (about **2**)

1½ cups diced red bell peppers (**1 large**)

1½ cups diced green bell peppers (**1 large**)

½ cup finely chopped parsley

¼ cup chopped jalapeño pepper (optional)

3 cups shredded purple cabbage

¾ cup scallions, chopped

ORANGE JUICE DRESSING

¼ cup orange juice

¼ cup apple juice

¼ cup apple cider vinegar

2 Tbsp fresh ginger, grated

1 tsp kosher salt

¾ tsp coarsely ground black pepper

TO COOK GRAINS

To cook quinoa: To a medium pot, add 1½ cups water, ½ teaspoon salt, and quinoa.
Bring to a boil, reduce heat to low, and cover.
Let simmer 15-20 minutes until fluffy.

To cook wheat berries (or other grain): To a medium pot, add 2 cups water, ½ teaspoon salt, and wheat berries.
Bring to a boil, reduce heat to low, and cover.
Let simmer 20-25 minutes until fluffy.
Once grain is fully cooked, drizzle with 2 tablespoons umami plum vinegar; stir to combine.

TO COOK EDAMAME

Place edamame in a nonstick pan over medium heat.
Cook, stirring often, until most of the steam evaporates.
Add garlic and soy sauce.

Cook for 1 minute.
Remove from heat; set aside to cool.

DRESSING

Combine all dressing ingredients in a jar with a tightly fitting lid; shake vigorously. This recipe makes a very light dressing. It makes a little more than you will need, but it can be enjoyed with other veggie combinations as well.

TO ASSEMBLE

Layer vegetables and grains in a large glass bowl. Make sure to alternate colors.

Pour dressing over top layer of salad, allowing it to flow all the way to the bottom.

TIPS + TRICKS

This salad can also be served in individual glasses for a personalized trifle look!

NOTE

I love a good crunch factor in a salad, so sometimes I fry a few wonton wrappers and then lightly crush them and top the salad with them!

sumac scented fennel & tangerine salad

I LOVE FENNEL. RAW, ROASTED, BRAISED … ANY WAY. IT MIGHT BE BECAUSE THE LICORICE-Y TASTE WAS IMPLANTED IN US AS SMALL CHILDREN WHEN MY GRANDMOTHER WOULD DIP THE CORNER OF A CLOTH INTO ARAK IF WE HAD A TOOTHACHE … MAYBE. EITHER WAY, I LOVE IT. IT'S CRUNCHY, FRESH, AND THE PERFECT SALAD ADDITION TO A TABLE FULL OF HEAVY DISHES (SHOUT OUT TO SHABBOS). THE ORANGE PAIRS PERFECTLY WITH THE FENNEL AND WHAT I LOVE MOST ABOUT THIS IS THAT THE SEASON FOR THIS BRIGHT, WAKE-UP-YOUR-TASTE-BUDS SALAD IS THE WINTER!

2 large fennel bulbs

2 tangerines (OR **1** blood orange OR tangelo OR orange)

1 small purple onion, thinly sliced

¼ cup rice vinegar

2 tsp sumac, or more to taste

¾ tsp kosher salt

¼ tsp freshly ground black pepper

2 tsp honey

¾ cup olive oil

6 cups baby arugula OR baby spinach

Trim fennel bulb root ends and cut woody stalks from the top of the bulbs.

Cut fennel bulbs in half. Using a mandoline or Asian slicer, carefully shave fennel into paper thin slices (should yield about 8 cups).
Place shaved fennel into a large bowl.

Segment tangerines: Cut polar ends off. Using a serrated knife, gently cut away peel, sawing away around the curvature of the fruit to remove the peel and pith.

Working over a second bowl, make a cut on either side of each membrane, then give a slight push to release the fruit segment into the bowl.
You should be left with a mass of membranes.

Squeeze the membranes over a bowl or measuring cup to extract as much juice as possible; discard membranes.
Pour accumulated juices into a measuring cup to measure ¼ cup (you can supplement with orange juice if you don't have enough).

Remove any pits from tangerine segments; add segments to the fennel.

Prepare the dressing: In a large bowl, combine reserved ¼ cup tangerine juice, rice vinegar, sumac, salt, pepper, and honey. Whisk to blend.
Whisking continuously, slowly drizzle in olive oil until well blended and emulsified.
Season to taste, as needed.

Before serving, add arugula to fennel and tangerines.

Toss with half of the dressing, adding more as needed to coat.

VARIATION

Considering adding leftover chicken to this dish to make it a complete meal. You can shred leftover roasted chicken, slice some leftover grilled chicken, or even add some roughly chopped pieces of a good store bought rotisserie chicken!

tuna salad à la moi

THIS IS MY FAVORITE LUNCH SALAD. I COULD EAT IT, ON REPEAT, EVERY DAY. I KNOW, MERCURY. OK, FINE. EVERY OTHER DAY. IT'S FILLING, THE FLAVORS ARE PUNCHY, AND IT'S MY ABSOLUTE FAVORITE WAY TO EAT TUNA. MAKE IT TODAY, DOUBLE THE RECIPE, AND STORE IT IN AN AIRTIGHT CONTAINER FOR TOMORROW. IT IS ACTUALLY BETTER THE SECOND DAY.

2 cups shredded purple cabbage

1 cup shredded radicchio

1 cup chopped scallions

1 cup chopped cucumber

1 cup finely chopped celery

½ cup diced purple onion

1 cup parsley, chopped

1 cup chopped preserved lemons (page 24)

½ cup chopped capers

15 oz canned tuna in water, drained, roughly chopped

juice of **1** lemon

2 tsp paprika

1 tsp cayenne pepper

1 tsp kosher salt

½ tsp coarsely ground black pepper

Place all ingredients into a large bowl.
Toss well to combine.

Let sit for 5 minutes.

Toss again.

bbq chicken rice salad

AAAAAH! I CAN'T BELIEVE I CAN FINALLY SHARE THIS SALAD WITH THE WORLD. THIS IS ELI'S FAVORITE SALAD AND, OF COURSE, IT HAPPENED BY ACCIDENT. ELI HAD TO RUN OUT TO A LUNCH SOMEWHERE AND I HAD AGREED TO SEND A SALAD, WHICH AS SOON AS I COMMITTED TO, I PROMPTLY FORGOT. I ONLY HAD 2 BAGS OF LETTUCE IN MY HOUSE, SOME LEFTOVER RICE, AND A PACKAGE OF CHICKEN CUTLETS IN THE FREEZER. I QUICKLY THAWED THE CHICKEN, ADDED THE RICE TO THE SALAD TO BULK IT UP, AND TOPPED OFF THE WHOLE THING WITH THE BEST CAESAR EVER. BOOM, SALAD, FIT FOR MEN. AND WOMEN. AND CHILDREN.

6 skinless, boneless chicken cutlets

1½ cups favorite BBQ sauce, divided

2 cups prepared, warm (not boiling hot) white rice

4 cups romaine lettuce, cut into 2 inch pieces

2 cups arugula

1 cup radicchio, cut into ½ inch strips

1 purple onion, halved and thinly sliced

Best Caesar Dressing Ever (page 44)

Preheat a grill pan over medium high heat.

Meanwhile, combine chicken and 1 cup BBQ sauce in a bowl. (Reserve remaining sauce.)
Toss to combine.

Cook chicken for 4 minutes on the first side and 3 minutes on the second side.
Remove chicken from pan and immediately brush with remaining BBQ sauce.
Set aside.

Place veggies into a large wide bowl; add warm rice.
Toss to combine.

Dress salad with Best Caesar Dressing Ever.

Slice chicken on a bias and fan out over the salad.
Drizzle with any accumulated juices.

Serve and enjoy!

brick roast salad
with creamy scallion dressing

THE BEST STEAK SALAD EVER WITH THE SOFTEST MEAT THANKS TO THE AMAZING ADVICE FROM RABBI YEHOSHUA FROM GOURMET GLATT WHO TAUGHT US TO SLICE A BRICK ROAST IN HALF AND GET 2 ROASTS FOR THE PRICE OF 1!

CREAMY SCALLION DRESSING

3 cloves garlic

1½ cups chopped scallions

½ cup parsley leaves

½ cup cilantro leaves

1 Tbsp fresh lemon juice

1 tsp low sodium soy sauce

1 tsp cider vinegar

1 tsp kosher salt

1 tsp coarsely ground black pepper

5 Tbsp mayonnaise

2 tsp honey

¼ cup avocado oil

BRICK ROAST

1 brick roast (ask your butcher to slice it in half crosswise for you; you will have 2 pieces)

1 head garlic, minced

4 tsp kosher salt, divided

4 tsp garlic powder, divided

4 tsp coarsely ground black pepper, divided

SALAD

1 cooked brick roast, sliced against the grain

1 batch Creamy Scallion Dressing

4 cups butter lettuce

4 cups arugula

1 purple onion, halved, thinly sliced

1 cup heirloom cherry tomatoes, halved

NOTES

If you want to serve this on Shabbos day, adjust the cooking time to 6 minutes on one side and 4 on the second. Put on the plata (hot plate) 1 hour before serving.

CREAMY SCALLION DRESSING

Process all ingredients except oil in the bowl of a food processor fitted with the "S" blade.

Once smooth, slowly drizzle in oil.

Transfer to an airtight container; will stay fresh in the fridge for up to 1 week.

Shake well before pouring.

BRICK ROAST

Divide the minced garlic into 4 equal portions.

Rub each side of the 2 pieces of brick roast with ¼ of the garlic, 1 teaspoon salt, and 1 teaspoon pepper. At this point both pieces of brick roast should be rubbed in spices on both sides.

(Wrap one piece of the brick roast in a few layers of plastic wrap and then 1 layer of foil. Freeze until the night before you want to make this salad again!)

Place marinated brick roast in the fridge to marinate for at least 3 hours or up to overnight.
A few hours before cooking, remove meat from fridge and allow to come to room temp.

Preheat barbecue grill or any heavy bottomed skillet (I use cast iron, but you can use any pan as long as it is NOT nonstick) over medium high heat.
Once pan is hot, add 1 tablespoon canola oil and the meat.

Sear for 7-8 minutes on one side and 5 minutes on the second side for medium rare meat.

Remove from pan. Cover meat loosely with foil; allow to rest for 8-10 minutes before slicing.

Slice against the grain and serve!

TO SERVE

On a large platter, toss together butter lettuce and arugula.

Top with onion and tomatoes.

Lay sliced roast over the salad.

Drizzle with dressing.

NOTES

If you live in Israel you want to ask for a roast that comes from the chuck. This will be the most similar. The roast may be cut thinner so don't ask to have it cut in half until you see it. You are looking for the meat to be about 1-1½ inches thick when you cook it.

VARIATION

Rub each side of brick roast with 2 tsp lime juice, 1 Tbsp onion soup mix, and 1 tsp olive oil. Grease a baking dish; add 3 thinly sliced onions, ¼ cup dry red wine, ½ tsp coarsely ground black pepper + pinch kosher salt. Place seasoned meat on top. Broil on low broil (400°F / 200°C) for 12 minutes on the first side and 10 minutes on the second side. Reduce heat to 350°F / 180°C, cover baking dish, and cook for 10 more minutes for rare-medium rare or longer until desired doneness! Slice against the grain and serve!

grilled chicken panzanella salad

I LOVE A GOOD PANZANELLA SALAD. SOMETHING ABOUT THAT GRILLED BREAD SOAKING UP THE VINAIGRETTE IS JUST SO SATISFYING TO BITE INTO. I ALWAYS FEEL THAT THE LACK OF PROTEIN IS A MISSED OPPORTUNITY, THOUGH. IF I'M GOING TO GO THROUGH THE EFFORT TO START GRILLING BREAD, I'M GOING TO ADD SOME CHICKEN ONTO THAT GRILL AND MAKE THIS A WHOLE MEAL, OR AT LEAST A SIGNIFICANT PART OF A BEAUTIFUL SHABBOS MEAL!

TOMATO VINAIGRETTE

4 medium (or **2 very large**) tomatoes, sliced crosswise

2 Tbsp red wine vinegar

3 shallots, finely chopped

5 Tbsp extra virgin olive oil

1 tsp kosher salt

1 tsp coarsely ground black pepper

CHICKEN

8 chicken cutlets

3 Tbsp olive oil

2 tsp kosher salt

1 tsp coarsely ground black pepper

3 cloves garlic, minced

SALAD

6 oz package beef fry

1 loaf whole wheat sourdough bread, crust cut away, sliced lengthwise to make two long slices of bread.

1 purple cabbage, diced into 1 inch cubes (or **1 lb** shredded purple cabbage)

2 kohlrabi, peeled and diced into 1 inch cubes

4 cucumbers, diced into 1 inch cubes

2 large red bell peppers, diced into 1 inch cubes

1½ cups yellow cherry tomatoes, halved

1 cup radishes, thinly sliced

1 purple onion, thinly sliced

4 scallions, thinly sliced

1 cup Kalamata olives, halved

1 Thai chili, thinly sliced

VINAIGRETTE

Using a box grater, grate cut sides of the tomatoes down to the skin; discard skin. Add remaining dressing ingredients to the tomato pulp; mix well.

Refrigerate till serving.

CHICKEN

Add chicken, olive oil, salt, pepper, and garlic to a zip top bag. Marinate in the fridge for at least 1 hour.

TO ASSEMBLE

Lightly oil grill pan; heat over medium heat.

Grill chicken cutlets until cooked through (2-3 minutes on each side). Set aside.

Lay strips of beef fry on grill (be careful, it splatters); grill until crispy. Set aside.

Drizzle olive oil and salt on bread; grill for 2 minutes on each side.

To assemble, thinly slice chicken, cut bread into 1-inch cubes, and crumble the beef fry.
Add vegetables, olives, and chili to a large bowl; add chicken, bread cubes, and beef fry.

Drizzle tomato vinaigrette over the salad before serving.

NOTE

This dressing stays fresh for only 2 days in the refrigerator.

modernized taco salad with grilled skirt steak

WE'RE BRINGING BACK THE TACO SALAD. ONLY THIS TIME AROUND, IT'S NOT A BUNCH OF SALAD LETTUCE, WITH BROWN CHOPPED MEAT, SALSA, AND SOME TORTILLA CRUMBS. NO NO NO. IT'S NOW COLORFUL, FRESH, CITRUSY, SLIGHTLY SPICY, TANGY, AND CRUNCHY. ALL THE ELEMENTS NEEDED FOR A PARTY SALAD. WHICH IS BASICALLY WHAT A TACO SALAD IS, BECAUSE IT'S JUST THIS HUGE PLATE OF YUMMINESS THAT'S PRETTY UNIVERSALLY LOVED!

ADOBO SKIRT STEAK

1 (3 lb/1.3 kg) skirt steak

2 Tbsp adobo paste (from a can of chilies in adobo, you can freeze the rest for later use)

juice of **1** lime

2 cloves garlic, minced

DRESSING

2 cloves garlic

1 Tbsp honey

1 tsp kosher salt

½ tsp coarsely ground black pepper

¼ cup freshly squeezed lime juice

1 cup cilantro leaves

½ cup canola oil

SALAD

4 cups lettuce

1 avocado, sliced

1 cup shredded purple cabbage

5 radishes, thinly sliced

1 tomato, diced

½ cup canned corn

½ cup sumac pickled onions (page 22, optional but recommended)

1 cup crushed tortilla chips

ADOBO SKIRT STEAK

Place skirt steak into a bowl; cover with cold water.
Soak steak for 1-2 hours. (This helps tenderize and remove some of the excess saltiness.)
Once skirt steak has soaked, remove from water and pat dry with paper towels.

Cut skirt steak into 3 inch pieces.

Combine remaining steak ingredients in a bowl or ziptop bag; mix well to combine.

Add skirt steak; toss to coat evenly. Cover bowl tightly with plastic wrap. Refrigerate for at least 2 hours or overnight.

To cook steak, place a grill pan over high heat.
Once pan is hot, grease lightly and add skirt steak pieces.
Cook for 2 minutes on each side for medium rare.

Remove from heat; allow to rest for 8 minutes.
Once meat is rested, use a sharp knife to cut pieces into slices against the grain.
Set aside.

CILANTRO LIME DRESSING

Place the first 5 dressing ingredients into a food processor fitted with the "S" blade.
Pulse till garlic is finely minced.

Add cilantro; with motor running, slowly drizzle in oil.

Transfer to an airtight container; refrigerate until serving.

TO ASSEMBLE

Place a bed of lettuce on a large platter.
Top with the vegetables in any way you like.
Top with skirt steak slices; drizzle with dressing.

Sprinkle with crushed tortilla chips to garnish.

or grilled shrimp

grilled chicken salad with facon vinaigrette

FACON TOOK THE KOSHER WORLD BY A STORM WITH ITS SUPER THINLY SLICED, SLIGHTLY SMOKY, FATTY BEEFINESS THAT CRISPS UP EVER SO PERFECTLY AND I AM ALL FOR IT. IT ADDS CRUNCH AND LAYERS OF FLAVORS TO ANYTHING IT'S ADDED TO, AND IT RELEASES JUST THE RIGHT AMOUNT OF FAT TO MAKE THIS SALAD DRESSING THE MOST LUSCIOUS, UMAMI PACKED DRESSING EVER.

FACON VINAIGRETTE

1 (6 oz) package Facon, cut into ½ inch pieces

2 small shallots (or **1 large**), finely minced

¼ cup red wine vinegar (OR apple cider vinegar or white wine vinegar)

1 Tbsp grainy Dijon mustard

1 Tbsp honey

⅛ tsp kosher salt

¼ tsp coarsely ground black pepper

½ cup avocado oil

GRILLED CHICKEN

6 thin chicken cutlets

3 Tbsp oil

5 Tbsp Montreal steak seasoning

SALAD

3 cups spinach

3 cups shredded kale

2 shallots, thinly sliced

2 pears, cut into thin wedges

Facon Vinaigrette, above

VARIATION
Swap out pears with peaches, nectarines, or plums.

FACON VINAIGRETTE

Prep all the ingredients and place next to the stove along with a whisk.

Place Facon in a cold pan over medium low heat.
Cook the Facon for 5-6 minutes, stirring often so that the Facon gets crispy and renders its fat.

When Facon is crisp, use a slotted spoon to transfer it to a plate, reserving the fat in the pan. There should be about 1½-2 tablespoons fat.

Turn off the heat; while the pan is still hot, add in the shallots. Stir.
After about 1 minute, add the vinegar.
Use the whisk to scrape up any bits that are stuck to the bottom.

Stir in mustard, honey, salt, and pepper.
While stirring, slowly drizzle in oil.

Add ½ the crispy Facon to the pan; transfer into a jar or airtight container.
Reserve remaining Facon bits.
Refrigerate till using.

Remove vinaigrette from fridge a few hours before serving so it can come to room temp, or gently reheat to serve.

GRILLED CHICKEN

In a bowl, combine all chicken ingredients.

Heat grill pan over medium high heat.

Grill chicken for 3 minutes on the first side and 2 minutes on the second side.
Remove from pan; set aside until ready to assemble salad.

TO ASSEMBLE

Combine greens in a wide, shallow bowl.
Top with shallots.

Slice grilled chicken into strips and lay over the top, together with pear wedges.

Shake reheated vinaigrette; spoon over the salad.

Garnish with reserved Facon bits.

asian chicken crumble salad

THIS IS WHAT I WANT FOR DINNER MOST NIGHTS. AFTER A LONG DAY OF COOKING BREAKFAST, LUNCH, AND DINNER, TESTING RECIPES, AND JUST GENERAL MOM-ING, I'M TIRED AND HUNGRY. I DON'T WANT SOMETHING HEAVY BECAUSE MY BODY IS TOO EXHAUSTED TO HANDLE ANYTHING LIKE THAT. I WANT SOMETHING LIGHT AND CRUNCHY BUT IT MUST HAVE A CHEWY, HOT AND COLD ELEMENT TO IT. THAT'S WHAT THIS IS. THE GROUND CHICKEN CRUMBLE, WHICH SOUNDS CRAZY BUT I GUARANTEE IS QUITE GENIUS, IS SO DELICIOUS AND SATISFYING AND TOGETHER WITH THE COLD PROPERLY CUT CUCUMBER (ALTHOUGH IF YOU DON'T PROPERLY CUT YOUR CUKES, I WON'T TELL ANYONE), AND THE UMAMI PACKED, PUNCHY VINAIGRETTE HITS JUST THE SPOT!

CHICKEN CRUMBLE

1 lb ground white or dark chicken

1 tsp freshly grated ginger

2 cloves garlic, grated

2 Tbsp soy sauce

1 Tbsp seasoned rice vinegar

1 tsp sesame oil

1 tsp sriracha

ASIAN DRESSING

3 Tbsp soy sauce

2 tsp sesame oil

1 tsp miso paste

2 tsp rice vinegar

1 clove garlic, grated

¼ cup water

SALAD

2 baby bok choy, chopped

4 cucumbers halved, seeded, chopped

6 radishes, sliced

1 Thai chili, thinly sliced

4 scallions, chopped

1 tsp black sesame seeds

CHICKEN CRUMBLE

Combine all chicken crumble ingredients in a medium bowl.

Heat a nonstick pan over medium high heat.
Add chicken mixture; cook, stirring often to break up mixture and create crumbles. This should take 6-7 minutes.
Once chicken is cooked through, turn off heat and set aside.

ASIAN DRESSING

Add all dressing ingredients to a bowl or a jar with a tightly fitting lid. Whisk or shake to combine.

Store in an airtight container in the refrigerator for up to 2 weeks.

SALAD

Add all the vegetables to a large bowl, along with chicken crumble.

Drizzle dressing over the top, starting with 3 tablespoons and adding 1 tablespoon more at a time till it is dressed how you like it.

Garnish with black sesame seeds.

VARIATION

If you're not a ground chicken lover (I'm looking, fine, talking, errrr, writing to you, Eli) you can absolutely swap out the same amount of ground chicken for turkey or beef.

salad toppers

WHAT IS A SALAD WITHOUT SOMETHING CRUNCHY TO THROW ON TOP? FINE, STILL A SALAD. BUT IN MY BOOK, A SALAD HAS TO BE NOT ONLY DELICIOUS BUT ALSO PACKED WITH DIFFERENT TEXTURES. IT'S WHAT TURNS OUR SALADS FROM RABBIT FOOD TO PEOPLE FOOD. HENCE THE SALAD TOPPERS: A BREAKAWAY FROM THE MOST TRADITIONAL TOPPER OF ALL...THE CROUTON. CROUTONS ARE NICE, AND I'M DOWN FOR THEM; BUT I ALSO LIKE TO HAVE NON BREAD, HEALTHIER OPTIONS TO ADD TO MY MORE HEALTHY SALAD. THESE SALAD TOPPERS ARE NOT A COMPROMISE BECAUSE THEY ARE PACKED WITH SO MUCH FLAVOR YOU WON'T EVEN MISS THE CROUTONS.

savory granola

2 cups rolled oats (can use gluten free)

1 cup slivered almonds

½ cup roughly chopped pecans

¼ cup extra virgin olive oil

3 Tbsp maple syrup

¼ cup honey

1½ tsp smoked paprika

1 tsp granulated garlic

1½ tsp kosher salt

Store granola for up to 2 weeks in a cool dry cupboard or in the freezer for up to 3 months!

Preheat oven to 350°F / 180°C. Line a baking sheet with parchment paper.

In a large bowl, combine oats and nuts.

In a small bowl combine remaining ingredients, mixing well.

Pour ALMOST all of the honey mixture over the oats, reserving about 2 Tbsp (which you can eyeball, it doesn't need to be exact!).
Use a spoon to mix the honey mixture really well into the oats and nuts until all are evenly coated.

Pour granola onto prepared baking sheet; spread into an even layer.
Bake for 15 minutes, then use a spoon to gently stir the granola around.
Spread granola out again into an even layer; return to oven for 10 minutes.

Remove pan from oven, mix granola one last time, then spread out again on the pan. Before returning pan to the oven, drizzle reserved honey mixture just over the top of the granola and immediately return to oven for 3-4 minutes.

Remove pan from oven; do not stir or mix granola; just set aside and allow to cool completely for 2 hours.
Then gently break up granola and transfer to a jar or container (don't break them too much, because clumps are the best and they will continue to break as you transfer to a jar or container!)

spiced nuts

Preheat oven to 400°F / 200°C.

Place seeds and nuts onto a small baking sheet; mix to combine.
Drizzle with oil and sprinkle with spices.

Mix everything well to combine.
(I like to put on disposable gloves and do this with my hands. I just find it easier.)

Bake for approximately 12 minutes, stirring every 4-5 minutes until seeds and nuts are nicely toasted.

Allow nuts to cool completely in the pan; transfer to an airtight container.

These nuts can stay fresh in your freezer for up to a month.

½ cup sunflower seeds

½ cup sliced raw almonds

½ cup pumpkin seeds

½ cup pine nuts

¼ cup sesame seeds

3 Tbsp canola oil

2 tsp paprika (or smoked paprika for fun!)

1 tsp granulated garlic

½ tsp granulated onion

¼ tsp mustard powder

you make miso happy

soup

3 freezer stocking stocks

IN MY OPINION, THE SOUP SECTION OF ANY COOKBOOK MUST START WITH A GOOD SOUP BASE. YES, ADDING WATER TO A SOUP CAN WORK. SHOULD IT BE YOUR GO TO, THOUGH? NO. EVERY TIME WE USE AN INGREDIENT IN COOKING, WE HAVE AN OPPORTUNITY TO ADD FLAVOR TO OUR FOOD. WATER, AN INGREDIENT IN MANY CASES, IS FLAVORLESS. ADDING A FLAVORLESS ELEMENT (WHICH IN A SOUP'S CASE IS A KEY INGREDIENT TO THE FINAL PRODUCT), IS COUNTERPRODUCTIVE TO WHAT YOU ARE INTENDING TO DO. HAVING AN ARSENAL OF STOCKS READY AT YOUR FINGERTIPS IS AS EASY AS DUMPING A BUNCH OF STUFF INTO A POT, LETTING IT COOK FOR A LONG TIME (WHICH IS A HANDS OFF PROCESS), STRAINING, DIVIDING, AND FREEZING. ONCE YOU HAVE A FREEZER WELL STOCKED WITH, WELL, STOCKS, THEN FLAVORFUL SOUPS, STEWS, GRAINS, AND SAUCES ARE NEVER OUT OF REACH!

beef/veal stock

OPENING MY FREEZER THE DAY I'VE LOADED UP ON SOME BEEF OR VEAL STOCK IS ONE OF THE BEST FEELINGS. THE POSSIBILITIES OF WHAT I CAN MAKE WITH A FORTIFIED, DELICIOUS, FLAVORFUL STOCK AT MY FINGERTIPS SENDS ALL THE CREATIVE NERVE ENDINGS IN MY BODY SHOOTING LIKE FIREWORKS. STEAK WITH A VELVETY PAN SAUCE, A HEARTY BEEF STEW, A MEATY ONION SOUP, AN UMAMI PACKED BROTH FOR DUMPLINGS, A RICH AND CREAMY MUSHROOM SAUCE ... THE POSSIBILITIES ARE ENDLESS AND THE FLAVOR IT CONTRIBUTES TO WHATEVER DISH YOU ARE MAKING IS SIMPLY UNBEATABLE.

YIELD: 6 QUARTS

15 lb (6.8 kg) beef or veal bones (I like to use a mixture of knee bones that still have meat on them and marrow bones)

1-2 Tbsp olive oil

4 large or **6 medium** carrots, peeled, trimmed, and cut into chunks

6 stalks celery, trimmed, and cut into chunks

2 onions, peeled, trimmed, and quartered

2 Tbsp tomato paste

8 quarts (2 gallons) cold water

1 Tbsp kosher salt

½ Tbsp black peppercorns

2 bay leaves

Preheat oven to 400°F / 200°C. Line 2 sheet pans with foil.

Arrange all beef/veal bones on prepared pans to fit tightly in 1 layer.
Roast for 45 minutes-1 hour, turning once during the cooking, until bones are nicely browned and caramelized.

Heat oil in large stock pot over medium high heat.
Add carrots, celery, and onions, turning to coat.
Sauté for 4-6 minutes, or until vegetables just begin to brown.

Add tomato paste, stirring to distribute; cook for 1-2 minutes until paste begins to darken in color (do not burn).
Add water, roasted bones, and any accumulated juices.
Add salt, peppercorns, and bay leaves.

Bring to a boil, then reduce heat to low.
Simmer, uncovered, for about 2 hours.
Skim foam off the surface as needed for clarity.

Cover pot; simmer for 4-6 hours.
Broth will be rich in color and aroma.
Remove from heat; cool slightly.
Strain through a fine sieve.

Discard solids. Skim excess fat off surface as needed.

When cool, stock can be portioned into containers and frozen for up to 6 months or refrigerated for up to 1 week.

PHOTO ORDER
CLOCKWISE FROM TOP
Beef Stock
Vegetable Stock
Chicken Stock

chicken soup + stock

I MAKE A 16 QUART POT OF CHICKEN SOUP. EVERY. SINGLE. WEEK. YES, IT'S A LOT. WE LOVE IT ON FRIDAY NIGHTS AND THE LEFTOVERS ON SUNDAY NIGHTS. KEEP IN MIND THAT IF YOU WANT YOUR SOUP LOADED WITH CHICKEN AND VEGGIES (AND WHO DOESN'T WANT THAT?), YOU NEED TO HAVE ROOM SO THAT YOU HAVE ENOUGH BROTH TO SERVE WITH ALL THAT GOOD STUFF. OH, AND, IF YOU'RE GOING THROUGH ALL THAT EFFORT (WHICH INCIDENTALLY IS REALLY NOT THAT MUCH EFFORT, BUT STILL...) THEN YOU MIGHT AS WELL BE ABLE TO LOAD UP YOUR FREEZER WITH SOME STOCK TO HAVE READY FOR WHENEVER YOU NEED! MAKE THE SOUP ON WEDNESDAY MORNING. LET IT COOK ALL DAY. POP IT IN THE FRIDGE AT NIGHT. THEN, ON FRIDAY MORNING, PULL IT BACK OUT FOR ITS SECOND BOIL AND SIMMER!

2 whole chickens cut into eighths (without skin)

5 carrots, peeled, cut into 2 inch pieces

2 yellow onions, peeled

1 leek, white and light green only, chopped

1 stalk celery, peeled, cut into 2 inch pieces

2 zucchini, cut into 2 inch pieces

1 kohlrabi, peeled

2 parsnips, peeled, cut into 2 inch pieces

1 celery root, peeled

2 cups fresh dill

2 cups fresh parsley greens

1 cup cilantro

2 Tbsp whole black peppercorns

3 Tbsp kosher salt

2 pieces flanken, optional

1 turkey neck, optional

SPECIAL EQUIPMENT

3-4 mesh soup bags

To the first mesh bag, add all the chicken.
To the second mesh bag, add all the vegetables.
To the third mesh bag, add dill, parsley, cilantro, and peppercorns.
(If using flanken and/or turkey neck, add that to the fourth bag.)

Place a very large pot (I use a 16 quart pot) over high heat.
Into the dry pot, place the bag with the chicken.
Sear chicken (and meat/turkey, if using) over high heat for 6-8 minutes, turning the bag every few minutes or so to sear on all sides.

Once chicken has browned, bring the pot to the sink and start filling with water. (The water should immediately become slightly golden due to the searing.)
Add the vegetable and herb bags to the pot while it's filling. Add salt.

Return pot to heat (do not cover yet!); bring soup to a boil.
Boil, uncovered, for about 40 minutes, skimming off any foam that accumulates. (I have a fine mesh skimmer that I use to make the job easier.)

After 40 minutes, reduce heat to the lowest setting (I actually move the pot to my smallest burner and then put it on low heat), cover the pot, and allow soup to simmer for 8 hours or overnight.

Remove from heat; allow soup to cool down slightly for 2 hours. Separate vegetables from soup (see Tips + Tricks).

After 2 hours, place the pot in the fridge.
Use a strainer to clarify soup; ladle cold soup into containers to use as stock.

If serving the soup on Friday night, take the pot out of the fridge 4 hours before Shabbos, bring the soup up to a boil, and then reduce heat and let the soup simmer until Shabbos!

TIPS + TRICKS

To serve: Remove bags from the pot and place all the vegetables into a shallow bowl. Shred chicken; add to the bowl. (If you added flanken or turkey, shred them as well.) Spoon 1 or 2 ladles of the broth over the veggies and chicken and bring that to the table so everyone can help themselves!

BONUS

If you do accumulate a few pints of chicken stock and are looking for ways to use them, try using the stock for rice, couscous, chicken dishes, meat braises, as a base for other soups, to thin out sauces, or just to have for the emergency feeling-under-the-weather-need-a-mug-of-soup situations.

NOTE

When adding matzah balls to the soup, here's what I do. I heat the soup up on Friday, then transfer all the bags to a 9x13 inch pan and add a few ladles of broth. That pan is covered and placed on the plata. I then portion out a few containers of broth so I have some plain stock in my freezer to use when I need them, and then I cook the matzah balls right in the pot. This way my frozen soup stays clear.

vegetable stock

SINCE WE DON'T MIX MEAT AND DAIRY, THERE ARE TIMES WHEN WE ARE IN NEED OF AN ALL-VEGETABLE BROTH. WHEN A CHICKEN OR BEEF STOCK CAN'T BE ADDED, EITHER BECAUSE THE SOUP IS DAIRY OR YOU'RE LOOKING TO CREATE A VEGETARIAN ONE, ADDING WATER TO YOUR POT INSTEAD OF A FLAVORFUL STOCK IS JUST A MISSED OPPORTUNITY. MAKE THIS BATCH, DIVIDE IT INTO PINT OR QUART CONTAINERS, FREEZE, AND NEVER EVER COMPROMISE ON FLAVOR AGAIN!

YIELD: 6 QUARTS

15 carrots, peeled, trimmed, and roughly chopped

15 stalks celery, trimmed, and roughly chopped

6 onions, peeled, trimmed, and roughly chopped

4 leeks, white and light green only, trimmed, cleaned thoroughly, and roughly chopped

2 Tbsp kosher salt, divided

4½ Tbsp olive oil, divided

1 head garlic, excess peel removed and top ⅛-inch cut off

6 Portobello mushrooms, cleaned and quartered

2 zucchini, scrubbed, trimmed, and roughly chopped

2 large tomatoes, quartered

½ tsp coarsely ground black pepper

½ cup dried porcini mushrooms

1 cup boiling water

1 Tbsp black peppercorns

1 bay leaf

5 quarts (20 cups) cold water

Preheat oven to 375°F / 190°C. Line 3 baking sheets with foil; set aside.

Combine carrots, celery, onions, and leeks in a very large mixing bowl.
Season with 2 teaspoons kosher salt; drizzle with 3 tablespoons olive oil. Toss to coat with oil.

Spread into an even layer on 2 prepared baking sheets.
Bake for 45 minutes, stirring occasionally, or until vegetables become slightly caramelized and are golden in color.

Combine garlic head, mushrooms, zucchini, and tomatoes in a large mixing bowl.
Season with 1 teaspoon kosher salt and ½ teaspoon black pepper; drizzle with 1½ tablespoons olive oil. Toss to coat with oil.
Spread into an even layer on remaining baking sheet.
Bake for 35 minutes, stirring occasionally, or until vegetables become very tender.

Meanwhile, soak dried mushrooms in boiling water to rehydrate and plump.

When the vegetables are done, transfer all vegetables and pan juices into a large stock pot.
Add reserved mushrooms (with the soaking water), peppercorns, bay leaf, remaining salt, and 5 quarts cool water.
Bring to a boil over medium high heat, then reduce heat to low.
Simmer, covered, for about 2 hours.
Broth will be rich in color and aroma.

Strain through a fine sieve. Discard solids.

When cool, stock can be portioned into containers and frozen for up to 6 months or refrigerated for up to 1 week.

roasted sweet potato, apple, and leek soup

THIS COMBO SCREAMS FALL AND RIGHTFULLY SO. IT'S JUST HEARTY ENOUGH TO WARM YOUR BONES ON THOSE NEWLY CRISP AUTUMN DAYS BUT STILL LIGHT ENOUGH TO EAT WHILE THE SUN STILL STICKS AROUND FOR DINNERTIME! ROASTING ALLOWS THE SWEET POTATO AND APPLES TO DEEPEN IN FLAVOR AND BRING OUT THESE REALLY LAYERED CARAMEL-Y NOTES THAT JUST TAKE THE SOUP OVER THE TOP!

6 sweet potatoes, peeled and cut into 1 inch cubes

3 green apples, peeled and cut into 1 inch pieces

5 Tbsp extra virgin olive oil, divided

1½ tsp coarse black pepper, divided

1 Tbsp kosher salt, divided

2 leeks, white and light green only, halved, thinly sliced

2 tsp curry powder

½ inch fresh ginger, minced

1 tsp tomato paste

8 cups vegetable broth (page 86)

2 cups almond milk

TO GARNISH

good quality olive oil

dehydrated apple chips

Preheat oven to 350°F / 180°C. Line 2 baking sheets with parchment paper.

Spread sweet potatoes and apples on the pans in a single layer, being sure not overcrowd them.
On each pan, drizzle 2 tablespoons olive oil and sprinkle with 1½ teaspoons pepper and 1 teaspoon salt.
Roast for 45 minutes.

Meanwhile, place a large pot over medium high heat.
Add remaining tablespoon olive oil, leeks, and remaining salt to the pot.
Cover; allow leeks to sweat for 3-4 minutes.

Remove cover and continue cooking for 25 minutes, stirring every 5 minutes so that leeks don't burn.

Once leeks have softened, add curry powder, ginger, and tomato paste; stir to combine and cook for 2 minutes.
Add roasted apples, sweet potatoes, and any accumulated pan juices.

Add stock. Bring soup up to a boil, uncovered.
Reduce heat, cover, and simmer for 30 minutes to 1 hour.

After simmering, add almond milk and "juzz" with an immersion blender until creamy.

Taste to adjust seasoning.

Serve hot and enjoy.

VARIATION

Go ahead and swap out the sweet potato for any orange vegetable you like. Just don't forget to roast it first. What's really nice is that if you use a vegetable that's difficult to peel (like acorn squash or pumpkin), you can go ahead and roast it with the skin and then easily just scoop out the flesh!

nondairy "dairy delicious" soup

IF YOU GREW UP IN THE FIVE TOWNS IN THE 1990'S YOU UNDERSTAND WHY THIS SOUP, WHICH IS ABSOLUTELY PAREVE, IS CALLED "THE DAIRY DELICIOUS" SOUP. ALTHOUGH EVERY FAMILY I KNEW HAD A DIFFERENT NAME FOR THAT RESTAURANT, ITS ONION ROLLS, RICE AND CHEESE, AND PEROGIES WERE FIVE TOWNS' STAPLES, ALONG WITH THEIR FAMOUS SOUPS! LONG GONE, THE MEMORIES OF THOSE DISHES STAND STRONG FOR BOTH ELI AND MYSELF. THAT IN AND OF ITSELF IS SOMETHING, SINCE ELI AND I DO NOT AGREE ON ALMOST ANYTHING FOOD RELATED! SO A FEW YEARS AGO WE SET OUT TO RECREATE ONE OF OUR FAVORITE SOUPS, THE VEGETABLE SOUP! IT SOUNDS CRAZY TO THINK THAT A VEGETABLE SOUP COULD GET KIDS IN THE 90'S SO EXCITED, BUT IT WAS, WELL, DELICIOUS (IF YOU'RE SENSING A THEME HERE, THEN YOU'RE CATCHING ON). AFTER A LOT OF CROWDSOURCING AND PICKING THE BRAINS OF OTHERS WHO GREW UP WITH A DEEP LOVE OF THIS SOUP, WE FINALLY RECREATED IT IN A WAY THAT SATISFIED BOTH OF US. ITS CREAMY TEXTURE FROM THE DUMPLINGS ADDS RICHNESS AND THE VEGETABLES ADD FLAVOR AND BODY.

2 Tbsp extra virgin olive oil

1 large onion, diced

2 large celery stalks, peeled, diced

3 large carrots, peeled, cut into 1 inch rounds

2 tsp + 1 Tbsp kosher salt, divided

1 tsp coarsely ground black pepper

1 tsp garlic powder

2 Tbsp flour

5 large potatoes, peeled, cut into 1¾ inch chunks

2 cups frozen, finely chopped cauliflower

2 cups frozen string beans (I use haricot vert)

10 cups water

DUMPLINGS

3 eggs

1½ tsp kosher salt

1 cup room temp water

2½ cups flour

Heat a large pot over medium heat.
Add oil, onion, celery, carrots, 2 teaspoons salt, and pepper.
Cook for 5-10 minutes until the veggies have softened and are translucent but have not browned.
Add garlic powder and flour; stir to combine.
Add remaining ingredients and remaining tablespoon salt; stir to combine.

Raise heat to high; bring soup to a boil.
Reduce heat to low; simmer, covered, for 1 hour.

Uncover; continue to cook, stirring every so often, until soup has slightly reduced and thickened.

Meanwhile, prep and cook dumplings; add to the soup.
Turn up heat; bring soup back to a boil.

At this point you can serve or you can cover and leave over lowest heat to keep warm!

DUMPLINGS

In a bowl, whisk together eggs and salt until slightly foamy.
Add water; whisk again.
Add flour; stir with a spoon to create a thick batter.

Bring the soup up to a boil 20 minutes before serving.

With a spoon, scoop up about 2 tablespoons of dough.
Use a second spoon to scrape teaspoons of batter from the spoon right into the boiling soup. Repeat with remaining batter.

After dumplings float to the top, cook for 3-4 minutes, serve the soup, and enjoy!

NOTE

If you make the soup in advance, I recommend cooking the dumplings in salted boiling water and only adding them to the soup pot 15 minutes before serving!

To do that, set a medium pot of water over high heat.

Meanwhile prep dumplings as above.

Add 1 teaspoon salt to the boiling water.
Using two spoons, as above, drop little scoops of dough into the boiling water.
Once they float to the top, allow to cook for 1 minute. Use a slotted spoon to transfer to a container until serving the soup.

red lentil soup

I LOVE TO USE RED LENTILS IN MY SOUP BECAUSE OF HOW FAST THEY COOK UP. THIS SOUP IS LOADED WITH FLAVOR AND THE SQUEEZE OF LEMON JUST TAKES IT OVER THE TOP. THE LABANE WHIP AT THE END IS JUST EXTRA, COMPLETELY OPTIONAL AND SHOULD BY NO MEANS LIMIT YOU FROM MAKING THIS SOUP IF YOU CHOOSE NOT TO INCORPORATE AND KEEP THE SOUP PAREVE! I USE THE BASIC RECIPE AS A BASE ALL WINTER LONG, ADDING JALAPEÑOS, THROWING IN A FEW CHICKEN BOTTOMS (AND THEN OF COURSE LEAVING OUT THE LABANE), AND EVEN SOMETIMES BLENDING THE WHOLE THING FOR A PUREED VERSION!

1 tsp olive oil

5 stalks celery, chopped (I like to peel mine also to remove the strings)

1 large onion, chopped

1½ tsp kosher salt, divided

1¼ tsp coarsely ground black pepper, divided

1 tsp sumac

1 tsp turmeric

1 tsp paprika

2 tsp minced garlic (about **4 cloves**)

1 Tbsp tomato paste

2 tsp preserved lime purée (page 24) (or juice of **2** limes)

1½ cups red lentils

4 cups vegetarian stock

6 cup water

juice of **1** lemon

OPTIONAL DAIRY GARNISH

1 cup labane (whisked for 2 minutes)

To a pot over medium heat, add oil, celery, onion, ½ teaspoon salt, and ¼ teaspoon pepper.
Cook, stirring often, for 20 minutes until vegetables have softened.
Add the spices, garlic, tomato paste, and lime.
Cook, stirring, for 2 minutes.

Add lentils, stock, water, remaining teaspoon salt, and remaining teaspoon pepper.

Bring to a boil.
Reduce heat to low; simmer for 1 hour, stirring every so often.

Squeeze in lemon juice.

Simmer for 20 minutes.

Serve hot with a dollop of whipped labane.

TIPS + TRICKS

To whip labane, simply place 8 ounces labane into a bowl and with an electric mixer, beat for 2-3 minutes. For extra fun flavor, try adding ¼ teaspoon sumac to the labane!

no cream cream of broccoli

I LOVE THE IDEA OF A CREAMY SOUP THAT DOESN'T ACTUALLY REQUIRE CREAM! THE WHITE BEANS THAT MAKE THE SOUP CREAMY COMPLETELY MELT AWAY, SO NO ONE WILL EVEN KNOW THEY'RE THERE. WHICH IS EXTREMELY IMPORTANT IN MY HOUSE!

2 Tbsp olive oil

1 onion, diced

1 Tbsp kosher salt

1 tsp coarsely ground black pepper

1½ (32 oz/.9 kg) bags frozen broccoli

½ (32 oz/.9 kg) bag frozen spinach (you can replace spinach with broccoli if you prefer)

32 oz vegetable stock (or any pareve stock)

6 cups water

1 (15 oz/425 g) can Great Northern white beans, drained and rinsed

1 bay leaf

Heat a large pot over medium high heat.
Add oil, onion, salt, and pepper.
Stir for 4-5 minutes until onions are translucent.

Add remaining ingredients.

Bring soup to a boil.
Reduce heat to low, cover, and simmer for 1-2 hours.

Remove from heat; remove and discard bay leaf.

"Juzz" soup with an immersion blender.
Be sure to "juzz" for a few minutes so that soup is fully blended and creamy!

Taste to adjust seasoning!

VARIATION

For dairy meals, substitute 1 tablespoon butter for 1 tablespoon of the olive oil.

meaty vegetable barley soup

THERE IS SOMETHING SO COZY AND COMFORTING ABOUT A BOWL OF SOUP THAT IS IN FACT A MEAL IN ITSELF. THE BONE IN THE MEAT CREATES A MAGICAL BROTH THAT TOGETHER WITH ALL THE VEGETABLES LAYS THE FOUNDATION FOR THE BARLEY TO SOAK UP ALL THESE DELICIOUS LAYERS OF FLAVORS THAT KEEP YOU COMING BACK TO THIS SOUP TIME AFTER TIME. I MAKE THIS SOUP AT THE BEGINNING OF THE LONG WINTER WEEKS, AND AGAIN DURING THE HOLIDAYS FOR THOSE LATE NIGHT MEALS WHEN NO ONE'S REALLY HUNGRY BUT YOU NEED TO SERVE SOMETHING AND IF YOU'RE GOING TO COOK ANYWAY, IT MIGHT AS WELL BE DELICIOUS!

2 pieces bone in flanken

1 Tbsp + 1½ tsp kosher salt, divided + more for sprinkling

2½ tsp coarsely ground black pepper, divided + more for sprinkling

2 Tbsp canola oil

4 carrots, diced

5 stalks celery, peeled and diced

1 large yellow onion, diced

1 leek, white and light green only, diced

1 kohlrabi, peeled and diced

2 zucchini, diced

1 Tbsp paprika

1 (15 oz/425 g) can tomato sauce

1½ cups dry red wine (I use cab)

20 cups water

½ cup chopped parsley

½ cup chopped cilantro (can use all parsley instead)

½ cup barley

kosher salt and coarsely ground black pepper for seasoning along the way

Heat a large pot over medium high heat.

Sprinkle salt and pepper on both sides of the flanken.
Add oil and flanken to the pot; brown meat on both sides (about 3 minutes per side).
Transfer flanken to a platter; set aside.

Add carrots, celery, onion, and leek to the pot; sprinkle with 1 teaspoon each salt and pepper.
Stir and cook until the onion and leek are translucent.

Add kohlrabi, zucchini, and ½ teaspoon each salt and pepper; stir to combine.

Cook for 5-7 minutes, stirring every 2-3 minutes.
Add paprika. Stir until combined; cook for 1 minute.
Add tomato sauce; cook for 3-4 minutes.
Add wine; use a wooden spoon to scrape up any bits from the bottom of the pot.

Return flanken to the pot; cook for 4-5 minutes.

Add water, parsley, cilantro, 1 tablespoon salt, and 1 teaspoon pepper.

Bring to a boil.
Reduce heat to low; cover and simmer for 2-3 hours, until meat is tender.

Remove meat from the soup; let it rest for 5-10 minutes.
Shred meat, discarding bones and fat; return meat to the pot.

Bring soup back to a boil, add barley, and cook until tender, about 40 minutes.
Taste to adjust seasoning.

TIPS + TRICKS

You can easily swap out the flanken for a whole chicken cut into eighths for a lighter but still delicious option.

FREEZING TIP

if you are planning to freeze the soup, after adding barley immediately take the soup off the heat. The barley will slowly cook in the residual heat. Refrigerate the soup overnight, then pour into containers to freeze the next day. When you reheat the soup, the barley will finish cooking without absorbing all the liquid.

miso vegetable soup

I LOVE A YEAR ROUND SOUP BECAUSE IN OUR HOUSE SOUP IS AN ALL SEASON FOOD! THE WAY I SEE IT, WE REALLY SHOULD BE EATING SOUP IN THE SUMMER ANYWAY, WHEN THE AIR CONDITIONING IS BLASTING AND YOU BASICALLY NEED AN INDOOR WINTER COAT AS OPPOSED TO THE WINTER WHEN YOU NEED, WELL, YOU KNOW ... THIS SOUP FITS THE BILL WHATEVER THE SEASON IS. THE DEPTH OF FLAVOR FROM THE UMAMI RICH MUSHROOMS, MISO, AND TOMATO PASTE, COMBINED WITH THE EVER SO SLIGHTLY ACIDIC VINEGAR AND THE SOFT, LUSCIOUS TOFU MAKE IT HEARTY ENOUGH FOR THE COLDEST WINTER NIGHTS AND LIGHT ENOUGH FOR THE HOT, STICKY SUMMER DAYS!

1 cup dried mushrooms

4 cups boiling water

1 Tbsp avocado oil

1 tsp toasted sesame oil

10½ oz (300 g) tofu cut into ½ inch cubes

2 Tbsp soy sauce, divided

1 onion, diced

1 leek, white and light green only, diced

3 carrots, peeled and diced

5 stalks celery, peeled and diced

3 cups sliced cremini mushrooms

¼ tsp kosher salt

2 zucchini, diced

5 scallions, chopped

3 Tbsp white miso

2 Tbsp ghojugang

1 Tbsp seasoned rice vinegar

1 Tbsp soy sauce

¾ tsp coarsely ground black pepper

6 cups vegetable stock or water

In a medium bowl, combine dried mushrooms and boiling water.
Cover bowl with plastic wrap; set aside.

Set a large pot over medium high heat.
Add oils, tofu, and 1 tablespoon soy sauce.
Stir often for 8-10 minutes so that tofu edges can crisp up.
Transfer crisped tofu to a platter; set aside.

Add onion, leek, carrots, and celery to the pot.
Cook, stirring often, for 12-14 minutes until onions and leeks begin to brown.
Add cremini mushrooms; stir to combine.
Cook for 5 minutes; stir in zucchini and scallions.
Return tofu to the pot.

Make a well in the center of all the vegetables, exposing the bottom of the pot; add miso and ghojugang.
Stir in the center of the vegetables and allow pastes to cook for 2 minutes.

Add vinegar, soy sauce, and black pepper.
Stir so that all the flavors are evenly distributed among the vegetables.

Strain dried mushroom liquid into a bowl, discard the rehydrated mushrooms, and add the mushroom liquid to the pot along with stock or water.
Stir to combine.

Bring soup to a boil.
Reduce heat to low and cover the pot.
Allow soup to simmer over low heat for 2-3 hours.

Serve hot and enjoy!

italian wedding soup

WHILE I WAS GROWING UP, THERE WERE A FEW DISHES THAT I SAW OVER AND OVER AGAIN IN MAGAZINES AND IN COOKBOOKS THAT JUST ALWAYS STOOD OUT. THE ITALIAN WEDDING SOUP, A FLAVORFUL BROTH FILLED WITH DELICIOUS MEATBALLS AND LOADED WITH RIBBON LIKE STRANDS OF LEAFY GREENS, IS ONE OF THEM. WHEN I FINALLY HAD MY OWN KITCHEN, IT WAS THE FIRST SOUP I SET OUT TO CREATE. FOR YEARS I KEPT ADJUSTING AND ADJUSTING UNTIL THE FLAVORS TASTED LIKE THEY DID IN MY MIND.

MEATBALLS

1 lb (453 g) lean ground beef

¼ cup unseasoned breadcrumbs (or gluten free crumbs)

1 egg, lightly beaten

2 cloves garlic, minced

1 cup fresh parsley, torn

½ tsp crushed red pepper flakes

2 tsp kosher salt

1 tsp coarsely ground black pepper

¼ tsp ground fennel seeds (optional)

1 Tbsp oil, for frying

SOUP

1 cup dried porcini mushrooms

4 cups boiling water

3 quarts chicken stock

4 cups baby kale, stems removed, cut into ribbons

In a large bowl, combine meatball ingredients except oil.
Form mixture into 1½ inch meatballs.

In a large Dutch oven or heavy bottomed pot over medium high heat, heat oil. Add meatballs in small batches; sauté meatballs, rotating each meatball so that it is seared on all sides.

Transfer to a platter; set aside.

SOUP

In a large bowl, steep dried mushrooms in boiling water for 30 minutes.

Into a second large bowl, strain mushroom liquid through a sieve lined with a cloth napkin.
Discard mushrooms.

Reserve 1½ cups mushroom liquid; transfer remaining liquid to a container and refrigerate for a different soup!

In the same pot you made the meatballs in, add reserved mushroom liquid and chicken stock.

Bring to a boil.
Reduce heat and simmer for 2 hours.

After 2 hours add meatballs and as much kale as you like (I like a lot!!!).

Serve hot and enjoy!!!

moroccan harira soup

THIS IS THE SOUP I DREAM ABOUT AT NIGHT.

IT'S THE SOUP OF MY CHILDHOOD. THE SOUP MY GRANDMOTHER MADE, THAT MY MOTHER MAKES, AND THAT I CRAVE. IT'S PACKED WITH NUTRIENT RICH VEGGIES, LENTILS, AND CHICKPEAS. FORTIFIED WITH SOME BEEF BONES, AND LIGHTENED UP WITH A MANDATORY SQUEEZE OF LEMON WHEN YOU EAT IT, IT'S PERFECTLY BALANCED.

TRADITIONALLY THIS SOUP IS SERVED BEFORE OR AFTER FASTS, TO NEW MOTHERS, AND TO THE SICK.

IT'S REALLY A COMPLETE MEAL. I IMAGINE THAT EVERY MOROCCAN FAMILY HAS A DIFFERENT VERSION OF THEIR HARIRA SOUP. THIS IS MINE. NORMALLY, YOU WOULD FIND TINY LITTLE VERMICELLI LIKE NOODLES IN THE SOUP, BUT I NEVER FOUND THEM NECESSARY, SO I LEAVE THEM OUT.

MY HOPE IS THAT YOU TAKE THIS SOUP, MAKE IT YOUR OWN, AND, LIKE MY GRANDMOTHER AND MOTHER, YOU TOO PASS IT DOWN.

2 Tbsp extra virgin olive oil

4 stalks celery, peeled and diced

1 yellow onion, peeled and diced

1 tsp kosher salt

1 tsp coarsely ground black pepper

4 tomatoes, peeled, seeds removed

1½ cups cilantro leaves, divided

1¼ cups parsley leaves, divided

1 cup brown or green lentils

2 tsp turmeric

½ tsp ginger

¼ tsp cumin

¼ tsp coriander

2 beef knee bones (OR **3** marrow bones), sprinkled with kosher salt and coarsely ground black pepper, roasted in a 400°F / 200°C oven for 40 minutes

1 cup frozen chickpeas (OR ½ cup dried chickpeas soaked overnight in an uncovered bowl in room temperature water, then rinsed and drained)

12 cups chicken or beef stock (or water)

lemon wedges, for serving

Heat a large pot over medium high heat.
Add oil, celery, onion, salt, and pepper.
Sauté for 6-8 minutes.

Meanwhile, in the bowl of a food processor fitted with the "S" blade, process tomatoes, 1 cup cilantro, and ¾ cup parsley until fully pureed. Set aside.

After onions and celery have softened, add lentils and remaining spices to the pot; stir for 2 minutes to combine.

Add roasted beef bones, tomato-herb purée, and chickpeas.
Stir to combine.

Add stock and remaining ½ cup each cilantro and parsley.

Bring soup to a boil.
Reduce heat, cover, and allow to simmer over low heat for 2 hours.

Serve hot with a squeeze of lemon and enjoy.

NOTE

Feel free to adjust spices to your liking, and add 1 cup of noodles or rice to the soup with the chicken stock. Just don't forget the lemon!

tom yum soup with salmon

TEN YEARS INTO OUR MARRIAGE, ELI AND I HAD THE AMAZING OPPORTUNITY TO TRAVEL TO THAILAND. WE GOT TO EXPLORE THE LAND AND MARKETS, SWIM IN ITS PIERCING BLUE WATERS, PULL ACTUAL RUBBER FROM RUBBER TREES, AND THE HIGHLIGHT, MEET SOME OF THE NICEST, MOST GRACIOUS PEOPLE IN THE WORLD. THAILAND AND ITS NATIVE PEOPLES ARE EXTREMELY ACCOMMODATING TO THE THOUSANDS OF JEWS WHO FLOCK THERE EVERY YEAR. THERE ARE MULTIPLE CHABAD HOUSES AND KOSHER RESTAURANTS, AND THEY WILL GO OUT OF THEIR WAY TO MAKE YOUR STAY AS COMFORTABLE AS POSSIBLE. WHILE WE WERE STAYING IN ONE OF ITS MANY BEAUTIFUL HOTELS, OVERLOOKING MILES OF CRYSTAL BLUE WATERS, A FAMOUS CHEF FROM THE REGION WAS VISITING. ELI SURPRISED ME AND ARRANGED FOR US TO SIT AND CHAT FOR A FEW MINUTES. AS SHE HAD NEVER BEEN EXPOSED TO THE LAWS OF KASHRUS, I GAVE HER A QUICK OVERVIEW OF WHAT WE EAT AND DON'T EAT. TOGETHER WE CAME UP WITH A KOSHER VERSION OF THIS FAMOUS, TRADITIONAL THAI SOUP. EVERY TIME I MAKE IT, I AM INSTANTLY TRANSPORTED BACK TO THE LAND OF SUN, EXOTIC ANIMALS, AND THE SWEETEST MANGO WE'VE EVER TASTED.

1 large shallot

3 cloves garlic

3-4 Thai chilies (depending how spicy you like it)

3 cups vegetable stock

3 stalks lemongrass, bottom of stem cut off, outer layer of leaves discarded, and then thinly sliced on an angle

4 kafir lime leaves (each stem contains what seems to be 2 leaves; they are attached and are only considered to be 1 leaf. Therefore you need 4 stems), stems removed

4 inches galangal, peeled, thinly sliced

3 button mushrooms, cleaned and quartered

5 cherry tomatoes, quartered

3 Tbsp sugar

1 Tbsp fish sauce (optional)

1 Tbsp soy sauce (if you are not using fish sauce, use **2 Tbsp**)

2 (2 inch) salmon fillets

2-3 limes, halved

¼ cup cilantro leaves

In a mortar and pestle, or in a food processor fitted with the "S" blade, combine shallot, garlic, and chilies to make a paste.
Set aside.

In a medium pot combine stock, lemongrass, kafir lime leaves, and galangal.

Bring soup to a boil.
Reduce heat; simmer for about 10 minutes until the soup becomes very fragrant.

Add mushrooms, tomatoes, and sugar.
Stir until sugar has dissolved and mushrooms have cooked through.

Add reserved chili paste, fish sauce (if using), and soy sauce; stir to combine.

Gently place salmon into the pot; simmer until the salmon is cooked to your liking.

Turn off heat and squeeze in lime juice.
Taste and adjust seasonings.

Serve in a shallow bowl with a piece of salmon in each and sprinkle fresh cilantro over the top.

Enjoy!

NOTE
Galangal and kafir lime leaves can easily be found in most Asian food markets and online!

hawaij beef soup

WAIT!!! STOP! DON'T TURN THE PAGE YET!

I KNOW. I KNOW, IT SOUNDS SCARY, BUT REALLY HAWAIJ IS JUST A YEMENITE SPICE BLEND, WHICH YOU BUY ALREADY MIXED (WOOHOO FOR TIME SAVERS!) AND IT IS ABSOLUTELY DELICIOUS. I ALREADY WENT THROUGH THIS WITH MY KIDS AND AFTER LITERALLY BRIBING THEM TO TASTE THE SOUP (YES, I'M NOT ABOVE THAT!) THEY NOW REQUEST IT ON A REGULAR BASIS. I LOVE IT BECAUSE IT'S NOT THE TYPICAL MEAT SOUP FLAVOR. THE HINT OF SOURNESS MAKES THE SOUP COMPLETELY IRRESISTIBLE, SPOON AFTER SPOON!

2½ lb (1.13 kg) stew meat (1 inch cubes chuck)

½ cup flour

2 tsp kosher salt, divided

2 tsp coarsely ground black pepper, divided

1 Tbsp canola oil

1 large yellow onion, diced

3 carrots, peeled, cut into ¾ inch rounds

6 stalks celery, peeled, cut into ¾ inch pieces

7 red potatoes, peeled, cut into 1 inch cubes

4 cloves garlic, peeled, halved

3 Tbsp hawaij for soup

2 Tbsp tomato paste

1 cup cilantro leaves + extra for garnish

10 cups water

rice, for serving

schug, for serving (page 32)

In a large bowl, combine meat, flour, 1 teaspoon salt, and 1 teaspoon pepper.

Place a large Dutch oven or heavy bottomed pot over medium high heat. Add oil and meat.

Brown meat on all sides (about 8 minutes total).

Add onion, carrots, celery, potatoes, and remaining 1 teaspoon each salt and pepper.
Stir to incorporate vegetables with meat; allow to cook for 3-4 minutes.
Add garlic, hawaij, and tomato paste. Stir to combine.

Cook for 3-4 minutes, stirring often. Add water.

Bring mixture to a boil; reduce heat to low.
Cover; simmer over low heat for 2-3 hours, mixing every once in a while.

Serve hot over rice with a dollop of schug, and enjoy!

VARIATION

Crockpot method: Turn crockpot to high. Add oil and meat mixture. Cover crockpot; cook for about 30 minutes, mixing meat every 10 minutes or so. (If lots of liquid accumulates at any point, just remove the cover until it evaporates). Add remaining ingredients except water. Stir to distribute spices and tomato paste evenly. Leave crockpot uncovered for 10 minutes, stirring every 2-3 minutes. Add water; cover the pot. Cook on high for 5-6 hours. If putting in the crockpot for Shabbos day, cook on high for 2 hours and then turn the crockpot to low.

mexican chicken soup

NO ROOM FOR BLURB. MAKE SOUP. PARTY IN YOUR BOWL. BYE.

2 chicken breasts, without skin

2 tsp kosher salt, divided

1 tsp coarsely ground black pepper

3 Tbsp canola oil, divided

1 large yellow onion, peeled and diced

1 carrot, peeled and diced

1 green bell pepper, diced

2 stalks celery, peeled and diced

1 jalapeño pepper, minced (optional)

1 cup fresh corn kernels (cut from 1-2 ears corn)

4 cloves garlic, minced

1 tsp smoked paprika

½ tsp cumin

1 Tbsp tomato paste

1 (15 oz/425 g) can black beans, rinsed well and drained

1 cup cilantro leaves

1 (15 oz/425 g) can crushed tomatoes (if you can get fire roasted, that's a bonus!)

juice of **1** lime

12 cups chicken stock

TORTILLA CRISPS

8 (7½ inch/20 cm) tortillas

1 tsp granulated garlic

1 tsp granulated onion

1 tsp smoked paprika

¼ tsp cumin

¾ tsp kosher salt

IF BAKING: **2 Tbsp** canola oil

IF FRYING: about **1 cup** canola oil

NOTE
Go ahead and leave out the chicken, replacing chicken stock with a vegetable stock for a pareve version that you can top with shredded cheddar cheese and sour cream!

Heat a large pot over medium high heat.

Season chicken with 1 teaspoon salt and pepper.
Add 1 tablespoon oil and chicken to the pot.
Sear chicken for 3-4 minutes on each side.
Transfer to a platter; set aside.

Add remaining 2 tablespoons oil, onion, carrot, green bell pepper, celery, jalapeño, and remaining teaspoon salt to the pot.
Cook for 10-12 minutes, stirring often, until vegetables have softened.

Add corn, garlic, smoked paprika, cumin, and tomato paste.
Cook for 3-4 minutes, stirring to distribute spices evenly.

Add black beans, cilantro, crushed tomatoes, and lime juice. Return chicken to the pot; add stock. Stir to combine.

Bring soup to a boil, uncovered.
Reduce heat to low, cover the pot, and simmer for 3 hours.

Remove chicken from the pot; shred, discarding bones.
Return shredded chicken to the soup. Add toppings you like and enjoy!

TORTILLA CRISPS

In a small bowl, combine all the spices. Arrange the tortillas in one pile. Cut pile in half. Next, cut each half into about 8 even strips.

IF BAKING

Preheat oven to 350°F / 175°C. Line a baking sheet with parchment paper. Place all the tortilla strips into a large bowl; drizzle with oil. Toss well to distribute oil evenly. Sprinkle spices over the tortilla strips; toss again to evenly distribute. Spread coated strips over the baking sheet, spreading them out as much as possible. Bake for 30 minutes, mixing them after 15 minutes. Transfer tortilla chips to cooling rack to stay crispy.

IF FRYING

Set up a cooling rack next to the stove with a piece of parchment paper or a few sheets of paper towel beneath it. Place a shallow pan over medium high heat. Add enough oil to cover the bottom of the pan and come up just a little bit. Add a few tortillas strip to the hot oil at a time. Working quickly, use tongs to flip tortilla strips over after about 25-30 seconds and fry the second side. Remove strips from the oil once both sides are lightly golden. (Keep in mind they will darken just a little bit more after you remove them from the oil.) Immediately sprinkle a light dusting of the spice mix over the fried tortilla strips. Continue until all the strips are fried.

SOUP TOPPINGS

crispy spiced tortilla strips • cilantro • diced avocado • sautéed corn kernels
lime wedges • sliced radishes • roasted jalapeños

spicy meat soup
(crockpot)

I LOVE A GOOD SINK-YOUR-TEETH-INTO HEARTY MEAT SOUP IN THE WINTER. A SOUP WHOSE SCENT IS SO POWERFUL IT LITERALLY CALLS YOUR FAMILY TO THE TABLE FOR YOU!

1 piece bone in flanken

1 onion, diced

5 stalks celery, peeled and diced

5 cloves garlic, minced

1 red Thai chili, minced
(**2**, if you like to live dangerously)

1 Tbsp miso paste

2 Tbsp tomato paste

2½ tsp kosher salt (divided)

1 tsp coarsely ground black pepper

1 (15 oz/425 g) can tomato sauce

45 oz (1.3 liter) water or stock
(that's refilling the empty
tomato sauce can 3x!)

¼ cup red wine

1 small sweet potato,
cut into ½ inch cubes

1 large zucchini,
cut into ½ inch cubes

TO GARNISH

freshly grated horseradish

Turn crockpot to high; spray very liberally with nonstick cooking spray.
Add meat, onion, celery, garlic, chili, miso paste, tomato paste, 1 teaspoon salt, and black pepper to the pot.
Stir loosely just to sort of distribute the tomato paste and miso. (Don't get too crazy about distributing it evenly!)
Cover the crockpot; cook for 2 hours.

After 2 hours, turn crockpot to low, uncover, and add remaining ingredients.
If your crockpot is a bit bigger than mine, you can add another can or two of water or stock! It will be fine.

Cover crockpot; cook on low for at least 6 hours.

If cooking overnight, right before Shabbos, remove crockpot insert from the base. Add a square tin, upside down, to the bottom of the base; place insert over it.
This will lift the insert about 1 inch from the bottom of the base, allowing the soup to cook more gently overnight so it doesn't burn!
There.
That's my trick!

Serve hot and enjoy!

pureed vegetable soup
(meat)

I AM NOT A PUREED SOUP LOVER. I REPEAT, NOT A PUREED FOOD FAN. I LIKE TO CHEW MY FOOD. LIKE AN ADULT. WITH TEETH. SO, WHY THIS SOUP? BECAUSE EVERY RULE HAS AN EXCEPTION AND THIS SOUP IS IT. YOU DO HAVE TO ROAST THE VEGGIES FIRST, AND THEN COOK AND THEN SIMMER, AND THEN BLEND, SO IT'S NOT THE DUMP AND MIX, EASY TYPE OF SOUP FOR WHEN YOU'RE IN A RUSH. IT IS WORTH EVERY EXTRA FLAVOR LAYERING STEP, BECAUSE ONCE FINISHED IT WILL BE THE BEST PUREED VEGETABLE SOUP YOU'VE EVER HAD!

5 carrots, peeled and diced

2 small leeks, white and light green only, chopped

2 large zucchini, diced

1 head celery, peeled and diced

1 kohlrabi, peeled and diced

2 yellow onions, peeled and diced

5 cloves garlic, peeled

3 tomatoes, halved

4 Tbsp + 1 tsp extra virgin olive oil, divided

4 tsp kosher salt, divided

2 tsp coarsely ground black pepper, divided

¾ cup dry white wine

12 cups chicken stock (can be bought or leftover chicken soup, strained)

TO GARNISH

a few sprigs fresh oregano or thyme

Preheat oven to 400°F / 200°C. Line 2 baking sheets with parchment paper.

Spread all the veggies in a single layer on prepared baking sheets.
Drizzle veggies on each baking sheet with 2 tablespoons olive oil; sprinkle 2 teaspoons salt and 1 teaspoon pepper over each.
Stir veggies on each baking sheet to coat all with oil, salt, and pepper.

Bake 35-40 minutes until the vegetables have softened and begun to caramelize. Set aside.

Heat a large pot over medium high heat.
Add remaining teaspoon olive oil and all the veggies to the pot.
Use a spatula to push any of the juices that have accumulated on the baking sheets into the pot. Cook veggie for 4 minutes, stirring often.
Raise heat to high; add wine. Stir immediately; cook for 2 minutes.
Add chicken stock; stir to combine.

Bring soup to a boil.
Reduce heat to very low, cover, and simmer for 2-3 hours. Remove from heat.
Use an immersion blender to puree soup.

Taste to adjust seasonings!

matzah balls

I MEAN, IT'S A MATZAH BALL. A REALLY GOOD MATZAH BALL, BUT STILL, A MATZAH BALL. DUMP, MIX, REFRIGERATE, ROLL, BOIL. WAIT. ONE SECOND. IN MY WORLD, MATZAH BALLS ARE NOT EXCLUSIVE TO CHICKEN SOUP. PUT THEM IN EVERYTHING; LET THEM SOAK UP THE FLAVORS OF OTHER SOUPS/DISHES LIKE MEME'S FRICASSEE AND THE DAIRY TOMATO SOUP. ADD IN CHOPPED HERBS, GARLIC, OR MINCED ONION. THIS RECIPE IS REALLY GOOD AS IS, BUT ALSO THE BEST PLACE TO START PLAYING WITH FLAVORS! YOU CAN HALVE, DOUBLE, OR TRIPLE TO SUIT YOUR NEEDS!

1 cup matzah meal
1 tsp baking powder
1 tsp kosher salt
4 eggs, beaten
¼ cup oil

In a medium bowl, combine matzah meal, baking powder, and salt.
Add eggs and oil.
Mix well to fully incorporate.
Place plastic wrap directly on the mixture to cover well; place in the fridge for at least 1 hour or overnight.

To make matzah balls, bring soup or salted water up to a boil.
Lightly oil your hands and then scoop up 2 tablespoons of the mixture.
Roll into a ball and drop into the boiling liquid.

Once all the matzah balls are in the liquid, reduce heat to low, cover the pot, and cook matzah balls 30 minutes, until cooked through.

NOTE

Matzah balls grow as they cook. Keep that in mind when you are rolling them!

moroccan matzah ball soup

THIS SOUP IS THE COVER OF THE BOOK BECAUSE IT BASICALLY ME IN A BOWL HALF MOROCCAN, HALF ASHKENAZ, INFLUENCED BY THE FLAVORS OF THE SHUK IN JERUSALEM WHERE I'VE DONE MY SHOPPING FOR THE PAST 13 YEARS, FULL OF FLAVOR, EASY TO PREPARE, AND APPROACHABLE ENOUGH THAT IT APPEALS TO THE YOUNGEST AND OLDEST AMONGST US!

1 Tbsp saffron

1 cup boiling water

1 Tbsp extra virgin olive oil

2 large onions, diced

5 carrots, peeled, cut into ¼ inch rounds

2 fennel bulbs, diced

4 cloves garlic, peeled and halved lengthwise

1 tsp ground coriander

1 tsp hawaij for soup

1 tsp kosher salt

½ tsp coarsely ground black pepper

2 tsp harissa

¼ cup + 2 Tbsp arak

12 cups chicken stock

1 cup dried chickpeas, soaked overnight in water (uncovered), drained and rinsed

1 batch matzah ball mixture (uncooked; page 116)

6 cups Swiss chard (or any leafy green))

GARNISH

cilantro leaves

mint leaves

purple radish, cut into thin strips (or any color radish!)

very light sprinkle of sumac

Combine saffron and boiling water in a cup. Set aside.

Set a medium pot over high heat. Add olive oil.
Add onions, carrots, fennel, and garlic; stir to combine.
Cook vegetables on high heat for about 6 minutes.

We are looking for a quick sear on high heat to develop a bit of char on the edges of the vegetables.
Once veggies are charred, add coriander, Hawaij, salt, and pepper.

Stir spices and harissa with vegetables for 2 minutes to extract natural oils from the spices.
Once spices become fragrant, add arak.
Use a wooden spoon to scrape up any bits stuck to the bottom of the pan.

Allow arak to reduce for 3 minutes. Add saffron water and stock.
Add drained chickpeas.

Bring mixture to a boil (uncovered), then lower heat, cover the pot, and simmer soup for 2 hours.

40 minutes before serving, bring soup to a boil again.

Using lightly oiled hands, form 2 tablespoons of matzah ball mixture into a smooth ball and add to the pot.
Repeat until all the matzah balls are in the pot.

Add Swiss chard.

Reduce heat back, cover the pot, and simmer for 30 minutes.

Serve hot soup with a matzah ball in each bowl, and garnish with what you like!

NOTE

I kept the salt and pepper amounts on the lighter said to account for the use of previously made or store bought stock, since each person's stock may be seasoned a bit differently. Be sure to taste the soup once it's prepared and adjust seasoning accordingly.

VARIATIONS

I chose to keep this soup free of actual chicken pieces so that it could be thrown together quickly at all times, without having to run to the grocery store (or your freezer) for chicken or meat. However, if possible, I highly recommend adding a few pieces of chicken into the pot with the carrots, onion, and fennel and turning this into a full on Moroccan chicken soup.

If you don't want to bother with raw chicken but want that bite of chicken anyway, you can always add already cooked shredded chicken to each bowl!

TIPS + TRICKS

For a more sophisticated and cleaner soup, do not add chickpeas. Cook the soup for the recommended 2 hours. Then, before adding matzah balls, strain the broth to remove the vegetables. Then return the broth to the pot, add the chickpeas, and simmer for 45 minutes until chickpeas have softened. Then proceed to add the matzah balls and chard!

fish

moroccan fish

IT IS MOST BEFITTING THAT MY FISH CHAPTER STARTS WITH MY ALL TIME FAVORITE FISH RECIPE. ALTHOUGH MY GRANDMOTHER IS MENTIONED MANY TIMES THROUGHOUT THIS BOOK, NO DISH BRINGS HER MEMORY FLOODING BACK TO ME LIKE THIS ONE. SCOOPING UP THE SAUCE WITH A PIECE OF CHALLAH WHILE NUDGING A PIECE OF THE TENDER FISH ONTO MY FORK IS ONE OF MY STRONGEST FOOD MEMORIES. I LOVED IT THEN AND I LOVE IT NOW. A FRIDAY NIGHT WITHOUT MOROCCAN FISH IS ALWAYS MISSING SOMETHING. THE COMBINATION OF THE INTENSELY FLAVORED SAUCE, THE SOFTENED HOT PEPPERS, THE FLAKY FISH, AND THE CHALLAH IS, AS WE SAY "MEI EIN OLAM HABA," OTHER WORLDLY, AND THEREFORE THE PERFECT FRIDAY NIGHT FOOD! TRADITIONALLY, MY GRANDMOTHER ALWAYS MADE HER MOROCCAN FISH WITH CHICKPEAS; HOWEVER, I COULD NOT LET THE NON-FISH LOVERS IN MY HOUSE MISS OUT ON THIS DISH, SO I'VE SEPARATED THE CHICKPEAS OUT INTO THEIR OWN RECIPE (PAGE 288). ALTHOUGH MY GRANDMOTHER DIDN'T DO THAT, I KNOW SHE WOULD APPROVE BECAUSE FOR HER, COOKING WAS A MEANS TO MAKING THOSE SHE LOVED FEEL COMFORTED, NURTURED, AND LOVED, SO ADAPTING TO THEIR LIKES AND DISLIKES IS COMPLETELY IN HER SPIRIT!

2 tsp saffron strands

2 cups boiling water

1 Tbsp olive oil

2 cups cilantro, stems and leaves separated

2 red bell peppers, seeded and quartered

2 jalapeño peppers, halved

8 cloves garlic, peeled and halved

2 red dried chilies, rinsed

8 fish fillets, skinless (sea bass, salmon, or any fish of choice as long as it's on the thicker side)

1 Tbsp tomato paste

2 tsp kosher salt

1 tsp coarsely ground black pepper

1 tsp paprika

garlic mayo (page 28), for serving

challah, for serving

In a large cup, combine saffron and 2 cups boiling water.
Use a spatula to press saffron against the side of the cup to help release its flavor.
Cover cup with plastic wrap; set aside.

To a large skillet, over low heat, add olive oil.
Sprinkle cilantro stems into pan.

Arrange red pepper quarters, skin-side down, over stems.
Place jalapeño halves, skin side up, randomly between pepper slices.
Fit garlic cloves and dried chilies in any spaces between peppers.
Raise heat to medium-high; cook for 3-4 minutes.

Place fish over peppers in a single layer. Sprinkle fish with salt and pepper.

Remove plastic wrap from the cup; add tomato paste, stirring to combine.
Pour the saffron mixture over the fish.
Sprinkle the fish with paprika and cilantro leaves.

Bring mixture to a boil, reduce heat to low, cover the pan, and simmer for 30 minutes.
Every 5-7 minutes, lift up cover and baste the top of the fish with the liquid.

Remove cover and allow liquid to reduce down just a bit (2-3 minutes).

Serve hot with garlic mayo and challah!

TIPS + TRICKS

If you would like to serve this dish on Shabbos day, I suggest letting it come to room temperature instead of reheating it.

chreyme
(moroccan fish balls)

IN MY HOUSE, THESE TOMATO-Y, VERY FLAVORFUL LITTLE FOOTBALL SHAPED PIECES OF FISH WERE SERVED ON YOM TOV. I'M NOT SURE WHY, BECAUSE THEY'RE ACTUALLY EASY TO MAKE BUT MAYBE BECAUSE THEY CAN SIT IN THE FRIDGE FOR A DAY OR TWO AND BE JUST AS GOOD REHEATED AS THEY WERE THE DAY THEY WERE PREPARED. I OPT TO SERVE THESE WITH A BIG DOLLOP OF A LEMONY MAYONNAISE TO DRAG YOUR FORK THROUGH AS YOU SCOOP UP THE FISH AND SAUCE TO REALLY TAKE THE FLAVOR OVER THE TOP!

FISH

2.2 lb (1 kg) ground fish (I like buri, but use whatever is freshest)

5 cloves garlic

⅔ **cup** cilantro

½ **cup** parsley

1 egg

1 tsp kosher salt

¼ **tsp** coarsely ground black pepper

2 tsp paprika

1 tsp preserved lemon puree (page 24)

SAUCE

3 Tbsp extra virgin olive oil

8 tomatoes, peeled and quartered OR **2 (15-oz) cans** crushed tomatoes

3 Tbsp tomato paste

3 cloves garlic, thinly sliced

1 jalapeño, roughly chopped

3 Tbsp capers

¼ **cup** parsley leaves

¾ **cup** cilantro leaves

1 tsp. kosher salt

¼ **tsp** coarsely ground black pepper

2 cups very hot water (add some strands of saffron to the water for a flavor boost)

FISH BALLS

In a large bowl, combine all fish ball ingredients.
Cover mixture with plastic wrap; refrigerate until sauce is ready.

SAUCE

In a large pan, combine all sauce ingredients except water.
Cook for 15 minutes, stirring often.
Once the tomatoes begin to blister and mixture becomes fragrant, add water; stir to incorporate.

Bring sauce to a boil, cover the pan, and reduce heat to low.
Simmer for at least 30 minutes until a chunky but still liquidy sauce has formed.

Return heat to high; bring mixture back to a boil.

Remove 2 tablespoons of fish mixture and form into an oval ball.
Gently drop into boiling sauce.
Repeat with remaining fish mixture, stirring so that all the balls are coated in the sauce.

Reduce heat, cover and simmer for 30 minutes, turning the fish balls once after 15 minutes.

Serve the fish balls hot, topped with plenty of the sauce to sop up with challah!

Enjoy!

salmon burgers

THERE'S A TIME AND PLACE FOR EVERYTHING. IN THE FULL SWING OF BURGER SEASON, AKA THE SUMMER, IT'S NICE TO BE ABLE TO BREAK UP THE MONOTONY OF BEEF BURGER AFTER BEEF BURGER WITH SOMETHING A LITTLE LIGHTER THAT DOESN'T SACRIFICE ONE BIT ON FLAVOR.

12 oz (340 g) skinless salmon

1 small purple onion, finely diced

1 tsp minced garlic

¼ cup parsley leaves, chopped

½ large red bell pepper, finely diced

1 jalapeño pepper, finely diced (you can remove seed and membrane if you don't want it to be too spicy)

1½ tsp kosher salt

1 tsp cracked black pepper

1 Tbsp lemon zest (from about **1** lemon)

1 tsp fresh lemon juice

1 Tbsp mayonnaise

1 tsp Dijon mustard

1 tsp Worcestershire sauce

½ cup panko breadcrumbs (unseasoned is best)

1 egg, lightly beaten

oil, for frying

buns, for serving, optional

CHIPOTLE LIME CREMA

½ cup vegan sour cream (You can definitely use regular dairy sour cream or even Greek yogurt)

2 Tbsp fresh lime juice

1 Tbsp adobo from a can of chipotles in adobo

¼ tsp kosher salt

Cut fish into 1 inch chunks; add to the bowl of a food processor fitted with the "S" blade.
Pulse until fish resembles the texture of ground beef.

Add ground salmon to a large bowl along with the remaining ingredients.
Mix until ingredients are well distributed and combined.

Cover the bowl with plastic wrap.
Refrigerate for 2 hours so that all the flavors can come together.

When ready to cook, heat a pan over medium high heat; add 2 tablespoons canola oil.
Form patties with your hands, using ¼ cup of the mixture for each patty.

Add several patties to oil; cook for 3 minutes on one side.
Then flip and cook 2 minutes on second side.
Transfer to a cooling rack while you fry the rest of the salmon.
You may need to add oil to the pan to prevent them from sticking.

Serve on buns or alone alongside the chipotle lime crema and some pickled onions or cabbage or anything you'd like to pile on that burger!

CHIPOTLE LIME CREMA

In a bowl, combine all crema ingredients, stirring till incorporated.

best "crab" cakes ever

NOT JOKING. THERE ARE NO VEGGIES HERE, FOLKS. I MEAN, THERE'S AN ONION, BUT COME ON, THAT DOESN'T COUNT. JUST A FEW SIMPLE INGREDIENTS, USED REALLY WELL TO BRING YOU MAXIMUM CRISPINESS AND MAXIMUM FLAVOR! WHENEVER I MAKE THESE, I TRIPLE THE RECIPE SINCE THE PROCESS IS A BIT INVOLVED, SO THAT I CAN LOAD UP MY FREEZER AND PULL THEM OUT WHENEVER I NEED. THEY NEVER TASTE FISHY AND REHEAT BEAUTIFULLY. PLUS, THE STEPS CAN BE BROKEN UP OVER A FEW DAYS, SO SPENDING JUST A LITTLE TIME EACH DAY WILL YIELD A FEW MONTHS' WORTH OF "CRAB" CAKES. WOOHOO!

EGG MIXTURE

1 large onion, roughly chopped

2 eggs

1-3 tsp cayenne pepper
(depending how spicy you want it)

1 tsp kosher salt

"CRAB" CAKE MIXTURE

2 packages mock crab, chopped

1 sleeve saltines, pulsed into crumbs

oil, for frying

TARTAR SAUCE

¼ cup mayo

2 Tbsp freshly squeezed lemon juice

3 Tbsp capers, chopped

3 Tbsp chopped cornichons

2-4 tsp Tabasco sauce, to taste

½ tsp kosher salt

1 tsp coarsely ground black pepper

TIPS + TRICKS

To break up the steps of this process so that you never spend too much time in the kitchen, here's what I do:

Day 1 (Sunday):
Make onion mixture.

Day 2 (Monday):
Make tartar sauce.

Day 3 (Tuesday):
Blend saltines for crumbs.

Day 4 (Wednesday): Make "crab" mixture and refrigerate.

Day 5 (Thursday):
Shape cakes and refrigerate.

Day 6 (Fryday! Get it!): Fry.

EGG MIXTURE

Puree onion in a food processor fitted with the "S" blade till it is very smooth.
Add eggs, cayenne pepper, and salt to the processor; pulse until combined.
Transfer mixture to a bowl.
Place a piece of plastic wrap directly on the onion mixture to prevent it from oxidizing.
Cover the bowl with another piece of plastic wrap; refrigerate.

This mixture should be refrigerated at least 1 day in advance but is even better if it sits in your fridge for 3 days!

"CRAB" CAKES

in a large bowl, combine mock crab, saltine crumbs, and egg mixture.
Mix well to combine.
Refrigerate for twenty minutes to allow mixture to firm up.

Line a large baking sheet with parchment paper.

I use a large ice cream scoop to keep the cakes the same size.
Form mixture into cakes, using either a large scoop or your hands, or use a metal ring to form into uniform cakes.
To make these easier to fry, refrigerate them overnight or even just for an hour. They will hold their shape better when frying!

Preheat a large pan over medium high heat.
Add enough oil to cover the cakes halfway.

Place a few cakes in the pan at a time, being careful not to overcrowd the pan. Cook on each side for about 2 minutes until cakes are golden and cooked through.

Serve with tartar sauce, if you like.

TARTAR SAUCE

In a small bowl, combine all tartar sauce ingredients.

Refrigerate until ready to use.

supermarket style fish sticks

WHEN I WAS GROWING UP, TUESDAY NIGHT WAS ALWAYS FISH STICKS AND PASTA (USUALLY BAKED ZITI). NOT BEING A HUGE FISH STICK FAN, I THREW DOWN THE FISH STICKS I HAD TO EAT SO THAT I COULD EAT THE PASTA. FAST FORWARD 20 YEARS AND MY KIDS ARE HUGE FISH STICK FANS! LIKE, THEY LOVE THEM AND CONSIDER FISH STICKS A SPECIAL TREAT! SINCE WE LIVE FAR AWAY FROM THE WORLD OF FROZEN, JUST HEAT-UP-AND-SERVE FISH STICKS, I HAD TO RECREATE THEM ON MY OWN. AND GUESS WHAT, I AM NOW A PROUD FISH STICKS FAN. WHICH BASICALLY MEANS I'VE BEEN A FISH STICKS SNOB SINCE AGE 8 AND I DIDN'T EVEN KNOW IT.

1 lb (453 g) ground fish (I use cod)

1 tsp fresh lemon juice

1¼ tsp kosher salt, divided

½ tsp coarsely ground black pepper

1 Tbsp flour + **1 cup** flour, divided

4 eggs, beaten

2 cups breadcrumbs

In a large bowl, combine fish, lemon juice, ½ teaspoon salt, pepper, and 1 tablespoon flour. Mix well.

Line an 8x5 inch pan or dish with plastic wrap.
Transfer fish mixture to pan, pressing it down to create one smooth, flat layer.
Cover with plastic wrap; place into freezer for 45 minutes.

Meanwhile, preheat oven to 350°F / 180°C. Coat a baking sheet very well with nonstick cooking spray or oil. Set aside.

In a bowl, combine remaining 1 cup flour with ¼ teaspoon salt.
Add eggs to a second bowl, beating in ¼ teaspoon salt.
In a third bowl, combine breadcrumbs with remaining ¼ teaspoon salt.

Remove fish from freezer; flip pan onto a cutting board so that you have a flat ground fish rectangle.
Using a sharp knife, cut rectangle into 18 strips.

Bread each strip by coating flour, then egg, then breadcrumbs.
Be gentle during this process as they are fragile until cooked.

Place on prepared baking sheet.
Spray the tops and sides of fish sticks with nonstick cooking spray.
Bake for 30 minutes till crisp.

Serve hot and enjoy!

purple cabbage salmon cups

EVERYTHING ABOUT THIS DISH IS RIGHT. THE VIVID COLORS, THE TOTALLY BALANCED FLAVORS, THE COMBINATION OF TEXTURES, IT'S ALL JUST SO ON POINT AND COMPLETELY MOUTHWATERING. SERVE THIS ON A SHABBOS DAY FOR A BRIGHT BEAUTIFUL, KNOCK THE SOCKS OFF YOUR GUESTS APPETIZER THAT SOMEHOW COMES TOGETHER WAY MORE EASILY THAN ANYONE WILL EVER GUESS.

DIPPING SAUCE

1 Thai chili, thinly sliced

3 scallions, thinly sliced

1 clove garlic, minced

1 stalk lemongrass, gently smashed with the back of a knife, then the tender part inside removed and minced

½ inch ginger, minced

3 Tbsp rice vinegar

1 Tbsp mirin

1 Tbsp hot water

1 tsp sesame oil

FISH

1 (8 inch) skinless salmon fillet

1 clove garlic, minced

3 Tbsp soy sauce

1 tsp minced ginger

1 tsp toasted sesame oil

juice of **1** lime

FOR SERVING

10 leaves purple cabbage

1 mango, thinly sliced

5 radishes, thinly sliced

1 bunch scallions, chopped

1 cucumber, seeds removed, julienned

1-2 chilies, sliced

2 shallots, thinly sliced

1 cup cilantro leaves

2 limes, quartered, for squeezing

DIPPING SAUCE

In a small bowl, combine all sauce ingredients. Refrigerate until serving.

FISH

Place salmon on a plate.

In a small bowl, combine garlic, soy sauce, ginger, sesame oil, and lime juice. Pour over salmon.
Marinate salmon for only 3 minutes (no more!)

Grill on well greased grill pan over medium heat for 5-6 minutes, flipping once.

TO ASSEMBLE

Wash and dry cabbage leaves.

Flake fish; place into cabbage leaf cups.

Top with mango slices and veggies.

Spoon dipping sauce over the top, squeeze on some fresh lime, and enjoy.

"crab" salad with scallion pancakes

HOW MANY WAYS CAN I SAY THAT I LOVE CHINESE FOOD. AMERICAN, NEW YORK, JEWISH STYLE, CHINESE FOOD TO BE EXACT. AND SCALLION PANCAKES ARE A STAPLE. BECAUSE THEY'RE FRIED, THEY'RE CRUNCHY, AND THEY'RE DELICIOUS. SO SERVE THEM ON THEIR OWN, OR TOP THEM WITH THE MOST DELICIOUS KANI SALAD EVER (WHICH, INCIDENTALLY, CAN ALSO BE SERVED OVER SUSHI RICE FOR A MORE GROWN UP VERSION OF A SUSHI SALAD) AND YOU'VE GOT YOURSELF A DELICIOUS BITE OF FOOD!

1 package mock crab sticks

5 cucumbers, julienned (drain strips on paper towels for 20-30 minutes to dry out)

4-5 large scallions, chopped

2 Tbsp soy sauce

2 Tbsp mayonnaise

1-2 Tbsp sriracha (I used 2)

1 Tbsp rice wine vinegar

1 tsp sesame oil

black sesame seeds, for garnish

SCALLION PANCAKES

1 cup flour

2 tsp kosher salt

½ cup hot water

1 cup chopped scallions

6 Tbsp oil + 4 tsp sesame oil, mixed together

oil, for frying

"CRAB" SALAD

Separate sticks of mock crab into strings.

In a large bowl, combine fish with julienned cucumbers and scallions. Mix (easier to mix with your hands) to combine.

Add remaining ingredients; mix well.

May be refrigerated for up to 4-5 days.

SCALLION PANCAKES

In a bowl, combine flour, salt, and hot water.
Mix with a spoon for 3-4 minutes until a dough forms.
Cover dough directly with plastic wrap; cover bowl with a kitchen towel.
Allow to rest for at least 35 minutes.

Divide dough into 5 balls.

On a well floured surface, roll 1 ball of dough into a round, as thin as possible (it's OK if it tears a little).
Spread 1 tablespoon of oil onto dough; add a handful of scallions.
Roll dough into a long rope.
Roll rope around itself into a spiral.

Once again, roll spiraled dough into a round pancake. (This whole process helps make the fried dough crunchy and flaky.)
Repeat with remaining dough balls.

Pour oil about ¼ inch up the side of a large pan, set over high heat.
Place pancake in the pan; fry on the first side for 1½ to 2 minutes.
Flip and cook for 45 seconds.

Transfer to a wire rack to cook. Repeat with remaining pancakes.

Cut into any shape you want.

TIPS + TRICKS

For a more sophisticated presentation, you can make mini scallion pancakes (as pictured) so that you don't need to cut the very large ones! It is more tedious (and I personally love the rustic look of cutting up a large one) but there is a time and place for everything!

NOTE

To reheat these, simply lay them in a pan in a single layer and heat, uncovered.

VARIATION

Replace scallions with 1 cup chopped kimchi for the most flavor bomb scallion pancakes ever. The dough is a drop more technically difficult to work with once you add the kimchi, but I have faith in you!

moroccan tuna borekas

I AM A TUNA LOVER. ALSO A LOVER OF THE DELICATE FRENCH PASTRY THAT IS FLAKY AND DELICIOUS AND EASY ENOUGH TO BUY OR MAKE, KNOWN AS PÂTE BRISÉE. MAKE LITTLE POCKETS OF THE INTENSELY FLAVOR PACKED TUNA AND YOU HAVE AN APPETIZER THAT WILL SERIOUSLY SURPRISE EVERYONE YOU KNOW. BONUS, YOU NEVER EVEN HAVE TO STEP FOOT IN A FISH STORE BECAUSE IT'S MADE WITH JUST 2 CANS OF TUNA!

1 package savory pie dough (OR ½ **batch** pâte brisée)

1½ cups green pitted olives

1 Tbsp harissa (page 30)

1 Tbsp mayo (if you have any homemade garlic mayo [page 28], that would be yum)

1 tsp Dijon mustard

1 Tbsp preserved lemon puree (page 24) OR zest of **2** lemons

⅛ tsp kosher salt

¼ tsp coarsely cracked black pepper

2 (5 oz/140 g) cans tuna

1 egg, for egg wash

paprika, for sprinkling

Preheat oven to 350°F / 180°C. Line a baking sheet with parchment paper.

Place olives, harissa, mayo, mustard, preserved lemon puree, salt, and pepper into the bowl of a food processor fitted with the "S" blade.
Pulse about 15 times. Mixture should be coarse but well chopped.

Transfer mixture to a large bowl, add tuna, and mix to combine.

Roll out dough; cut into 4 x 1½ inch rectangles.
Place 2 tablespoons of tuna mixture diagonally on the lower half of each rectangle.
Fold over; seal edges with a fork.

Place on prepared baking sheet; brush with egg wash.
Sprinkle a tiny pinch of paprika from high up over the top of the borekas.

Bake for 40 minutes, until golden and crisp.
Transfer to cooling rack.

Once cooled, freeze or refrigerate for up to 1 week!

BONUS RECIPE: pâte brisée

2½ cups all-purpose flour

1 tsp kosher salt

1 tsp sugar

1 cup unsalted butter or nondairy butter substitute, chilled and cut into small pieces

¼-½ cup ice water

In the bowl of a food processor fitted with the "S" blade, pulse together flour, salt, and sugar.
Add butter; process until the mixture resembles coarse meal, 8 to 10 seconds.
With machine running, add 2 tablespoons ice water in a slow, steady stream through feed tube.
Pulse until dough holds together without being wet or sticky; be careful not to process more than 30 seconds.

To test, squeeze a small amount together: If it is crumbly, add more ice water, 1 tablespoon at a time.

Divide dough into two equal balls.
Flatten each ball into a disk; wrap in plastic.
Transfer to the refrigerator; chill at least 1 hour.

Dough may be stored, frozen, up to 1 month.

ERROR333ok

cajun salmon tacos with persimmon salsa

THIS SALMON IS THE BOMB. LITERALLY. SO MUCH FLAVOR IT EXPLODES IN YOUR MOUTH. ALTHOUGH THE SALSA CAN ONLY BE MADE THE FEW MONTHS OF THE YEAR THAT PERSIMMONS ARE AROUND, OR AT LEAST WORTH EATING, IT IS A DISH WORTH WAITING FOR. IT'S AN UNEXPECTED BUT ABSOLUTELY WONDERFUL MARRIAGE OF A SWEET AND SOUR SALSA, PAIRED WITH A HEAVILY SPICED HEARTY SALMON. AND REALLY, WHO DOESN'T LOVE A TACO?

CAJUN SALMON

3 Tbsp garlic powder
2 Tbsp paprika
2 Tbsp oregano
1 Tbsp onion powder
1 Tbsp smoked paprika
1½ tsp coarsely ground black pepper
4 Tbsp sugar
1 Tbsp cayenne pepper
4 Tbsp kosher salt
1 whole side salmon
1 lime or lemon

PERSIMMON SALSA

1 persimmon, peeled and diced (I like smaller ¼-½ inch cubes)
1 cup quartered yellow cherry tomatoes (or any color you find!)
½-1 jalapeño pepper, finely diced (optional but recommended)
2 shallots, finely chopped
½ cup cilantro, chopped
2 Tbsp extra virgin olive oil
½ tsp kosher salt
¼ tsp coarsely ground black pepper
juice of **1** lime

TACO SHELLS

1 pack wonton wrappers or store-bought mini tacos
oil, for frying

SPECIAL EQUIPMENT

taco mold tongs

CAJUN SALMON

In a bowl, combine all the spices; mix well until thoroughly combined.

Preheat oven to 350°F / 180 C. Coat a baking sheet with nonstick cooking spray.

Place side of salmon on prepared baking sheet.
Squeeze juice from the lime over fish.
Sprinkle a generous amount of spice mix over the salmon.

Bake for around 25 minutes and allow to rest for 10 minutes.
Cooking time will vary depending on thickness of your salmon.

Serve hot or cold and enjoy!

PERSIMMON SALSA

Place all salsa ingredients except lime into a large bowl; squeeze lime juice over the top.
Mix till well blended.

You can eat it right away or let it sit in your fridge for up to 4 days.
In my opinion it gets better the longer it sits!

TACO SHELLS

If not using store-bought mini tacos, set a medium pot over medium high heat.

When oil gets to 350°F / 180°C or a wooden spoon handle inserted upside down in the oil creates bubbles around the edges, begin to fry wonton wrappers.

Using taco mold tongs, place wonton wrapper into the mold, and squeeze the handles to press wrapper into taco shape. Immerse in oil for 45-50 seconds.

Transfer to cooling rack to cool.

Repeat until all wrappers are fried.

ASSEMBLE

Divide salmon between taco shells; top with persimmon salsa.

VARIATION

Use the spice rub to make any type of Cajun fish. Serve alongside a lemony salad or slaw for another delicious dish!

asian style halibut en papillote

A COOKED FISH DISH THAT LEAVES YOU WITH NO DISHES TO WASH? YES, PLEASE!

6 halibut or salmon fillets, without skin

6 heads baby bok choy

6 cups fresh broccoli florets

12 cloves garlic, minced

2-inch piece ginger, minced

3 Thai chilies, thinly sliced

3 cups chopped scallions

1 cup + 2 Tbsp soy sauce

1 Tbsp mirin

2 tsp sriracha

1 tsp sesame oil

Preheat oven to 350°F / 180°C. Cut 6 large pieces of parchment paper.

Place leaves of 1 head bok choy and 1 cup broccoli on each piece of parchment paper.
Top with halibut; sprinkle minced garlic and ginger over fish, distributing it as evenly as possible.
Sprinkle scallions and chilies over fish; drizzle with soy sauce, mirin, sriracha, and sesame oil.

Seal each piece of parchment by folding in the edges.
Place packets on a baking sheet.

Bake 15-20 minutes.

Careful when opening pouch!

NOTE
Use whatever thicker piece of fish is freshest at the market that day! And not just for this recipe, ALWAYS!

tahini + tamarind glazed salmon with kadaif topping

CREAMY, EARTHY TAHINI, SWEET AND SOUR TAMARIND PASTE, FLAKY RICH SALMON, AND THEN THE CRISPY, PARTY-IN-YOUR-MOUTH KADAIF MAKE THIS FISH THE MOST UNEXPECTED YET UTTERLY SATISFYING DISH! COMBINING FLAVORS THAT SPAN MANY REGIONS, IT'S AN UNEXPECTED COMBINATION THAT JUST TOTALLY WORKS! YOU CAN GO AHEAD AND MAKE AN ENTIRE SIDE OF SALMON WITH THIS RECIPE, BUT BECAUSE THE KADAIF CRISPS UP, I LIKE TO COOK THIS IN FILLET FORM SO THAT WHEN EACH PERSON GETS SERVED I DON'T HAVE TO CUT THROUGH THE CRISPY TOPPING AND RUIN THE PRESENTATION.

8 (1½ inch) fillets of salmon (with or without skin)

1½ tsp kosher salt

½ tsp coarsely ground black pepper

½ cup tahini paste

2 Tbsp + 1 tsp tamarind concentrate

2 Tbsp maple syrup

2 Tbsp olive oil

½ cup pomegranate seeds, for garnish

TOPPING:

4 cups frozen kadaif, defrosted

2 Tbsp olive oil

Preheat the oven to 350°F / 180°C. Line a baking sheet with parchment paper.

Place salmon fillets on prepared baking sheet and sprinkle with salt and pepper.

In a bowl, combine tahini, tamarind, maple syrup, and olive oil.
Spread 1 tablespoon tahini mixture over each salmon fillet. (I like to use a gloved hand here to make the process easier.)

To a large bowl, add kadaif; drizzle with olive oil.
Gently toss the kadaif in the bowl 2-3 times just to spread the oil.

Top each salmon fillet with about ⅓ cup kadaif strands, creating a sort of nest on the fish.

Bake for 18-20 minutes until fish is just cooked through and kadaif is golden and crunchy!

Garnish with pomegranate seeds.

Serve hot or cold and enjoy!

NOTE
Since all ovens are not created equal, you may need to broil the salmon for the last 2 minutes of cooking to get the maximum crunchability out of your kadaif!

NOTE
Kadaif topping on fish to bring another textural addition to your plate should not be limited to this recipe only. Don't like tahini or tamarind? Maybe shmear some honey mustard on there and then top with the kadaif. Maybe you're like me and don't love a sweet fish? How about sprinkling Montreal steak seasoning over your salmon instead of salt and pepper and then add a layer of white horseradish sauce or the horseradish mayo from this book (shameless plug — not embarrassed) on your fish and then top with the kadaif? I think you catch my drift. Kadaif on fish is an excellent idea and should not be limited to this exact recipe. Go, play, have fun, and then tell me what you did, so I can do it too!

NOTE
I really prefer to use the frozen kadaif for this recipe (and in general). However, if you only have access to the dried kadaif that comes in a bag, you can use that.

seared ahi tuna with tuna "juice"

FINE. DON'T CALL IT JUICE IF IT BOTHERS YOU. JUST MAKE IT ANYWAY, BECAUSE I GUARANTEE THE COMBINATION OF THE FRESH, PERFECTLY COOKED TUNA COMBINED WITH THE REALLY BALANCED INTENSELY FLAVORED JUICE WILL LEAVE YOU NOT CARING ONE BIT WHAT IT'S CALLED!

TUNA "JUICE"

3 scallions, thinly sliced (whites + greens)

1 clove garlic, minced

1 Thai chili, thinly sliced

¼ tsp minced ginger

1 juicy lime, juiced

1 Tbsp sesame oil

6 Tbsp low sodium soy sauce

½ cup water

1 Tbsp honey

⅛ tsp kosher salt

TUNA

1 (2 inch thick) piece sushi grade tuna

1 Tbsp low sodium soy sauce

1 tsp sesame oil

½ cup black and white sesame seed mix

1 tsp oil

¼ tsp kosher salt

TUNA "JUICE"

In a bowl, whisk together all juice ingredients.

Refrigerate until serving.

TUNA

Preheat a heavy skillet over high heat.

Rub soy and sesame oil all over the fish.

Place sesame seeds on a plate and gently lay fish on top.
Turn fish over so that all sides are coated in seeds.

Add 1 teaspoon neutral oil to the pan; add fish.
Cook for 35-45 seconds on 1 side, then flip over and cook for 39 seconds.

Remove from heat immediately.

TO SERVE

Using a very sharp knife, slice fish against the grain into thin slices. Drizzle tuna "juice" around the fish and then a little over the slices. Serve immediately and enjoy!

moroccan fried fish with sauce

THE SAUCE IS MY FAVORITE PART OF THE FISH! IT WAS ALWAYS MY JOB TO JUICE THE LEMONS ON MY MOTHER'S ALUMINUM JUICING BOWL AND I LOVED IT! MY MOTHER WOULD TAKE THE FISH AND SAUCE OUT OF THE FRIDGE EARLY ON SHABBOS MORNING SO THEY COULD COME TO ROOM TEMPERATURE. IT SEPARATES A LOT BECAUSE IT'S REALLY MORE A VINAIGRETTE THAN A SAUCE, SO MIX IT VIGOROUSLY AND THEN SPOON IT ALL OVER YOUR FRIED FISH!

FISH

12 fish fillets (whatever is the thinnest and freshest that day!)

4 eggs

1½ tsp kosher salt, divided

¾ tsp coarsely ground black pepper, divided

3 cups panko breadcrumbs

1-2 cups oil, for frying

cilantro, finely chopped, for garnish (OR finely chop **½ cup** cilantro and add to sauce)

SAUCE

(These measurements yield just enough to spoon a little sauce over each piece of fish. If you're anything like me and the fish is just a vehicle for the sauce ... double it!)

⅓ cup fresh lemon juice (about **1 large**, juicy lemon)

1 Tbsp white vinegar

3 tsp Moroccan paprika in oil (I like to use 2 tsp sweet + 1 tsp spicy)

¼ cup extra virgin olive oil

9 cloves garlic, finely minced

½ cup finely chopped fresh cilantro leaves (unless using as garnish)

In a wide, shallow bowl, beat together eggs, 1 teaspoon salt, and ½ teaspoon black pepper.

In a second wide, shallow bowl, combine panko bread crumbs with remaining ½ teaspoon salt and ¼ teaspoon pepper.

Set a large frying pan over medium high heat; add ¾ -1 cup oil.
(The amount will vary depending on the size of your pan. The wider the pan, the more the oil will spread and the more you will need. The oil should cover the bottom of the whole pan and come up about halfway on the fish when it is placed inside.)

Prepare a cooling rack next to the stove with a piece of parchment paper or a few paper towels beneath it.

Place all the fillets into the egg mixture; mix to coat every piece of fish.
Remove one fillet at a time and place into bowl of panko breadcrumbs.
Coat fish on both sides.
Add breaded fish to hot oil.
Cook only 2-4 pieces of fish in the pan at a time so as not to overcrowd them.

Cook for about 1 minute on the first side, then very gently flip fish over and cook for 1 minute.
Once crisp and golden on both sides, transfer fish to cooling rack.

Repeat until all the fillets are cooked through.

Garnish with chopped cilantro if you didn't add it to the sauce.

Serve hot, cold, or room temperature and enjoy!

SAUCE

In a jar or medium bowl, combine all sauce ingredients, mixing well.

Shake or whisk vigorously before pouring over fish.

NOTES
The sauce is best made a few hours or even a day or two in advance so that the flavors can come together. However, it is still delicious if made and eaten on the spot!

pan seared whole fish

IF THERE IS A WHOLE GRILLED FISH ON THE MENU, MY MOTHER IS ORDERING IT. IT WAS A REGULAR DAY WHEN YOU SAW MY MOM EATING A PIECE OF FISH DOWN TO THE VERY LAST MORSEL AND HAVING ONLY A PERFECT CLEAN FISH SPINE ON HER IMMACULATE PLATE. WATCHING HER ENJOY THE FISH FROM HEAD TO TAIL IS PROBABLY WHAT INSTILLED IN ME A DEEP LOVE OF A WHOLE FISH. ITS FLAVOR IS UNBEATABLE AND REALLY THE FISH JUST STAYS THE MOISTEST THAT WAY. IF YOU ARE A FISH LOVER LIKE ME (AND MY MOTHER), I DARE YOU TO TRY THIS. I BET YOU'LL NEVER GO BACK TO FILLETS!

1 whole fish (striped bass, red snapper ...)

2 tsp preserved lime puree (page 24) or the juice of **2** limes + **½ tsp** kosher salt

1 tsp lemongrass vinegar or apple cider vinegar (see Note)

1 tsp turmeric

1 clove garlic, minced

1 tsp minced fresh ginger

½ tsp coarsely ground black pepper

1 bulb fennel, halved, thinly sliced, fronds discarded

1 shallot, thinly sliced

½ cup rice flour

½ tsp kosher salt

½ tsp coarsely ground black pepper

3 Tbsp canola oil

In a bowl, combine lime puree, vinegar, turmeric, garlic, ginger, and pepper.

Spread ⅓ of the mixture into the fish cavity.
Rub remaining mixture all over both sides of the outside of the fish.
Stuff fennel and shallot into the fish.

Heat a large pan (large enough to fit fish) over medium high heat.

In a large, shallow dish, combine rice flour, salt, and pepper.

Carefully dip fish on both sides into the flour mixture.
Gently tap off any excess flour.

Drizzle oil into hot pan; carefully add fish.
Cook for 4 minutes on 1 side.
Using 2 spatulas, gently flip fish to second side; cook for 3 minutes.

Remove fish from oil, serve, and enjoy!

NOTE

To make your own lemongrass vinegar, which I highly recommend you do, simply cut stalks of lemongrass (tough exterior layer removed) into 2 inch pieces and combine with 2 cups white vinegar in a clean and dry jar with an airtight lid. Place on a cool shelf, away from direct sunlight, for 1-2 weeks. The vinegar will develop a beautiful pink hue and be absolutely delicious in everything from this recipe to vinaigrettes!

TIPS + TRICKS

The best advice I can give you regarding this recipe is go to the store, ask your fishmonger which is the freshest (you can throw in wild caught for bonus points), and use that fish!

salmon en croute with spinach and mushrooms

THIS IS MY GO TO FISH FOR THE SECOND OR THIRD DAY OF A LONG HOLIDAY. I DON'T LOVE THE IDEA OF FREEZING FISH AND DEFINITELY DON'T WANT TO KEEP RAW FISH IN MY FRIDGE FOR 2 DAYS BEFORE I COOK IT. THIS RECIPE IS THE SOLUTION TO THAT, BECAUSE IF YOU USE REALLY FRESH FISH TO BEGIN WITH, IT WILL DEFROST AND REHEAT BEAUTIFULLY.

2 Tbsp olive oil

1 large leek, white and light green only, halved, sliced

1 lb (453 g) sliced assorted mushrooms (any variety you like)

1½ cups defrosted and squeezed frozen spinach

1 tsp kosher salt, divided

¾ tsp coarsely ground black pepper

1 cup tomato sauce

1 piece puff pastry

3 (2 inch/5 cm thick) skinless salmon fillets

1 egg, beaten

⅛ tsp paprika (optional)

Place a large pan over medium high heat.
Add oil and leek. Cook for 5-6 minutes, stirring often, until leek begins to soften.

Add all the mushrooms.
Stir often for 20-25 minutes until the mushrooms cook down and release their juices, and the liquid completely evaporates.
Cook for 3-4 minutes, stirring constantly.

Add spinach, salt, and pepper; stir to combine.
Add tomato sauce; stir to combine.

Cook just until tomato sauce is heated through, then remove from heat.
Set pan aside so mixture can cool.

TO ASSEMBLE THE LOAF

Preheat oven to 350°F / 180°C. Line a baking sheet with parchment paper.

Place your three pieces of salmon in a "train," one after the other, with the thin ends slightly overlapping, so that you have one long piece of salmon with roughly the same thickness all the way through.

Roll out puff pastry to be the length of the "fish train," plus an additional 1½ inches on each side to use to seal the roll after filling it.

Place pieces of fish on the center of the puff pastry in a long train-like line.
Spoon the spinach mushroom mixture over the fish.
Lift one side of the pastry dough and fold it over the fish.
Next, lift the other side of the puff pastry and bring it over, sealing the fish completely.
Gently nudge the long roll of fish up, and tuck the edge of the puff pastry under the roll so that the seam is on the bottom.

Place roll, seam side down, onto prepared baking sheet.

Brush roll with beaten egg; sprinkle paprika over the top.

Bake for 45 minutes until puff pastry is golden brown.

Serve hot, with garlic mayo or horseradish mayo and enjoy!

FREEZER TIP

To freeze this dish, cool it completely first. As soon as it's totally come down to room temperature, wrap it in 2 layers of plastic wrap and then a few layers of foil. Place it into the freezer and freeze for up to 1 month. To serve it, remove the roll from freezer, unwrap immediately, and place on baking sheet. Once defrosted, reheat uncovered to recrisp.

smoked whitefish toast with radish butter

I AM ALMOST AS EXCITED TO WRITE THIS BLURB AS I WAS TO EAT THE DISH. BASICALLY, THIS DISH WAS ON MY COOKBOOK RECIPE LIST FOR MONTHS. THEN AFTER WHITTLING AND WHITTLING THE LIST DOWN, IT WAS SADLY REMOVED. EVERYONE AGREED THAT NO ONE WOULD EVER MAKE IT AND I WAS JUST INCLUDING IT FOR MYSELF. WHICH I WAS. BUT ALSO, THE SPACE IN THE BOOK BECAME A THING AND I FINALLY GAVE IN. THEN SOMETHING CRAZY HAPPENED. ON THE FIRST DAY OF OUR COOKBOOK PHOTO SHOOT, ERIC, MY CUTE, YOUNGER BROTHER, BROUGHT BRUNCH OVER FOR EVERYONE. BEING EXTRA NICE, HE OF COURSE BOUGHT AN ENTIRE SMOKED WHITE FISH. LITERALLY THE ONE STARING AT YOU IN THIS PHOTO. ALL DAY LONG EVERYONE PICKED AT IT, BECAUSE IT WAS DELICIOUS, AND AT THE END OF THE DAY IT GOT WRAPPED UP AND PUT IN THE FRIDGE. THE NEXT DAY, SOMEONE OPENED THE FRIDGE AND SAID, DANIELLE DO YOU HAVE ANY RECIPES WE CAN USE THIS IN, IT WOULD BE SO SAD TO WASTE IT. I COULDN'T BELIEVE MY EARS AND SCREAMED VERY LOUDLY (WHICH IF YOU KNOW ME, YOU KNOW WHAT MY EXCITED SCREAM SOUNDS LIKE, SO PICTURE THAT), THAT IN FACT, I HAD THE PERFECT RECIPE FOR THIS LEFTOVER SMOKED WHITE FISH! AND THAT, MY FRIENDS, IS WHY YOU ARE LUCKY ENOUGH TO HAVE MY FAVORITE BRUNCH RECIPE EVER. HASHEM ALWAYS SENDS US EXACTLY WHAT WE NEED AT EXACTLY THE RIGHT TIME!

1 cup butter

6-8 small red radishes, grated

¼ cup grated fresh horseradish

½ tsp kosher salt

¼ tsp coarsely ground black pepper

1 long, crusty baguette, sliced in half lengthwise

1 good quality smoked whitefish, flaked

¾ cup micro greens, to garnish

In a small bowl, combine butter, radish, salt, and pepper.

Place baguette on a serving tray.

Spread inside of baguette with radish butter.
Add flaked whitefish to the baguette.

Top with micro greens; serve on a large platter with a serrated knife so everyone can help themselves to a piece and enjoy!

TIPS + TRICKS
If you don't have a good, crusty on the outside, chewy on the inside baguette to work with, you can lightly toast what you have to add that texture.

NOTE
Radish butter is also delicious as a dip for crudité. I know, dip vegetables in butter? That doesn't sound right. Oh, but it is.

VARIATION
Replace smoked white fish with any variety of smoked fish or lox you like! You can even be wild and use herring!

an apron

is

just a

capon

backwards

poultry

easy chicken marinades

THESE RECIPES ARE ALL ABOUT MAKING YOUR LIFE EASIER. FIND A POCKET OF TIME, THINK 30–35 MINUTES OR SO, TO PREP ALL 7 MARINADES, ADD IN WHATEVER TYPE OF CHICKEN YOUR FAMILY LIKES, THEN POP IT INTO THE FREEZER. PULL OUT THE BAG IN THE MORNING TO DEFROST THEN ADD THE CONTENTS TO A 9X13 INCH PAN, BAKE, AND YOU'RE DONE. IT'S THAT EASY.

HERE ARE MY BEST TIPS FOR GETTING THIS DONE PROPERLY

Make sure you have all the ingredients and set them out on your counter.

Prep all the chicken and place each portion on a piece of foil so that it's ready to pop into the marinades.

Label each ziptop bag with the name of the marinade and the date.

Double each recipe so that now your freezer is stocked with 14 ready to cook chicken dinners!

NOTE

For all these recipes, you can use any chicken on the bone: 8 bottoms, 8 breasts, 16 drumsticks, or 1 whole chicken, cut up. Bake the same way!

pomegranate teriyaki chicken

1 whole chicken, cut into eighths (see Note)

MARINADE

¼ **cup** pomegranate molasses

¼ **cup** soy sauce

4 cloves garlic

¼ **tsp** cardamom

1 tsp kosher salt

½ **tsp** coarsely ground black pepper

1 Tbsp honey

Place chicken pieces into a ziptop bag.
Mix all marinade ingredients together in a bowl.
Pour marinade into the bag over the chicken.
Place bag flat into a 9x13 inch pan; place into the freezer.

Once frozen, bag can be removed from pan and replaced in the freezer in a vertical or horizontal manner to save space!

Freeze for up to 4 weeks.

TO COOK

Transfer chicken from freezer to the fridge the night before you want to cook it.

Preheat oven to 350°F / 180°C. Coat a 9x13 inch baking pan with nonstick cooking spray.
Place defrosted chicken with its marinade into prepared pan.
Cover pan tightly with foil.

Bake for 1 hour and 20 minutes.
Uncover pan; bake for 15-25 minutes, basting the chicken every 7 minutes.

sticky buffalo chicken

Place chicken pieces into a ziptop bag.
Mix all marinade ingredients together in a bowl.
Pour marinade into the bag over the chicken.
Place bag flat into a 9x13 inch pan; place into the freezer.

Once frozen, bag can be removed from pan and replaced in the freezer in a vertical or horizontal manner to save space!

Freeze for up to 4 weeks.

TO COOK

Transfer chicken from freezer to the fridge the night before you want to cook it.

Preheat oven to 350°F / 180°C. Coat a 9x13 inch baking pan with nonstick cooking spray.
Place defrosted chicken with its marinade into prepared pan.
Cover pan tightly with foil.

Bake for 1 hour and 20 minutes.
Uncover pan; bake for 15-25 minutes, basting the chicken every 7 minutes.

1 whole chicken, cut into eighths (see Note)

MARINADE

2 cups hot sauce, such as Frank's

1¼ **cups** brown sugar

PHOTO ORDER
CLOCKWISE FROM
TOP LEFT CORNER
Scallion lime,
Apricot Soy,
Harissa Lemon Olive,
Fig and Balsamic,
Sticky Buffalo,
Apricot Soy, Caesar

caesar chicken cutlets

Place chicken pieces into a ziptop bag.
Mix all marinade ingredients together in a bowl.
Pour marinade into the bag over the chicken.
Place bag flat into a 9x13 inch pan; place into the freezer.

Once frozen, bag can be removed from pan and replaced in the freezer in a vertical or horizontal manner to save space!

Freeze for up to 4 weeks.

TO COOK

Transfer chicken from freezer to the fridge the night before you want to cook it.

Preheat grill, or grill pan.
Once pan is very hot, add chicken.

Grill for 2-3 minutes on each side until cooked through.

16 pieces thinly sliced chicken cutlets

MARINADE

1 recipe Best Caesar Dressing Ever (page 44)

2 Tbsp flour

fig and balsamic chicken

1 whole chicken, cut into eighths (see Note on page 156)

MARINADE

5 tsp fig jam

¼ cup balsamic vinegar

1 Tbsp soy sauce

1 Tbsp kosher salt

1 Tbsp coarsely ground black pepper

4 cloves garlic

1 onion, halved, sliced

Place chicken pieces into a ziptop bag.
Mix all marinade ingredients together in a bowl.
Pour marinade into the bag over the chicken.
Place bag flat into a 9x13 inch pan; place into the freezer.

Once frozen, bag can be removed from pan and replaced in the freezer in a vertical or horizontal manner to save space!

Freeze for up to 4 weeks.

TO COOK

Transfer chicken from freezer to the fridge the night before you want to cook it.

Preheat oven to 350°F / 180°C. Coat a 9x13 inch baking pan with nonstick cooking spray.
Place defrosted chicken with its marinade into prepared pan.
Cover pan tightly with foil.

Bake for 1 hour and 20 minutes.
Uncover pan; bake for 15-25 minutes, basting the chicken every 7 minutes.

harissa lemon olive chicken

Place chicken pieces into a ziptop bag.
Mix all marinade ingredients together in a bowl.
Pour marinade into the bag over the chicken.
Place bag flat into a 9x13 inch pan; place into the freezer.

Once frozen, bag can be removed from pan and replaced in the freezer in a vertical or horizontal manner to save space!

Freeze for up to 4 weeks.

TO COOK

Transfer chicken from freezer to the fridge the night before you want to cook it.

Preheat oven to 350°F / 180°C. Coat a 9x13 inch baking pan with nonstick cooking spray.
Place defrosted chicken with its marinade into prepared pan.
Cover pan tightly with foil.

Bake for 1 hour and 20 minutes.
Uncover pan; bake for 15-25 minutes, basting the chicken every 7 minutes.

1 whole chicken, cut into eighths (see Note on page 156)

MARINADE

3 Tbsp harissa (page 30)

3 Tbsp preserved lemon puree (page 24)

2 cups pitted green olives

4 cloves garlic, minced

1½ cups tomato sauce

¼ cup extra virgin olive oil

½ tsp kosher salt

½ tsp coarsely ground black pepper

apricot soy chicken

1 whole chicken, cut into eighths
(see Note on page 156)

MARINADE

3 cloves garlic, minced

10 oz apricot jam

¼ cup hot sauce, such as Frank's

¼ cup soy sauce

1 Tbsp fish free Worcestershire sauce

¼ tsp kosher salt

½ tsp coarsely ground black pepper

Place chicken pieces into a ziptop bag.

Mix all marinade ingredients together in a bowl.
Pour marinade into the bag over the chicken.
Place bag flat into a 9x13 inch pan; place into the freezer.
Once frozen, bag can be removed from tin and replaced in the freezer in a vertical or horizontal manner to save space!

Freeze for up to 4 weeks.

TO COOK

Transfer chicken from freezer to the fridge the night before you want to cook it.

Preheat oven to 350°F / 180°C. Coat a 9x13 inch baking pan with nonstick cooking spray.
Place defrosted chicken with its marinade into prepared pan.
Cover pan tightly with foil.

Bake for 1 hour 20 minutes.
Uncover pan; bake for 15-25 minutes, basting the chicken every 7 minutes.

Serve hot and enjoy!

scallion lime chicken

Place chicken pieces into a ziptop bag.
Mix all marinade ingredients together in a bowl.
Pour marinade into the bag over the chicken.
Place bag flat into a 9x13 inch pan; place into the freezer.

Once frozen, bag can be removed from pan and replaced in the freezer in a vertical or horizontal manner to save space!

Freeze for up to 4 weeks.

TO COOK CUTLETS

Transfer chicken from freezer to the fridge the night before you want to cook it.

Preheat grill, or grill pan.
Once pan is very hot, add chicken.
Grill for 2-3 minutes on each side until cooked through.

TO COOK WHOLE CHICKEN

Transfer chicken from freezer to the fridge the night before you want to cook it.

Preheat oven to 350°F / 180°C. Coat a 9x13 inch baking pan with nonstick cooking spray.
Place defrosted chicken with its marinade into prepared pan.
Cover pan tightly with foil.

Bake for 1 hour and 20 minutes.
Uncover pan; bake for 15-25 minutes, basting the chicken every 7 minutes.

16 thinly sliced chicken cutlets,
or **1 whole** chicken cut into eighths
(see Note on page 156)

MARINADE

4 cloves garlic, minced

4 scallions, roughly chopped

2 Tbsp lime zest

½ cup olive oil

1 tsp kosher salt

1 tsp coarsely ground black pepper

spinach artichoke chicken burger

YECHEZKEL MEIR, WHO JUST LIKE HIS FATHER IS SUUUUPER PICKY ABOUT PROTEINS (ONLY WELL DONE, NO BONE, NO SKIN … YOU GET THE POINT), IS A GIANT FAN OF THE CHICKEN BURGER! SO, I MAKE THEM ALL THE TIME TO ENSURE THAT HE NEVER FORGETS THAT HE LIKES THEM! I CAME UP WITH THIS RECIPE AS A WAY OF ADDING MORE FLAVOR TO THE CHICKEN BUT ALSO AS A MEANS TO KEEP THE BURGER MOIST! BONUS: THEY ARE ALSO FILLED WITH EXTRA NUTRIENTS THAT NO LITTLE PERSON WILL OBJECT TO BECAUSE THEY ARE DELICIOUS!

1 tsp oil

2 onions, thinly sliced

1¼ tsp kosher salt, divided

¾ tsp coarsely ground black pepper, divided

1 clove garlic, minced

1 tsp balsamic vinegar

1 lb ground white meat chicken

1 small onion, puréed
(I do this in the food processor)

¼ cup thawed frozen spinach

2-3 artichoke hearts
(if frozen, defrost), chopped

1 Tbsp Dijon mustard

½ tsp cayenne pepper (optional)

To a pan set over the lowest heat, add oil, onions, ¼ teaspoon salt, and ¼ teaspoon pepper.
Cook for about 1 hour, stirring frequently until deeply golden and sticky.

During the last minute of cooking, add garlic and balsamic vinegar.
Set aside to cool for 5 minutes.

In a large bowl, combine remaining ingredients with remaining 1 teaspoon salt and remaining ½ teaspoon pepper.
Add ¾ of the onion mixture (reserving remaining ¼ to top your burger).
Mix thoroughly to combine all the ingredients.

Preheat a cast iron skillet or pan over medium heat.
Once pan is hot, add oil just to coat the bottom.

Use your hands to grab a scoop of the chicken mixture and drop into the hot pan to form a patty.
Cook for 2-3 minutes on the first side and another 2 minutes on the second side.

Top with reserved onion mixture. Serve hot and enjoy!!!

dumplings — 1 filling, 3 ways

HI. MY NAME IS DANIELLE AND DUMPLINGS ARE MY ALL TIME FAVORITE FOOD ON THE PLANET. FOR REAL. I CAN EAT THEM IN A HOUSE, I CAN EAT THEM WITH A MOUSE, IN A BOAT, WITH A GOAT, I CAN EAT THEM HERE OR THERE, I CAN EAT THEM ANYWHERE. WHICH IS WHY I INCLUDED ONE BASE RECIPE AND THREE SAUCES. YOU KNOW, BECAUSE MOODS.

PHOTO ORDER
TOP TO BOTTOM
Spicy Peanut Sauce
Light Asian Broth
Pan Fried

dumplings

1 lb ground chicken

1 lb ground turkey (for moisture)

5 whole scallions, thinly sliced

4 cloves garlic, grated

1 inch fresh ginger, grated

2 Tbsp soy sauce

1 Tbsp rice vinegar

2 tsp toasted sesame oil

2 packages wonton wrappers (circle or square, your choice!)

In a large bowl, mix together all ingredients very well.

Place 1 large spoonful of mix onto the middle of each wonton wrapper.
Dip your finger into a little water and spread around the edge of the dough.
Seal dumpling any way you like. (I like to make pleats on one side.)

Cook as indicated in each recipe.

spicy peanut sauce

½ cup peanut butter

3 Tbsp low sodium soy sauce

2 Tbsp chili flakes

1 clove garlic, minced

1 tsp minced ginger

1 tsp sesame oil

¾ cup water

1 batch dumplings cooked in salted boiling water for 4-5 minutes until cooked through

TO GARNISH

1 cup chopped scallions

Add sauce ingredients to a blender or a food processor fitted with the "S" blade. Process for 1 minute to combine. Scrape down the sides; process again.

Pour sauce over hot dumplings. Garnish with chopped scallions.

pan fried dumplings

DIPPING SAUCE

2 Tbsp sugar

¼ cup boiling hot water

3 Tbsp + 2 tsp low sodium soy sauce

¼ cup chopped scallions

NOTE

This is not the most authentic way to pan fry dumplings, but I think it makes the process easier.

Bring water to a boil in a large pot. Add salt. Add dumplings, a few at a time.
Cook for 3-4 minutes, then transfer to a rack to dry. Repeat with remaining dumplings.

Once dumplings have dried, place a frying pan over high heat. Add a little bit of oil; add dumplings. Don't overcrowd the pan! The dumplings should get crispy after 30-45 seconds.

Remove from pan and continue with the rest! Serve with Dipping Sauce (below).

DIPPING SAUCE

In a bowl, combine sugar and water. Stir until sugar has dissolved. Add soy sauce and scallions.

Serve warm, cold, or room temperature

dumplings in a light asian broth

BROTH

6 cups stock (I like **3 cups** chicken stock + **3 cups** beef stock)

1½ inches ginger, peeled, sliced into 4 long pieces

5 cloves garlic, halved

2 Tbsp chopped scallions

2 Tbsp low sodium soy sauce

1 Tbsp mirin (optional)

1 batch dumplings, cooked in salted boiling water for 4-5 minutes until cooked through, **¼ cup** cooking water reserved

Add all broth ingredients to a pot; bring to a boil.
Once boiling, add ¼ cup of the reserved dumpling cooking water.
Boil for 1 minute, then reduce to a low simmer. Cook, covered for 30 minutes.

To serve, return broth to a boil and add dumpling for 1 minute to heat through.
Add dumplings and a little broth to each bowl; top with scallions.

NOTE

Think ravioli in a simple, clear, yet complex flavored broth, only Asian.

mexican chicken and rice

ALTHOUGH I DID NOT GROW UP EATING RICE — HENCE MY INABILITY TO COOK IT PROPERLY — IT IS A STAPLE DISH IN MY HOME NOW. NO MEAL IS COMPLETE FOR ELI AND THE KIDS WITHOUT RICE (I MEAN, COUSCOUS, PTITIM, OR SOMETHING OF THE SORT ARE ALL OPTIONS, BUT RICE IS NUMBER 1). AND OF COURSE, THE RICE MUST BE FRESH. WHICH MEANS THERE ARE NIGHTS WHEN LEFTOVER RICE IS INEVITABLE. EITHER A LARGE AMOUNT OR A FEW SMALL AMOUNTS THAT HAVE ACCUMULATED INTO A NICE SUM OF LEFTOVER RICE. THAT IS HOW THIS RECIPE CAME TO BE. TOO MUCH LEFTOVER RICE, NO DINNER PLANNED, WANT SOMETHING FLAVORFUL AND HEARTY, BUT ALSO DON'T WANT TO WORK THAT HARD BECAUSE, WELL, LIFE.

12 chicken cutlets, thinly sliced

4 chorizo sausages, thinly sliced

2 purple onions, sliced

1 leek, white and light green only, chopped

2 red bell peppers, sliced

1 cup cooked corn kernels (or canned)

1 cup cooked black beans (or canned)

½ cup cilantro leaves, torn

2 chilies, finely chopped

¼ cup sprouts

3 cloves garlic, chopped

2 chilies in adobo

8 oz beer

1 cup chicken/beef/veg stock (or water)

6 cups cooked rice.

MARINADE

2 tbsp oil

2 tsp kosher salt

2 tsp coarsely ground black pepper

2 tsp smoked paprika

2 tsp garlic powder

TO GARNISH

1 cup cilantro

1-2 limes, each cut into 4 wedges

Add marinade ingredients to a bowl or ziptop bag.
Add chicken.

In a very large pot, sauté sausage over medium high heat, stirring often, until the edges begin to crisp up (6-8 minutes).
Remove sausage slices; set aside.

Add chicken with its marinade to the pot.
Sauté until chicken is cooked through. Remove chicken; set aside.

Add onions, leek, and peppers to the pot. Cook for 10 minutes until softened.

Add corn, beans, cilantro leaves, sprouts, chilies, and garlic. Cook for 2 minutes while stirring.

Return chicken and sausage to the pot.
Add chilies in adobo; stir to combine.

Add beer and stock; use a wooden spoon to scrape up any brown bits from the bottom of the pot.
Bring to a boil; cook for 5 minutes.

Add cooked rice; stir to combine.
Cook for 3 minutes.

Garnish with cilantro and lime wedges.
Serve and enjoy.

tiny shnitSel

THIS IS BY FAR THE MOST ANTICIPATED RECIPE IN THIS ENTIRE BOOK, WHICH IS JUST TOO FUNNY, BECAUSE OF ALL THE RECIPES I'VE EVER CREATED, THIS IS THE ONLY ONE YOU DON'T EVEN REALLY NEED TO FOLLOW A RECIPE FOR! IT'S MORE ABOUT TECHNIQUE THAN ANYTHING ELSE. SO I'M GOING TO DIVERGE FROM THE STANDARD RECIPE WRITING TECHNIQUES YOU'VE SEEN IN THE BOOK SO FAR, TELL YOU WHAT YOU NEED, AND THEN GO INTO DETAIL ON HOW TO GET IT DONE! THE AMOUNTS WILL VARY DEPENDING ON HOW MUCH CHICKEN YOU USE, SO I'LL GIVE THE AMOUNTS I USE TO MAKE 1 BATCH FOR 1 SHABBOS MEAL WITH COMPANY.

12 very thin chicken cutlets, partially frozen (or partially defrosted if they were frozen)

canola or avocado oil, for frying

FLOUR MIXTURE

2 cups all purpose flour

1 tsp kosher salt

1 tsp coarsely ground black pepper

EGG MIXTURE

7 eggs, very well beaten

½ tsp kosher salt

BREADCRUMBS

5 cups original panko breadcrumbs (no weird flavors allowed), divided

½ tsp kosher salt

POPPER SAUCE

1 cup hot sauce, such as Frank's

¼-½ cup honey (depending on how sweet you like it)

The first thing you are going to want to do is put on gloves. Get out a plastic cutting board and a medium bowl, and put on disposable gloves.
Next, using a very, very sharp knife, cut the partially frozen chicken, horizontally, into tiny little ¼ inch wide strips.
(They're bigger after you coat them in the breadcrumbs, so if you want them to look like mine, cut them a bit thinner than you see in the photo.)

BREADING

Place flour, salt, and pepper into a ziptop bag.
Add chicken strips, seal bag, and shake well to coat every strip.

In a large bowl, combine eggs and salt.

To a medium shallow dish, add 1½ cups breadcrumbs, adding more as needed. (I like to add only a little at a time; this way if I have leftover breadcrumbs, I can return them to the container. Any breadcrumbs remaining after you have coated all your chicken must be discarded.)

Prepare a third large bowl to hold the breaded raw chicken.

Wearing gloves, pull out a handful of flour coated chicken and gently shake your hand over the bag to allow excess flour to fall through your fingertips like a sifter.

Add a handful of chicken to egg mixture.
Toss gently to coat.

Remove the chicken from the egg mixture with your second hand, holding your hand over the bowl for a moment to allow excess egg to drip off, and place chicken pieces into breadcrumbs.

Using the hand that you used for the flour, toss the chicken in the breadcrumbs.
Gently place breaded chicken into prepared large bowl.

Once all your chicken has been breaded, it is time to fry!

FRYING

Set up a cooling rack over a large piece of foil.

Pour 1 inch of oil into a large high walled frying pan.
Place pan over medium high heat.
Once oil reaches 350°F / 180°C or the handle of a wooden spoon inserted in the oil bubbles around the edges, your oil will be ready for frying.
(You can always just drop one piece of chicken into the oil if you are uncertain.)

Add enough breaded chicken pieces to fill the pan without being crowded so that each piece can properly fry and crisp up.

This method of breading is called the "wet hand, dry hand" method. It basically means one hand is used for flour and breadcrumbs and the other hand goes in the egg mixture. It keeps the breading process cleaner and easier.

Keep an empty bottle of oil to pour the oil you fried the chicken in, instead of pouring the used oil down your drain. Simply let the oil cool completely, then use a funnel to pour it into the bottle. Close the bottle and discard.

You can absolutely use the exact same method for regular size shnitsel!

For poppers, I like to replace half the panko mixture with cornflake crumbs.

Premade cornflake crumbs are fine. The same way raisins are fine: NOT FINE AT ALL. Buy a box of cornflakes, grind them in the food processor, and use those.

Feel free to fully substitute panko with cornflake crumbs for a completely gluten free option. Just add 2 tablespoons cornstarch to the cornflake crumbs.

If you live in Israel, where honey costs as much as a car and cars cost as much as a home, you can swap out honey for sugar. If you are not using the popper sauce right away, though, and it is not properly reheated, the sugar will crystallize, giving the poppers a sandy texture.

To serve tiny shinitsel on Shabbos day, do not pour the sauce over right away. When you wake up on Shabbos morning, remove sauce from fridge and allow it to come to room temperature. To reheat the tiny shnitsel, simply put the baking sheet, uncovered, on the hot plate or in the warming drawer 1 hour before serving.

Fry each batch of tiny shnitsel for 4-5 minutes, gently moving them around the pan as needed.

Once shnitsel is golden brown, use a slotted spoon to remove from oil and place immediately on cooling rack.

Continue cooking the chicken in batches and removing pieces to the rack. (If the cooling rack fills up, transfer the already cooled pieces of chicken to a pan or serving dish.)

Once all your chicken is fried and cooled, your job is done!

POPPER SAUCE

Add hot sauce and honey to a small nonstick pot.
Stir to combine.
Place over medium heat.
Once bubbles form around the edges of the pan, remove from heat.

Pour sauce right over tiny shnitsel or allow mixture to cool in the pot and then transfer to a container.

Store in the fridge for up to 1 month.

chicken mole fajitas

I LOVE MEXICAN FLAVORS. THE FOOD HAS DEPTH FROM ALL THE DIFFERENT SPICES, IS COLORFUL FROM THE VEGETABLES, ACIDIC FROM THE CITRUS, AND JUST SO INSANELY DELICIOUS. WHEN YOU HAVE A RECIPE THAT'S BASICALLY A ONE POT DINNER WITH ALL THOSE COMPONENTS, THAT'S A DEFINITE DINNER WIN!

16 super thin chicken cutlets, cut into thin, tiny pieces (or **8** thick boneless chicken cutlets)

2 tsp garlic powder

2 tsp onion powder

¼ tsp coriander

½ tsp kosher salt

¼ tsp coarsely ground black pepper

½ tsp smoked paprika

1 Tbsp canola oil

2 cloves garlic, chopped

1 oz (25 grams) dark chocolate (usually that's ¼ bar)

1 (15 oz) can tomato sauce

⅓ cup chicken stock (or **1 cup** if using thick chicken cutlets)

2-3 chipotles in adobo (optional)

1 Tbsp adobo sauce

10-12 flour tortillas

Combine all the spices in a bowl; sprinkle over chicken.

Preheat a large pan over medium high heat.
Add canola oil.

Add chicken and garlic to the pan. (If using thick pieces, just brown on both sides and remove from pan.)
Once chicken is cooked through, add chocolate, stir, and then immediately stir in tomato sauce and chicken stock.
Stir in chipotles and adobo sauce.

Bring mixture to a boil.
(If using thick, not cut up cutlets, return them to the sauce at this point. Reduce heat to low and allow chicken to simmer till soft. Then remove from sauce, cut up chicken, and return it to the pot.)

Serve hot over Avocado Crema (below) on a charred tortilla.
To char tortillas, use tongs to hold each tortilla over an open flame for about 20 seconds, moving tortilla in a circular motion so that it chars evenly.
If you don't have an open flame or cannot do that for kashrut reasons, heat a nonstick pan over high heat.
Add tortilla to the pan (without oil) and cook for 30 seconds on each side.

For extra yumminess, top with sumac pickled onions (page 26) and cilantro!

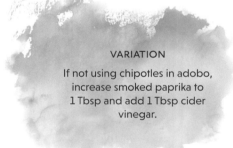

VARIATION

If not using chipotles in adobo, increase smoked paprika to 1 Tbsp and add 1 Tbsp cider vinegar.

BONUS RECIPE: avocado crema

2 avocados

2 Tbsp vegan sour cream

¼ cup fresh lime juice

½ tsp kosher salt

¼ tsp coarsely ground black pepper

Place all crema ingredients into a food processor fitted with the "S" blade.
Process until smooth and creamy!

beer battered chicken nuggets

I.E., AN EASIER WAY TO MAKE TINY SHNITSEL FOR THOSE DAYS WHEN YOU JUST DON'T HAVE TIME!

12 chicken cutlets, cut into ½ inch pieces

oil, for frying

2 cups all purpose flour

1 Tbsp + 1 tsp kosher salt

1 tsp coarsely ground black pepper

2 Tbsp paprika

1 Tbsp granulated garlic

2 tsp mustard powder

12 oz light beer

½ cup water

Pour 3 inches oil into a medium pot; place over medium high heat.
While oil is heating, add flour, salt, pepper, and spices to a bowl.
Stir to combine.
Slowly pour in beer and water. Stir till a thick pancake-like batter forms.
Add chicken; stir really well to make sure each piece is coated!

Once oil is hot, add chicken in small batches to the pot.
Don't overcrowd them or they'll stick together!
Fry for 2 minutes total, only stirring after 1 minute.

Use a slotted spoon to remove and place on cooling rack.

Serve hot and enjoy.

NOTE

I like to serve these with a dipping sauce, such as the popper sauce (page 166), honey mustard, or curried mayo (page 28)!

artichoke chicken

THIS IS THE FIRST CHICKEN RECIPE I EVER DEVELOPED ON MY OWN. IT'S BEEN 12 YEARS AND I STILL MAKE A VERSION OF THIS CHICKEN AT LEAST ONCE A MONTH. I LOVE THE BRIGHT FLAVORS, THE CREAMY ARTICHOKE, AND HOW THE FLOUR FROM THE CHICKEN EVER SO SLIGHTLY THICKENS THE SAUCE. IT'S MY GO TO FOR SHABBOS WHEN I DON'T KNOW WHAT I'M IN THE MOOD FOR, BECAUSE AS SOON AS I SMELL IT AS IT COMES OUT OF THE OVEN, ALL I WANT TO DO IS EAT IT!

6 artichokes, or **1 bag** frozen artichoke hearts

1 lemon

12 thin chicken cutlets

1 cup flour

1 tsp kosher salt

1 tsp coarsely ground black pepper

2 Tbsp canola oil

1 Tbsp minced garlic

½ Tbsp crushed red pepper flakes (optional)

1 cup dry white wine

½ cup chicken stock

1 handful fresh parsley (optional)

ARTICHOKES

(If using frozen artichokes, defrost, cut away any rough parts, and skip to preparing the chicken.)

To a large pot, add artichokes; cover with water.

Cut lemon into 8 pieces, squeeze the juice into the water, and add lemon wedges into the water.

Bring mixture to a boil, reduce heat, and simmer for 2 hours.

Remove artichokes and set aside for 30 minutes until cool enough to handle.

Peel leaves off the artichoke to expose the heart. (Don't discard the leaves; they are delicious dipped into any salad dressing or dip and eaten.)

Remove the spikes and cut heart into 4 pieces. Set aside.

CHICKEN

Preheat oven to 350°F / 180°C. Coat a 9x13 inch pan with nonstick cooking spray.

In a large bowl, combine flour, salt, and pepper; toss with chicken.

In a large frying pan, heat oil on medium high heat and brown chicken cutlets on both sides, 2-3 minutes per side. (Chicken will still be a little raw inside.)

Place chicken pieces in a single layer into prepared pan.

In the same skillet, sauté artichoke heart pieces, garlic, and crushed red pepper flakes for 1 minute, being careful not to burn the garlic. (If not enough oil is left in the pan, drizzle in a tiny bit.)

Add white wine while scraping all the bits off the bottom of the pan.

Allow alcohol to cook off for 2-3 minutes.

Add chicken stock; season with salt and pepper to taste.

Pour sauce over chicken; bake for 30 minutes.

If adding the fresh parsley, sprinkle on top during the last 2 minutes of baking.

NOTE

Use this recipe as a jumping off point. Swap the artichoke for any vegetable or add in capers, mushrooms, etc.

NOTE

If you don't want to use wine, you can sub 1 cup white wine with an additional ½ cup chicken soup and an additional lemon.

Enjoy!

potato chip shnitsel

THIS IS, TO A FEW MEMBERS OF MY FAMILY, THE BEST VERSION OF SHNITSEL. IF IT WEREN'T FOR THE FACT THAT THE CRUMBS WERE MADE OF DEEP FRIED POTATOES, I WOULD MAKE THIS ALL YEAR LONG. I LOVE THE IDEA OF A COLD, CRUNCHY SALAD OVER A HOT, JUICY, RIGHT OUT OF THE OVEN PIECE OF SHNITSEL, BUT YOU CAN EASILY SEPARATE THIS RECIPE'S COMPONENTS AND SERVE THEM ON THEIR OWN. I PROMISE, THEY ARE THAT GOOD!

CHICKEN

12 thin chicken cutlets

4 cups potato chip crumbs (salty potato chips crushed by hand or in a food processor until they resemble fine breadcrumbs)

3 cups potato chips gently crushed by hand (they should look like broken potato chips, not crumbs)

2 cups potato starch

3 eggs, beaten

1 Tbsp garlic powder

1 tsp black coarsely ground black pepper

¼ tsp kosher salt

oil, for frying

SLAW

4 nectarines or peaches (slightly firm), halved and thinly sliced

3 cups shredded purple cabbage

1 purple onion, diced

1 cup roasted, salted cashews, roughly chopped

½ cup lime juice

3 Tbsp sugar

1-2 Thai chilies, finely chopped OR any small spicy red pepper (optional)

½ cup cilantro leaves, finely chopped

1 tsp kosher salt

¼ tsp coarsely ground black pepper

In a large bowl, combine all potato chips and potato starch.

In a second bowl, combine eggs, garlic powder, pepper, and salt.

Dip each cutlet in egg mixture and then into potato chip mixture, using your hands to help press the potato chips onto the chicken.

Heat 1-2 inches of oil in a frying pan.
When oil is hot, add 2-3 pieces of shnitsel to the pan.
It is important not to overcrowd the pan or the shnitsel will steam and not get crunchy!

Fry for 2-3 minutes on the first side and then flip and fry for 1-2 minutes on the second side.
Transfer from pan to a cooling rack to allow any excess oil to drip off.

SLAW

In a large bowl, toss together sliced peaches, cabbage, onion, and cashews.

In a small bowl or jar with a tightly fitting lid, combine remaining ingredients.

Mix or shake well to dissolve the sugar.

Toss with slaw; marinate for 4-5 minutes.

To serve, place ¼ cup slaw over each piece of shnitsel.

lemon and black pepper chicken

I LOVE ALL FORMS OF SPICY HEAT. BLACK PEPPER, ALTHOUGH USUALLY USED AS SEASONING, IF USED WELL, CAN BRING ITS OWN BEAUTIFUL, SPICY, AND DELICIOUS FLAVOR TO THE PARTY. ADD IN A LITTLE BIT OF LEMON TO BRIGHTEN THE BLACK PEPPER AND WHOA, I'M SOLD!

12 thinly sliced chicken cutlets or pargiyot (dark meat chicken cutlets)

⅓ cup minced garlic (**1-1½ head**s garlic)

1 tsp kosher salt

3 tsp coarsely ground black pepper

1 Tbsp olive oil

1 large lemon (or lime!), halved

Optional: Use only **2 tsp** coarsely ground black pepper and add **1** Thai chili minced with the garlic!

In a bowl, combine all ingredients except lemon.

Preheat cast iron skillet or grill pan on high heat for white meat chicken or medium high for pargiyot.
Once pan is hot, lightly grease it; place chicken on pan.

THIN CHICKEN CUTLETS

After 35-40 seconds, carefully squeeze a little of the lemon juice over the uncooked side.
After another 20-30 seconds, flip chicken over and squeeze on more lemon juice while the second side cooks.

PARGIYOT OR THICKER CUTLETS

After 1½ minutes, add lemon juice.
Cook another 30 seconds, then flip, squeeze on more lemon juice, and cook for 2 minutes.

Cook until chicken is cooked through.

Serve hot, room temp, or cold and enjoy!

confetti pepper chicken

WHEN I WAS FIRST MARRIED, MY MOTHER GAVE ME A RECIPE FROM HER CLOSE FRIEND, NAOMI, TO MAKE FOR SHABBOS. IT WAS A VERSION OF THIS CHICKEN THAT I TWEAKED AND TWEAKED OVER THE YEARS TO CREATE THIS EASY BUT FLAVORFUL CHICKEN. WHAT I REALLY LOVE ABOUT THIS DISH IS THAT IT'S A COOKED CHICKEN THAT YOU CAN REHEAT OR SERVE AT ROOM TEMPERATURE FOR SHABBOS LUNCH BECAUSE IT IS NOT SAUCY!

12 chicken cutlets

1 cup flour (I use spelt)

2 tsp kosher salt, divided

2 tsp coarsely ground black pepper, divided

3 Tbsp oil, divided

4 bell peppers (**1** red, **1** yellow, **1** orange, **1** green), cut into ½ inch dice

1 onion, diced

4 cloves garlic, minced

½ cup sherry or white wine

1¼ cups chicken stock

Heat oven to 350°F / 180°C. Coat a baking dish with nonstick cooking spray.

In a large bowl, combine flour, 1 teaspoon salt, and 1 teaspoon pepper.

Dip each cutlet into flour, shaking off excess.

Heat a large pan over medium heat.
Add 2 teaspoons oil; working in batches, brown chicken on both sides for 1 minute. Don't cook through. Add oil as needed for each batch.
Transfer chicken to prepared baking dish. Set aside.

Once all the chicken has browned, add remaining oil to the pan along with peppers, onion, remaining teaspoon salt, and remaining teaspoon pepper.
Cook, stirring, for about 10 minutes, until pepper and onions have softened and released their juices.
Add garlic; stir for 1 more minute.
Add wine; simmer for 4 minutes. Stir in chicken stock.

Pour all the veg and pan juices over the chicken in the baking dish.

Bake about 35 minutes until the edges of the peppers slightly char.

Serve hot and enjoy.

crispy baked chicken fingers

DINNER AGAIN? I KNOW. IT'S CRAZY. NO MATTER HOW MANY TIMES YOU GO THROUGH IT, IT COMES BACK AGAIN AND AGAIN. IT'S ALMOST LIKE LAUNDRY. ONLY YOU CAN'T EAT YOUR LAUNDRY, SO AT LEAST THERE'S THAT. THIS IS FOR THOSE DAYS. AND SINCE THOSE DAYS HAPPEN MORE THAN WE'D LIKE TO ADMIT, I GAVE YOU 3 VERSIONS SO THAT YOU CAN CHANGE THINGS UP. YOU'RE WELCOME.

CRISPY ASIAN BAKED SHNITSEL

1 package chicken tenders (about **18 pieces**) OR **12** thin cutlets

1 cup mayo

2 Tbsp minced garlic

2 Tbsp honey

1-2 tsp sriracha (depending how spicy you like it!)

1 Tbsp white miso

¼ cup soy sauce

3 cups panko breadcrumbs

BARBECUE CRISPY CHICKEN

1 package chicken tenders (about **18 pieces**) OR 12 thin cutlets

¼ cup mayo

¾ cup favorite barbecue sauce

1 tsp granulated garlic

1 tsp granulated onion

3 cups panko breadcrumbs

HONEY MUSTARD CRISPY CHICKEN

1 package chicken tenders (about **18 pieces**) OR **12** thin cutlets

¼ cup mayo

¼ cup Dijon mustard

3 Tbsp honey

3 cups panko breadcrumbs

Preheat oven to 350°F / 180°C.
Coat a baking sheet liberally with nonstick cooking spray.

In a large bowl, combine flavoring ingredients (aside from chicken and breadcrumbs) in selected recipe.
Add chicken to wet mixture; mix to coat.

Dip coated chicken into breadcrumbs, then place flat on prepared baking sheet.
Spray the top of the chicken pieces with a little more nonstick spray.

Bake for 30-40 minutes, until chicken is cooked through.

taste the rainbow chicken skewers

HERE'S MY THEORY — WELL, YOU SEE IT. I DON'T REALLY NEED TO EXPLAIN IT. BUT I WILL. IT MAKES ZERO SENSE TO PUT ALL DIFFERENT VEGETABLES AND PROTEINS ON ONE SINGLE SKEWER. IT JUST DOESN'T. I GET IT THOUGH. YOU WANT EVERYONE TO TAKE THEIR OWN ENTREE SKEWER AND EAT IT. BUT REALLY THINK ABOUT IT? TO GIVE PEOPLE A FULLY COOKED PIECE OF CHICKEN OR MEAT MEANS YOU'RE GIVING THEM MUSHY OR BURNT ONIONS AND TOMATOES. SO, LET'S SAY YOU GO VEGETARIAN, WELL NOW YOU'RE SERVING THEM UNDERCOOKED ZUCCHINI AND PEPPERS. NO! FOR THE LOVE OF FOOD. STOP. SEPARATE EACH ITEM ONTO ITS OWN SKEWER. COOK IT PROPERLY WHILE HELPING YOURSELF BY SAVING TIME STANDING OVER THE GRILL AND FLIPPING ONLY 5 OR 6 SKEWERS INSTEAD OF A TON OF INDIVIDUAL ITEMS AND PAT YOURSELF ON THE BACK WHEN YOU SERVE A BEAUTIFUL, COLORFUL PLATTER OF PERFECTLY COOKED FOOD!

MARINADE

¼ cup finely chopped garlic

6 Tbsp chopped scallions

2 tsp smoked paprika

2 tsp kosher salt

1 tsp coarsely ground black pepper

zest and juice of **6** limes

1 Tbsp honey, optional

SKEWERS

4 thick chicken cutlets, cut into 1 inch cubes

12-15 cherry tomatoes

1 yellow bell pepper, cut into 1 inch squares

1 orange bell pepper, cut into 1 inch squares

3 long spicy green peppers, cut into 1 inch cylinders

1 large zucchini, cut into ½ inch thick rounds

2 purple onions, cut into 1 inch squares

Process marinade ingredients in a food processor fitted with the "S" blade, or use an immersion blender to blend until combined.

Thread all the chicken and vegetables onto skewers, with each type on its own skewers!

Pour ½ the marinade over the skewered chicken.
Pour remaining the marinade over both sides of the skewered vegetables.

Grill chicken within 10 minutes of adding the marinade!
Grill chicken for 2 minutes on each side.

Grill vegetables on all sides till charred.

Serve hot and enjoy!

Actually, hot or cold!!!

It's good both ways!

spicy baked pargiyot

THIS IS MY FAVORITE TYPE OF CHICKEN TO HAVE AS LEFTOVERS THE NEXT DAY. IN FACT, I OFTEN MAKE IT AT THE BEGINNING OF THE WEEK AND JUST POP IT INTO MY FRIDGE TO HAVE LATER! THE FLAVOR IS SO DELICIOUS AND THE CHICKEN CAN BE THROWN INTO A SALAD AND DRESSED WITH ANY SALAD DRESSING YOU HAVE ON HAND!

4 boneless, skinless chicken thighs, halved

MARINADE

3 Tbsp olive oil

1 Tbsp hot Moroccan paprika in oil

1½ tsp kosher salt

1 tsp coarsely ground black pepper

2 tsp granulated garlic

2 tsp granulated onion

1 tsp dried parsley flakes

juice of **1** lemon

Preheat oven to 350°F / 180°C.

In a medium bowl, combine all marinade ingredients. Add chicken.
Marinate chicken for only 10 minutes.

Place chicken with its marinade in a lightly greased baking dish or Pyrex baking dish.
Bake, uncovered for 50 minutes – 1 hour, until edges of the chicken begin to slightly crisp up.

Serve hot, with a drizzle of techina!

grilled rosemary pargiyot

ONCE UPON A TIME, I WAS TESTING THIS CHICKEN FOR A COOKBOOK, THEN PROCEEDED TO MAKE IT FOR EVERY SHABBOS FOR MANY, MANY WEEKS BECAUSE I COULDN'T GET ENOUGH OF IT. TRUE STORY.

4 boneless, skinless chicken thighs, halved

4 cloves garlic, minced

3 Tbsp avocado oil

1 Tbsp Dijon mustard

1 Tbsp minced fresh rosemary (about **1 large** sprig)

1½ tsp kosher salt

1 tsp coarsely ground black pepper

1 tsp canola oil

In a medium bowl, combine all ingredients.
Mix well to evenly coat chicken pieces.

Set a grill pan over medium high heat.
Once pan is hot, lightly grease with 1 teaspoon canola oil.
Add chicken to the pan. Discard remaining marinade.

Cook for 6 minutes on one side, then flip and cook for 5 minutes on the second side.

Serve hot or cold and enjoy!

braised pargiyot with celery and peas

THERE ARE FEW FOODS THAT CAN HOLD THE TITLE OF ALL SEASON DISHES. FOR ME, THIS IS ONE OF THEM. IT'S HEARTY AND COMFORTING BUT BECAUSE OF THE LEMON IT'S STILL BRIGHT AND FRESH. SERVE THIS TO ME ON ANY FRIDAY NIGHT OF THE YEAR WITH SOME COUSCOUS OR RICE TO SOP UP ALL THAT DELICIOUS SAUCE AND MAYBE ADD A DOLLOP OF SCHUG AND A DRIZZLE OF TECHINA. I AM A HAPPY CAMPER!

8 pargiyot (boneless, skinless chicken thighs)

2 Tbsp neutral oil

1¼ tsp kosher salt, divided

1 tsp coarsely ground black pepper

1 onion, halved and thinly sliced

8 stalks celery, peeled, cut into 3 inch pieces

1 cup frozen peas (I like to use the smallest peas)

4 cloves garlic, minced

2 tsp turmeric

3 Tbsp dry white wine

1 lemon, halved

1½ cups chicken stock

2 Tbsp celery leaves, rinsed

¾ cup fresh cilantro leaves, divided

Heat a large pan over medium high heat. Add oil.

Season pargiyot on both sides with salt and pepper.
Add to the skillet and cook for 4 minutes on each side until golden.
Remove from pan; set aside.

Add onion and celery to the pan with remaining salt.
Cook, stirring often, for 2 minutes.
Once softened, add peas, garlic, and turmeric. Stir for one minute.
Add wine, scraping up any bits from the bottom of the pan.
Squeeze lemon juice right into the pan and then add the lemon halves to the pan.
Add chicken stock, celery leaves, and ½ the cilantro.

Return chicken to the pan, dipping each piece in the juices on both sides before nestling it in beneath the vegetables.
Top with remaining cilantro; bring mixture to a boil.
Once boiling, turn heat to low, cover the pot, and cook for 1 hour.

Bonus points if you baste the chicken pieces every 15-20 minutes!

Serve hot and enjoy!

all purpose poultry marinade

THIS CHICKEN IS COMPLETELY ADDICTIVE AND I'LL TELL YOU WHY: BECAUSE OF THE MULTIPLE FORMS OF ACIDITY IN THE MARINADE. IT'S BRIGHT, FRESH, FLAVORFUL, AND HEARTY AT THE SAME TIME. I DARE YOU TO MAKE IT ONLY ONCE!

1 chicken cut into 8 or 10 pieces (OR 4 chicken bottoms, thighs and drumsticks separated OR **12** thighs OR **1** spatchcocked chicken OR **12** pargiyot OR **12** chicken cutlets OR **2** boneless turkey breasts)

MARINADE

½ **small** yellow onion

12 cloves garlic

zest and juice of **1 large** lemon (about ¼ **cup** juice)

2 Tbsp red wine vinegar

1 tsp kosher salt

½ **tsp** coarsely ground black pepper

1 jalapeño, optional, for a little heat!

¼ **cup** packed herbs (I used all parsley, but think cilantro, mint, dill, even a combo)

2 Tbsp olive oil

MARINADE

In a food processor fitted with the "S" blade, process onion, garlic, zest, lemon juice, vinegar, salt, pepper, and jalapeño (if using), until very puréed.
Add herbs; with motor running, drizzle in oil.
Blend until herbs are very finely chopped.

Pour marinade over chicken and cook within 10-15 minutes or store marinade in fridge for up to 3 days and pour over poultry before cooking.

TO COOK

BONE IN CHICKEN

Set grill pan to medium low heat and allow to get very, very hot.
Then add chicken to the pan. For BBQ, place on a cooler spot on the grill so that the inside can have time to cook before the outside.
You'll know the chicken is ready to turn when it pulls off easily from grill pan or grill. Turn to cook on all sides.

The whole process should take 20-30 minutes, depending on the size of each piece of chicken!

CUTLETS

Grill for 2-3 minutes on the first side and 1-2 minutes on the second side over medium high heat.

PARGIYOT

Grill for 5 minutes on the first side and 4 minutes on the second side over medium high heat.

NOTE
You can double or triple the marinade recipe and freeze in individual portions to have ready all summer! Just remove the marinade from the freezer and place in the fridge the night before you want to use it. Or defrost it on the counter for 5-6 hours.

onion, maple + balsamic chicken

THE CHICKEN YOU MAKE WHEN YOU HAVE PICKY EATERS OR GUESTS COMING OVER AND YOU DON'T KNOW THEIR PREFERENCES. IT'S A UNIVERSAL CROWD PLEASER.

1 whole chicken, cut into 10 pieces (with or without skin)

kosher salt, for sprinkling

coarsely ground black pepper, for sprinkling

ONIONS

1 Tbsp canola oil

5 large onions, halved, thinly sliced

½ tsp kosher salt

½ cup maple syrup

⅓ cup + 1 Tbsp balsamic vinegar

2 Tbsp soy sauce

ONIONS

Heat a large pot over medium heat. Add oil and onions.
Cook onions, stirring constantly for 30-40 minutes, until they are soft and melty.
(If you want to walk away from the pot, turn the heat to very low and stir every 7-8 minutes. It will take longer, though.)

Once onions are deeply golden, add remaining ingredients. Remove from heat.

If making in advance, allow mixture to cool, then store in the fridge for up to 5 days.

CHICKEN

Preheat oven to 350°F / 180°C. Coat an oven to table baking dish with nonstick cooking spray.

Place chicken into prepared baking dish; season with a sprinkle of salt and pepper.
Top chicken with onion mixture, creating almost a crust over the chicken.
Pour any onion juices right on top.

Coat a large piece of foil with nonstick cooking spray.
Place foil sprayed side down over chicken and seal dish tightly.
Bake for 1 hour 25 minutes, covered, then remove foil and bake for 15-20 minutes.

Serve hot and enjoy!

shabbos chicken

WHAT MAKES THIS SHABBOS CHICKEN? IT'S SOMETHING ABOUT THE SWEET AND SOUR FLAVORS AND THE DARK MEAT CHICKEN BOTTOMS THAT GIVE ME ALL THESE ASHKENAZI FRIDAY NIGHT SHABBOS CHICKEN VIBES. ESPECIALLY WITH THE CABBAGE THROWN IN THERE; YOU CAN SERVE SOME RICE ON THE SIDE AND CALL IT A WHOLE MEAL. WHETHER YOU ACTUALLY MAKE THIS FOR A WEEKNIGHT DINNER, A SHABBOS MEAL, OR, I DON'T KNOW, SAY A SNACK MAYBE (WE DON'T JUDGE HERE), I THINK YOU'LL FIND THE CHICKEN DELICIOUS AND THE CABBAGE ABSOLUTELY IRRESISTIBLE!

SAUCE

4 cloves garlic, minced

1 cup apricot jam

5 heaping Tbsp tomato paste (**100 g**)

3 Tbsp soy sauce

2 Tbsp apple cider vinegar

2 Tbsp honey (optional, if you like more sweet, less sour)

2 tsp dried minced onion

2 tsp fish free Worcestershire sauce

1 tsp granulated garlic

½ tsp granulated onion

½ tsp coarsely cracked black pepper

¼ tsp kosher salt

CHICKEN

6 chicken bottoms with skin (leg and thigh attached)

1 whole cabbage, cut into 8 wedges

In a nonstick pot over medium heat, stir together all sauce ingredients. Cook for 3-4 minutes until well combined.

Preheat oven to 350°F / 180°C. Coat a large Pyrex baking dish lightly with nonstick cooking spray.

Place chicken into prepared baking dish; add wedges of cabbage between chicken pieces.
Wearing a disposable glove, gently nudge the skin off the chicken to create a pocket.
Spoon a little bit of the sauce mixture under the skin of each piece of chicken.
Pour the rest of sauce over the chicken and the cabbage.

Cover dish tightly with foil; bake for 1 hour.
Remove foil after 1 hour and return dish to the oven, making sure to baste the juices over the chicken and cabbage every 6 minutes for 25 minutes.
When you take the chicken out of the oven, immediately baste one more time.

Serve hot and enjoy!

fifle tomatese

I CAN LITERALLY SMELL THIS DISH SIMMERING AWAY IN MY MOTHER'S KITCHEN. I CAN PICTURE THE KITCHEN OF THE HOUSE WE LIVED IN WHEN I WAS A LITTLE GIRL. MY GRANDMOTHER STANDING BY THE STOVE ADDING INGREDIENTS TO THE POT, USUALLY USING LEFTOVER SIMPLY ROASTED CHICKEN THAT SHE WAS REPURPOSING BECAUSE NO MOROCCAN WOMEN WOULD EVER SERVE YOU THE SAME FOOD TWO NIGHTS IN A ROW (GASP, THE HORROR). THE BED I WAS SITTING ON, IN THE ROOM RIGHT NEXT TO THE KITCHEN, WAS CALLED "GRANDMA'S ROOM," AS THE CHICKEN–VEGGIE PACKED, LIGHT TOMATO BROTH SOUP SCENT WAFTED OUR WAY. THAT'S WHAT THIS DISH IS ABOUT. HOME.

CHICKEN

1 chicken, cut into eighths

1 tsp kosher salt

1 tsp coarsely ground black pepper

1 Tbsp olive oil

STEW

1 onion, quartered

2 carrots, peeled, cut into thirds

4 celery stalks, peeled, cut into 2 inch pieces

2 red potatoes, peeled and quartered

3 Tbsp tomato paste

½ cup white wine, optional

1 cup halved string beans

2 tomatoes, halved

1 Tbsp kosher salt

2 tsp coarsely ground black pepper

CHICKEN

Season chicken with salt and pepper.
Heat olive oil in a large pot; brown chicken on both sides, approximately 7 minutes total.
Remove chicken to a platter; set aside.

STEW

To the pot, add onion, carrots, celery, potatoes, and tomato paste.
Cook, stirring often, for 8 minutes.

Add white wine (if using).
Allow wine to cook out, then add string beans and tomatoes.

Return chicken to the pot. Add water to just cover.
Season with salt and pepper.

Bring to a boil and then reduce heat, cover pot, and simmer for 1½ hours.

sriracha lime drumsticks

#5IVEINGREDIENTFRIDAY

16 chicken drumsticks

MARINADE
juice of **6** limes
¼ cup soy sauce
¼ cup honey
2-3 tsp sriracha
2 cloves garlic, minced

In a bowl, combine all marinade ingredients.

Put chicken into a ziptop bag; add ¾ of the marinade, reserving the last ¼ for basting.
Marinate for at least 2 hours in the fridge, turning the bag once after 1 hour.

Heat grill or grill pan; grill chicken for about 20 minutes, basting with remaining sauce halfway through.

Serve hot and enjoy!

VARIATION

To prepare in the oven, preheat oven to 400°F / 200°C. Prepare the marinade and marinate as directed. Place chicken with its marinade into a greased baking dish. Bake, uncovered, for 40-45 minutes, basting every 10-12 minutes until the outside of the chicken is sticky and slightly charred.

moroccan chicken tagine

A TAGINE IS A TRADITIONAL MOROCCAN COOKING VESSEL. IT'S A SHALLOW CERAMIC BOWL SHAPED PAN WITH A CONICAL CERAMIC LID. THE INSIDE OF THE LID COLLECTS STEAM THAT RISES UP FROM THE HOT FOOD AND DROPS THE CONDENSATION BACK DOWN ON THE FOOD TO YIELD THE MOISTEST RESULTS. TODAY, MOST PEOPLE DON'T HAVE TAGINES IN THEIR HOMES (UNLESS YOU'RE MY MOTHER AND YOU HAVE 6), BUT MANY OF US DO HAVE HEAVY DUTCH OVENS. IF YOU DON'T HAVE A DUTCH OVEN, CONSIDER DOING THIS LOW AND SLOW IN YOUR CROCK POT! THE RESULTS OF THE LOW TEMPERATURE AND SLOW COOKING PRODUCE THE SOFTEST, MOST FLAVORFUL CHICKEN!

1 whole chicken, cut into 10 pieces, skin on

1¼ tsp kosher salt, divided

2 Tbsp canola oil

1 onion, halved and sliced

2 carrots, peeled, quartered, and cut into 3 inch sticks

4 fennel bulbs, quartered

½ tsp coarsely ground black pepper

1 tsp paprika

1 Tbsp tomato paste

6 dried apricots, halved horizontally then each piece halved again

4 prunes, pitted and halved

4 cloves garlic, peeled

½ cup dry white wine or sherry

1 tsp saffron, dissolved in **1½ cups** hot water

Preheat a Dutch oven over medium high heat.
Season chicken pieces with ¾ teaspoon salt.
Add oil and chicken, skin side down, to the pot.
Brown the chicken for 4 minutes on each side.
You may have to do this in batches so that you don't overcrowd the pan.
Remove chicken and set aside.

Add onion, carrots, and fennel to the pan with remaining ½ teaspoon salt and the pepper.
Cook for about 5 minutes, until vegetables begin to soften and become fragrant.
Add paprika and tomato paste, stirring to coat vegetables.
Add apricots, prunes, and garlic.
Cook for 2 minutes so fruit can begin to soften.

Add wine, using a wooden spoon to scrape up any bits from the bottom of the pan (don't skip this step!)
Cook for 1-2 minutes to allow flavors to begin to marry.
Add saffron and its water.

Return chicken to the pan, tucking the chicken pieces under the vegetables.
Bring mixture to a boil, then reduce heat to low, cover the pot and cook chicken low and slow for 1½ hours.

Serve hot, with couscous, if desired, and enjoy!

braised chicken in dijon white wine sauce with zucchini & spinach

THIS DISH IS AN ODE TO MUSTARD. MUSTARD IS SO UNDERUSED. IT IS SO MUCH MORE THAN JUST A SPREAD. IT'S AN EXCELLENT EMULSIFIER, A MILD FORM OF ACIDITY ADDING JUST A SLIGHT TANGINESS WHEN USED RIGHT, AND, WELL, ITS FLAVOR IS JUST, DELICIOUS! THE COMBINATION OF THE DEEPLY FLAVORED STOCK, WITH THE TANGINESS AND HEAT OF THE MUSTARD, TOGETHER WITH THE CHICKEN AND THE ZUCCHINI … SOOOOO GOOD!

10 pieces chicken
(I used without skin)

1 cup flour

1 tsp kosher salt

1 tsp coarsely ground black pepper

1 Tbsp olive oil

2 onions, sliced

3 cloves garlic

4 Tbsp Dijon mustard
(I used whole grain and smooth)

1½ cups white wine

1½ cups chicken stock

2 zucchini, julienned

1 cup fresh spinach

½ cup fresh parsley, optional

Preheat oven to 350°F / 180°C.

In a bowl, combine flour with salt and pepper.
Dip each piece of chicken in flour mixture, shaking off excess flour.

In a large ovenproof pot, heat oil over medium heat.
Add chicken in two batches, browning on both sides.
Remove from pot. Set aside.

Add onions and garlic to the pot. Sauté for 3 minutes.
Add mustard and wine; mix well.
Cook for 2-3 minutes. Add chicken stock.
Bring to a boil.

Return chicken to pot, cover and bake for 1½ hours.

Add zucchini and spinach, tucking them under and around chicken.
Replace lid; return to oven for 10 minutes.

Sprinkle with fresh parsley and serve right away.

best roast chicken

THERE IS NOTHING BETTER ON THE PLANET THAN A CRISPY ON THE OUTSIDE, JUICY ON THE INSIDE, BEAUTIFULLY GOLDEN PIECE OF ROAST CHICKEN. IT SOUNDS WAY MORE INTIMIDATING THAN IT ACTUALLY IS AND IN MY MIND IT IS THE MOST SHOW STOPPING DISH YOU CAN BRING OUT TO YOUR TABLE. I PREFER TO SERVE IT DURING THE WEEK WHEN IT CAN GO RIGHT FROM THE OVEN TO THE TABLE SO EVERYONE CAN EAT IT WHEN IT'S AT ITS MOST PERFECT. HOWEVER, LEFTOVER ROAST CHICKEN IN THE FRIDGE IS LIKE GOLD. THE POSSIBILITIES OF WHAT TO DO WITH PERFECTLY MOIST, ALREADY COOKED CHICKEN ARE ENDLESS.

1 whole chicken (about 5 lbs.)

1 Tbsp kosher salt, divided

2 tsp coarsely ground black pepper, divided

4 cloves garlic, halved

1 lemon, sliced into ½ inch thick slices

2 sprigs thyme

butchers string

3 Tbsp extra virgin olive oil

Preheat oven to 450°F / 230°C.

Pat chicken very, very dry, inside and out.
Holding chicken upside down with cavity facing you, sprinkle in 1 teaspoon salt and 1 teaspoon pepper.
Add garlic, lemon, and thyme to the cavity.
Use butchers string to tie the ends of the legs together to close cavity.

Place chicken, breast side up, in a lightly greased heavy bottomed roasting pan.
Drizzle oil all over the chicken.
From high up, use your hand to sprinkle remaining salt and pepper all over the chicken, making sure to get it under and on the sides as well.

Place pan into the oven; immediately lower the temperature to 400°F / 200°C.
Roast for about 1 hour until the skin is golden and crispy and juices run clear when a knife is inserted in the thigh.

Allow chicken rest for 12 minutes before carving.

VARIATIONS

Add any vegetables you like (potatoes, onions, sweet potatoes, string beans, fennel, carrots ...) to the roasting pan and place chicken on top for a one pan meal!

TIPS + TRICKS

if you're uncertain whether or not your chicken is cooked, invest in a meat thermometer. Insert the thermometer into the thickest part of the thigh. When the thermometer reads 165°F / 74°C, the chicken is done.

WAYS TO USE LEFTOVER ROAST CHICKEN

Shred and add to a salad, sandwich, or wrap

Shred and make a chicken salad by adding minced onion, finely diced celery, granulated garlic, a drop of mustard or horseradish, and enough mayo to hold it all together. Taste and season with kosher salt and coarsely ground black pepper! Use the remaining chicken bones to create a chicken stock by boiling them in water along with a few carrots, onion, and celery.

Use as a filling for kreplach.

Add to a sauté pan with veggies, minced garlic, and ginger. Season with a little soy sauce, wrap in egg roll wrappers, and bake.

Add shredded chicken to a stir fry.

Toss shredded chicken into a taco shell or charred tortilla and top with salsa and avocado!

Chop and use to make chicken pot pie (page 210).

Add to a quick soup.

apples & honey mustard chicken

BEFORE + AFTER. ROSH HASHANAH EDITION.
FOR ALL YOU JEOPARDY/WHEEL OF FORTUNE FANS OUT THERE. THIS WAS A SHINING MOMENT FOR ME.

HONEY MUSTARD

½ cup honey (spray the measuring cup with nonstick spray before measuring the honey; it will slide right out!)

⅓ cup Dijon mustard

3 Tbsp mayo

CHICKEN

1 large yellow onion, halved and thinly sliced

1-2 green apples, peeled, cored, and thinly sliced

1 whole chicken, cut into **10 pieces** (or 8-10 pieces of whatever you like)

kosher salt and coarsely ground black pepper, for seasoning the chicken

1-2 cups panko breadcrumbs

Preheat oven to 350°F / 180°C. Coat a large Pyrex baking dish or 9x13 inch pan with nonstick cooking spray.

In a bowl, combine the ingredients for the honey mustard; set aside.

Place sliced onions and ½ the sliced apples into the pan.
Top with chicken pieces.
Sprinkle chicken liberally with salt and pepper.

Use a spoon to coat all the chicken pieces with the honey mustard.
Sprinkle the breadcrumbs over the honey mustard till the chicken is fully coated.

Place remaining apple slices in the little nooks and crannies all around the chicken.

Spray the breadcrumbs with nonstick cooking spray.

Cover the baking dish tightly with foil. Bake for 1 hour 20 minutes.
Remove foil; continue baking until the top is crispy and the chicken is cooked to your taste.

Serve hot and enjoy!

spatchcocked chicken – 2 ways

HERE'S A STORY ABOUT A GIRL WHO MOVED FAR AWAY FROM NEW YORK AND ALL SHE WANTED WAS A WHOLE ROASTED CHICKEN. NO MATTER WHOM SHE ASKED OR WHERE SHE LOOKED COULD SHE FIND A WHOLE CHICKEN, WITH A HECHSHER HER FAMILY ATE, THAT WAS NOT CUT DOWN THE BACKBONE. SO, SHE DID WHAT ANY MILLENNIAL WOULD DO AND GOOGLED, "WHAT CAN YOU DO WITH A WHOLE CHICKEN THAT IS CUT DOWN THE BACKBONE?" KEEP IN MIND THIS STORY TAKES PLACE WAY BACK IN THE GOOD OL' DAYS OF 2007/2008 WHEN THERE WERE ONLY A FEW THOUSAND COOKING BLOGS OUT THERE, UNLIKE NOW, WHEN THE NUMBER IS INFINITE. AFTER A LITTLE DIGGING, THE GIRL FOUND JUST THE RECIPE. IT SPOKE ABOUT A CHICKEN THAT'S INTENDED TO BE CUT. IT WAS CALLED "A SPATCHCOCK" CHICKEN. ITS FLAT, EVEN LAYER WOULD ENSURE MORE EVEN COOKING AND YIELD A JUICY, TENDER CHICKEN. OF COURSE, THE GIRL TRIED IT AND LOVED IT. NOW, 13 YEARS LATER, SHE IS STILL SPATCHCOCKING HER CHICKENS ON A WEEKLY BASIS AND THESE ARE TWO OF HER FAVORITE RECIPES!

PRESERVED LIME AND TURMERIC

2 whole chickens, backbone removed

4 Tbsp preserved limes (page 24)

4 cloves garlic, minced

½ inch piece fresh turmeric root, minced on a microplane

1 tsp freshly cracked black pepper

2 Tbsp olive oil

2 tsp paprika

½ cup roughly chopped cilantro leaves

CRANBERRY + ORANGE CHICKEN MARINADE

3 Tbsp minced garlic

zest of **1** tangerine (reserve tangerine for the pot!)

2 Tbsp honey

1 Tbsp paprika

2 tsp kosher salt

1 tsp coarsely ground black pepper

CHICKEN

1 whole chicken, backbone removed

5 mini or **2 large** acorn squash, halved and sliced

1 purple onion, diced

1 cup fresh cranberries

½ tsp coarsely ground black pepper

¾ tsp kosher salt

2 Tbsp honey

½ cup Marsala wine

zested tangerine, from marinade

olive oil, for drizzling

FOR BOTH RECIPES PREPARE CHICKEN THE SAME WAY

Coat 2 baking sheets with nonstick cooking spray.
Place chickens flat on the prepared baking sheets, skin-side up.
Place both hands on top of the chicken, over the breastbone.
Apply pressure until the breastbone cracks, allowing you to lay the chicken completely flat.

Use your fingers to gently separate the skin from the flesh.

PRESERVED LIME AND TURMERIC

Preheat oven to 375°F / 190°C.

Rub preserved limes, garlic, and turmeric directly onto the flesh.
Sprinkle in some black pepper.
Replace skin over the flesh so that as little flesh as possible is exposed.
Drizzle olive oil over the top of both chickens.
Sprinkle paprika, a little more black pepper, and cilantro leaves over the top.

Bake for about 45-60 minutes until the chicken is golden brown and the skin is crispy!

CRANBERRY + ORANGE

In a bowl, combine all marinade ingredients to form a paste.

Rub the marinade under the skin of the chicken, on the bottom of the chicken, and onto the skin.
Yes, marinade everywhere!

Place into a ziptop bag and marinate in the fridge overnight or for a few hours.

Preheat oven to 350°F / 180°C. Coat a baking sheet lightly with nonstick cooking spray.

Place chicken skin side up on prepared baking sheet.
Place squash, onion, and cranberries around the chicken.
Sprinkle with salt and pepper; drizzle honey over the veggies.

Sprinkle with wine and squeeze the juice of the tangerine over the chicken and veg. Drizzle with olive oil.

Bake for 60-75 minutes until chicken is golden and cooked through.

Serve hot and enjoy!

hoisin-sriracha chicken egg rolls

OK. LET'S BE REAL ABOUT THIS RECIPE. I NEVER EVER COOK CHICKEN SPECIFICALLY FOR THESE EGG ROLLS. I TAKE WHATEVER CHICKEN ON THE BONE I HAVE LEFT IN MY FRIDGE AFTER SHABBOS, CHOP IT UP, ADD THESE AMOUNTS OF HOISIN, SRIRACHA, AND SOY AND I REPURPOSE IT INTO CRISPY, BAKED EGG ROLLS BECAUSE THAT LIMITED AMOUNT OF WORK SAVES ME FROM UNLIMITED LEFTOVERS WHINING. YOU ARE WELCOME.

CHICKEN

12 chicken drumsticks

¾ cup hoisin sauce

¼ cup sriracha

2 Tbsp oil

½ cup soy sauce

EGG ROLLS

1 (1 lb/½ kg) package egg roll wrappers

1 Tbsp canola oil

1 onion, sliced

2 cups shredded cabbage

3 cloves garlic, minced

1 Tbsp minced fresh ginger

shredded chicken with pan juices

CHICKEN

Preheat oven to 350°F / 180°C.

In a large bowl, combine all chicken ingredients.
Transfer chicken to a greased roasting pan; bake, covered, for 1 hour.

Uncover, spoon some pan juices over, and bake for 30 minutes.

When chicken has cooled slightly, shred it with 2 forks; discard bones. Set aside chicken and pan juices.

EGG ROLLS

Preheat oven to 425°F / 220°C. Coat a baking sheet well with nonstick cooking spray.

Heat oil in a large skillet over medium heat.

Add onion; sauté till translucent, 2-3 minutes.
Add cabbage, garlic, and ginger.
Sauté for 3 minutes.

Add shredded chicken and pan juices.
Mix until everything is combined and heated through.

Place ½ cup filling on one corner of 1 egg roll wrapper.
Dip your finger in a bit of water and wet the edges of the corner to moisten.
Fold the edge into egg roll, by rolling in that corner halfway.
Next, fold two adjacent corners into the middle and then continue rolling until sealed.

Repeat with remaining filling and wrappers.

Place filled egg rolls onto prepared baking sheet. Brush with oil.
Bake for 20 minutes. Serve hot.

chicken pot pie

THIS IS ONE OF THE FIRST DISHES I STARTED WORKING ON AFTER I WAS MARRIED. ELI INFORMED ME EARLY ON THAT HE WAS A HUGE CHICKEN POT PIE LOVER. SO NATURALLY I SET OUT TO MAKE THE BEST VERSION EVER. FAST FORWARD 13 YEARS LATER AND ELI WILL TELL YOU THIS EXACT RECIPE IS HIS FAVORITE CHICKEN POT PIE EVER. AND NOT JUST 'CAUSE HE'S MARRIED TO ME. FINE. MAYBE THAT DOES CONTRIBUTE. ANYWAY, THE KEY HERE IS THE WINE. IT ADDS DIMENSION AND BODY TO THE POT PIE MIXTURE SO THAT IT FEELS LIGHT IN YOUR MOUTH.

3 Tbsp canola oil, divided

3 carrots, diced

4 stalks celery, diced

1 onion, diced

1 large zucchini, diced

½ cup flour

1 cup dry white wine

4 cups chicken stock or leftover soup (just strain out veg)

4 cups shredded cooked chicken (can be leftover chicken from the soup, or just roast a whole chicken in the oven with olive oil, kosher salt, and coarsely ground black pepper, till done)

1 cup frozen peas (I like the tiny ones, but use what you find!)

1 roll puff pastry, thawed

1 egg, lightly beaten

1 Tbsp paprika

Preheat oven to 400°F / 200°C.

In an ovenproof pot, heat 1 tablespoon oil over medium high heat.
Add carrots, celery, and onion.
Sauté, stirring, for about 5 minutes until onion becomes translucent.
Stir in zucchini and remaining oil.
Add flour; mix well.

Raise heat to high; add wine.
Mix to incorporate flour into the wine and then cook for 3 minutes, stirring frequently.
Add stock and shredded chicken.

Bring mixture to a complete boil. (At this point the sauce should have thickened.)
Stir in the peas.
Remove from heat.

Roll and cut puff pastry to be 1 inch larger all around than the pot.
Lay pastry over the pot to cover.
(You may need to brush a thin layer of beaten egg on the rim of the pot to help the dough adhere to the rim.)
This will create the chicken pot pie crust.

Brush puff pastry with beaten egg; use a sharp knife to make a few cuts in the dough for the steam to escape.
Sprinkle paprika over the top.

Bake for 45-60 minutes until the puff pastry is golden brown and crispy.

Serve hot and enjoy!

NOTE

if you do not have an ovenproof pot or do not want to make this in a pot, you can make the chicken mixture, pour it into a greased 9x13 inch pan or Pyrex baking dish, and top with puff pastry.

Also, feel free to add in any other veggies you like. Think potatoes, sweet potatoes, cauliflower, broccoli ....

meme's chicken fricassee

THE FIRST TIME MY MOTHER MADE FRICASSEE, I WAS A LITTLE GIRL AND VERY CONFUSED. WHY ON EARTH WAS MY VERY MOROCCAN MOTHER SERVING ME A DISH SO ETHNICALLY ASHKENAZ AND REALLY, IN MY MIND, CAMP FOOD? ALSO, WHY WERE THERE GIZZARDS AND NECKS IN MY BOWL?!?!? WELL, 20 YEARS LATER AND I CANNOT ANSWER EITHER OF THOSE QUESTIONS. WHAT I CAN TELL YOU, THOUGH, IS THAT IT IS THE NUMBER ONE MOST REQUESTED DISH FROM MY CHILDREN, WHICH IS NOT SURPRISING AT ALL, BECAUSE ANY TIME MY MOTHER TREATED US WITH FRICASSEE ON A COLD FRIDAY NIGHT, THE POT WAS DEVOURED. WELL, MOSTLY DEVOURED. NO ONE TOUCHES THE GIZZARDS. EVER. THEY'RE JUST THERE FOR DECORATION. AND FLAVOR.

2 lb (1 kg) ground beef

1 egg

¾ cup breadcrumbs

1 tsp granulated garlic

1 tsp granulated onion

1 Tbsp kosher salt, divided

2 tsp coarsely ground black pepper, divided

1 tsp oil

1 onion, diced

3 cloves garlic, minced

3 cups chicken stock (or water; stock is best, though)

20 oz tomato sauce (about **2 cans**)

1¼ lb (½ kg) chicken gizzards

1½ lb (8 kg) chicken necks

2 lb (1 kg) chicken drumsticks or chicken wings

3 Tbsp brown sugar

1 bay leaf

1 batch prepared matzah ball mixture (not formed, just mixed and refrigerated) (page 116)

FREEZER TIP

Fricassee freezes really well. Double or triple the recipe, just don't add the matzah balls. Allow fricassee to cool completely, divide into containers, and freeze. To defrost, place in the fridge overnight to thaw, then add to a pot over gentle heat, stirring often. Once boiling, add matzah balls, reduce heat to low, cover, and cook for 35-40 minutes before serving.

Preheat oven to 350°F / 180°C. Line a baking sheet with parchment paper.

In a medium bowl, combine beef, egg, breadcrumbs, granulated garlic, granulated onion, 1 teaspoon salt, and 1 teaspoon pepper.
Form mixture into balls, using 2 teaspoons of mixture for each.
Place raw meat balls on prepared baking sheet, leaving ½ inch between each one.

Bake for 35 minutes until the outside is slightly crispy. (Meatballs may still be undercooked, but don't worry, they will finish cooking in the pot!)
Set meatballs aside.

Heat a large pot over medium high heat.
Add oil and onion; sauté, stirring often, for 8-10 minutes.
Once onion is translucent, add garlic; stir for 2 minutes to brown.

Add stock and tomato sauce.
Bring mixture to a boil.
Add gizzards, necks, drumsticks, brown sugar, and bay leaf.
Cook for 20 minutes, skimming off any foam that accumulates at the top.

Add meatballs.
Reduce heat to low, cover the pot, and simmer for 2 hours.

45 minutes before serving, turn heat to high and bring fricassee back to a boil.
Form matzah balls using 2 teaspoons matzah ball mixture for each.
Add matzah balls to pot.

Reduce heat to low, cover, and let matzah balls cook (about 35-40 minutes) until ready to serve!

savory stovetop turkey

THIS RECIPE IS AN ODE TO MY FATHER. MY FAVORITE TURKEY LOVER OUT THERE. MY DAD DOESN'T EAT LOTS OF RED MEAT, SO I'M ALWAYS ON THE LOOKOUT FOR GOOD TURKEY RECIPES. WHAT I NEVER SAW WAS A TURKEY ROAST RECIPE, WHERE I FELT LIKE THE TURKEY WAS TREATED LIKE A PROPER BEEF ROAST. THAT IS WHAT I WAS AIMING FOR HERE. TURKEY THAT WAS DEEPLY SAVORY, MOIST, AND EXTREMELY SATISFYING.

1 large whole deboned turkey breast

1 Tbsp kosher salt

1 tsp coarsely ground black pepper

1½ tsp granulated garlic

1½ tsp paprika

1 Tbsp neutral oil

1 onion, thinly sliced

4 cloves garlic, minced

2 Tbsp tomato paste

1½ cups dry white wine

2 bay leaves

1 Tbsp white vinegar

2 cups chicken broth

¼ cup duck sauce

In a small bowl, combine salt, pepper, garlic, and paprika.
Season turkey breast with mixture on all sides.

Heat a pot over medium heat. Add oil; place turkey top side down and sear for 4 minutes on each side.
Remove turkey from pot; set aside.

Add onion; cook for 12 minutes.
Add garlic and tomato paste to the pot. Cook for 2 minutes until fragrant.
Add wine, bay leaves, and vinegar, stirring to scrape up any bits on the bottom of the pan.

Cook for 2 minutes; add chicken broth and duck sauce.

Return turkey to the pot, spooning some of the mixture over the top.

Bring mixture to a boil, cover pot, and reduce heat to low.
Cook for 1½ hours, basting every 20 minutes or so.

Serve hot and enjoy.

TIPS + TRICKS

If making in advance, slice turkey when it's cold, return to sauce, and reheat gently.

NOTE

This is a great turkey recipe for Seder night when many people have a custom not to eat roasted foods!

miso + apricot roasted turkey breast

MISO AND APRICOT GO TOGETHER LIKE, HMM ... LIKE, UM ... WELL, LIKE PEAS AND CARROTS! (SEE WHAT I DID THERE?) IT'S A HISTORIC COMBINATION BECAUSE THE SWEETNESS OF THE APRICOTS TOTALLY ROUNDS OUT THE SALTY SAVORINESS THAT THE UMAMI PACKED MISO BRINGS TO THE PARTY! WHAT I LOVE ABOUT THIS RECIPE IS THAT I INTEND IT TO BE PREPPED ON A DAY YOU HAVE SOME EXTRA TIME AND FROZEN FOR A DAY WHEN YOU HAVE LESS TIME BUT STILL NEED TO COOK! BUY A FEW TURKEY ROASTS, DOUBLE OR TRIPLE THE RECIPE, AND POP 'EM ALL IN THE FREEZER FOR RAINY DAYS!

1 large turkey roast
(you can use white or dark meat)

1 tsp kosher salt

1 tsp coarsely ground black pepper

2 cloves garlic, finely minced

¼ cup white miso

4 oz apricot jam

TO COOK

2 yellow onions,
thinly sliced into rings.

Sprinkle salt, pepper, and garlic all over turkey roast.
Rub miso all over the turkey, being sure to get it on all sides.
Rub apricot jam over the miso.

Wrap turkey in 2 layers of plastic wrap, then wrap in a single layer of foil.

Freeze until ready to use.

Remove turkey from freezer and place the fridge the night before you want to cook it.
In the morning, remove it from the fridge and allow it to come to room temp.

Preheat oven to 425°F / 220°C. Coat a 9x13 inch baking pan with nonstick cooking spray.

Place onions into prepared pan.
Place roast on onions.
Bake, uncovered, for 20 minutes.

Remove pan from the oven, spoon any juices over the top of the turkey.
Coat a large piece of foil with nonstick cooking spray.
Place the foil, sprayed side down, over the turkey; cover tightly.

Reduce oven temperature to 350°F / 180°C.
Bake, covered, for 1 hour.

Serve hot and enjoy!

VARIATION

This rub is easy and delicious. If you don't like turkey or want to change things up, think about doing this with any type of chicken or veal!

a
pleasure
to
meat
you
my
friend

meat

pastella
(moroccan shepherd's pie)

THIS DISH IS PROBABLY ONE OF THE MOST MEANINGFUL TO ME. IT WAS A WEEKLY DINNER STAPLE AND NO ONE MADE IT BETTER THAN MY GRANDMOTHER. I THINK IT IS ONE OF THE BEST EXAMPLES OF MOROCCAN COOKING IN THAT IT SEEMS SO SIMPLE. IT'S MEAT AND POTATOES. REALLY, THOUGH, HIDDEN INSIDE THESE INSTRUCTIONS ARE LITTLE BITS OF TECHNICAL COOKING WISDOM THAT SOMEHOW EVERY MOROCCAN COOK JUST KNOWS. FOLLOW THE EASY ALTHOUGH DESCRIPTIVE DIRECTIONS FOR THE BEST RESULTS!

POTATO LAYER

5 lb (2 kg) Yukon gold potatoes, peeled, quartered
1 Tbsp + 2 tsp kosher salt
1 tsp turmeric
2 egg yolks, beaten

MEAT LAYER

2 Tbsp canola oil
1 small yellow onion, finely diced
2.2 lb (1 kg) chopped beef
1 tsp kosher salt
1 tsp granulated garlic
1 tsp cumin
1 tsp coriander
1 bay leaf
1 Tbsp seasoned rice vinegar

1 egg yolk, beaten
(for brushing on top)

TIPS + TRICKS

Putting the potatoes back into the hot, dry pot helps extra steam evaporate, for a better mashed potato consistency.

The vinegar in the meat is everything. It adds so much depth of flavor. If you don't have rice vinegar, swap it for apple cider vinegar!

Any time you make mashed potatoes, add any spices in with the potatoes before ricing, eliminating the need for extra mixing after they are already mashed!

Traditionally the meat is put through a meat grinder, after cooking, to give it a smoother texture. it tastes good either way!

POTATO LAYER

In a large pot, combine potatoes and salt; add enough cold water to cover the potatoes.
Place pot over high heat; bring to a boil.
Allow potatoes to boil, uncovered, for 15 minutes, or until fork tender.

Drain potatoes and then return the potatoes to the hot, dry pot.
Add turmeric; use a potato ricer, rice potatoes to make the creamiest mashed potatoes.

Once all the potatoes are mashed, pour in egg yolks and mix until mixture is smooth and creamy (don't over mix!).

Set aside.

MEAT LAYER

Heat a large pan over medium high heat.
Add oil and onion; sauté for 5-6 minutes, stirring often, until onion is translucent.

Add meat, all the spices, and the bay leaf.
Using a wooden spoon, continuously break up the clumps of beef to create a fine mince.

Once all the liquid from the meat has evaporated, add vinegar.
Cook for 2 minutes, stirring and continuously breaking up meat.

Remove from heat, discard bay leaf, and set meat aside.

ASSEMBLE

Preheat oven to 350°F / 180°C. Coat a baking dish or 9x13 inch pan with nonstick cooking spray.

Spread half the mashed potato mixture evenly into the pan.
Add all the meat in an even layer over the potatoes.
Finally, add remaining potato mixture. I like to do this by scooping up about a cup of potatoes with my hand (gloved, of course), gently patting it into a flat layer, and then placing it onto the meat.

Continue until all the meat is coated and the top layer of potatoes reaches from edge to edge of the pan.
Gently brush egg yolk over the top; then use a fork to create a pattern.

Bake for 40 minutes until top is crisp!

Serve hot and enjoy.

meat borekas + mushroom sauce

HAVE YOU EVER BEEN TO AN ISRAELI WEDDING? OR BAR MITZVAH? OR BRIS? OR BUSINESS MEETING? JUST KIDDING, I'VE NEVER BEEN TO AN ISRAELI BUSINESS MEETING EITHER. YOU GET THE POINT, THOUGH. NO ISRAELI SOCIAL GATHERING THAT INVOLVES PEOPLE SITTING DOWN TO A TABLE WITH A MULTI COURSE MEAL IS EVER COMPLETE WITHOUT SOMETHING-WRAPPED-IN-DOUGH-SMOTHERED-IN-MUSHROOM-SAUCE DISH. FOR YEARS I DIDN'T GET IT AND THEN ONE DAY, WHILE SITTING AT MY OWN MULTI COURSE MEAL WITH ELI AND MY FATHER, I BROUGHT UP THE MUSHROOM-SAUCE-SMOTHERED DOUGH-FILLED-WITH-SOMETHING AND THEY BOTH INFORMED ME THAT IT IS THEIR FAVORITE PART OF ANY ISRAELI MEAL! SO, THEN THIS HAPPENED AND NOW I'M FULLY ON BOARD.

BOREKAS

1.1 lb (½ kg) lean ground beef

1 tsp kosher salt + more for sprinkling

½ tsp coarsely ground black pepper

2 tsp garlic powder

2 tsp paprika

1 tsp mustard powder

1 egg, beaten (+ another egg for egg wash)

1 package puff pastry, defrosted

CREAMY MUSHROOM SAUCE

4 Tbsp extra virgin olive oil, divided

1 onion, diced

6 cups thinly sliced assorted mushrooms (I used portobello & shitake)

2 cloves garlic, chopped

1-2 tsp kosher salt (depending on how salty the stock is)

1 tsp coarsely ground black pepper

¼ cup flour

¾ cup white wine

3-4 cups chicken stock

BOREKAS

Preheat oven to 350°F / 180°C. Line a baking sheet with parchment paper.

In a bowl, combine meat with spices and egg.
Mix till just combined. Don't over work or meat will toughen.

Cut puff pastry into 2 inch squares.
Place 2-3 tablespoons of meat mixture onto the center of each square.
Fold one corner over to the opposite corner to form a triangle.
Seal edges by pressing with a fork.
Place borekas on prepared baking sheet.
Brush borekas with beaten egg; sprinkle with salt.
Bake for 30-40 minutes until borekas are golden!

MUSHROOM SAUCE

Heat a large pot over medium high heat.
Add 2 tablespoons oil and onion. Cook until onion is translucent.
Add mushrooms. Cook, stirring often, until all the liquid evaporates (12-15 minutes).

Continue to cook for 3-5 minutes, stirring often, till mushrooms begin to brown.
Add garlic; cook for 1 minute.
Add remaining 2 tablespoons olive oil, salt, pepper, and flour.
Stir constantly for 2 minutes.

While stirring, add wine. Stir to break up any lumps.
Once the flour has absorbed all the wine, slowly stir in chicken stock.

Bring mixture to a boil, then reduce heat and cook for 2 minutes (yup, still while stirring).
Remove from heat; allow to cool for 10 minutes.

Sauce will thicken as it cools!

TIPS + TRICKS

If I ever need a festive themed dish, I use an appropriately shaped cookie cutter to cut the puff pastry into those shapes, add mixture, place another cutout on top, seal edges, and bake! It's super cute and a delicious way to start off a festive meal. Think dreidels for Chanukah, flowers for Shavuos, Torahs for bar mitzvahs ....

FREEZER TIP

The sauce also freezes really well. To reheat, thaw in fridge overnight, then add to a small pot over low heat and stir till hot. Alternatively, place defrosted but cold sauce into a small heatproof container, cover, and place on your hot plate before Shabbos.

FREEZER TIP

The borekas can be filled and frozen raw, then defrosted overnight in the fridge and egged and baked fresh. Alternatively, you can make the whole thing, cool completely, and freeze.

15 minute prep chili

15 MINUTES? NO WAY? YES WAY! I MEAN, THERE IS THAT 1 HOUR OF SIMMERING. BUT AFTER THE FIRST 15 MINUTES, YOU LITERALLY JUST WALK AWAY. SO GO, GRAB A CUP OF COFFEE, PUT YOUR FEET UP, AND RELAX. HAHAHA, WHO ARE WE KIDDING? GO FOLD SOME LAUNDRY; DINNER WILL BE READY WHEN YOU'RE DONE.

2 Tbsp canola oil

1 large yellow onion, diced

2⅛ tsp kosher salt, divided

3 cloves garlic, minced

1 tsp smoked paprika

1 Tbsp paprika

1 chipotle + **1 Tbsp** adobo sauce (or 1 **full Tbsp** smoked paprika)

1 Tbsp fire roasted green chilies (optional)

2 lb (1 kg) lean ground beef

2 (15 oz/425 g) cans tomato sauce

2 tsp kosher salt

2 (14 oz/400 g) cans dark red kidney beans, rinsed and drained

1 (15 oz/425 g) can black beans, rinsed and drained

Heat a large pot over medium heat.
Add onion and ⅛ teaspoon salt.
Sauté for 4 minutes until onion is translucent.

Add garlic, both paprikas, chipotle, adobo, and chilies (if using). Cook for 2 minutes.

Add meat, using a spoon to break into chunks and incorporate all the spices. Once meat is cooked through (about 8 minutes), add remaining ingredients.

Stir to combine.
Bring to a boil, then reduce heat to low; simmer for 1 hour.

Serve hot and enjoy.

FREEZER TIP

Make dish in its entirety, then place into a freezer container, add a layer of plastic wrap directly on the chili, then close with airtight lid. Freeze for up to 1 month.

TIPS + TRICKS

Once in a while I like to have a fun Mexican meal on Shabbos day. So I take the frozen chili out of the freezer only a few minutes before Shabbos, transfer to a pot, and place it on the plata. By Shabbos day, the chili is piping hot and ready to serve along with guacamole, salsa, and chips!

meat sauce

THERE ARE 4 IMPORTANT FACTORS TO REALLY GOOD MEAT SAUCE. 1. USE GOOD QUALITY GROUND BEEF. 2. THE RED WINE IS NOT OPTIONAL. 3. TOMATO SAUCE, NOT MARINARA SAUCE. 4. THE CLUMPS OF MEAT ARE EVERYTHING. WHEN THE MEAT HITS THE POT, STIR THE MEAT JUST ENOUGH TO BROWN IT BUT NOT SO MUCH THAT THE PIECES OF GROUND MEAT TOTALLY BREAK UP.

1 Tbsp canola oil

1 yellow onion, diced

2-3 cloves garlic, minced

3 lb (1½ kg) ground beef
(a little more or a little less won't affect the recipe)

1 Tbsp kosher salt

2 tsp coarsely ground black pepper

1 tsp crushed red pepper (optional)

¾ cup dry red wine

3 (15 oz/425 g) cans tomato sauce

2 bay leaves

In a large pot over medium heat, add oil and onion.
Cook for 7-8 minutes, stirring frequently, until they are soft and just begin to slightly color.
Add garlic; cook for 1 minute.

Add meat, salt, pepper, and red pepper flakes.
Break up meat very gently, not overworking the meat.
It will continue to break up as you stir, but you WANT clumps.

Once the meat is cooked and most of the liquid has evaporated, add wine.
Cook for 2 minutes until wine has slightly reduced.
Add sauce and bay leaves.

Bring mixture to a boil; reduce heat to low.
Simmer for 1 hour, covered.

Serve hot, by itself, over pasta or rice, or even stuffed into a pita, and enjoy.

VARIATION

Take the best meat sauce ever, add pasta, and turn it into the best meat lasagna! Here's how: Cook one package of lasagna noodles according to the box (do not use the no-cook type, they absorb all the sauce and leave the lasagna dry!). Make meat sauce. Transfer 2 cups meat sauce to a large bowl; add 1 cup nondairy whipping cream, ½ tsp kosher salt and 2 Tbsp nutritional yeast, stirring to combine. Preheat oven to 350°F / 180°C and grease a 9x13 inch pan. Add half of a 15 oz can of tomato sauce to the pan; cover with a layer of cooked noodles, slightly overlapping. Add reserved, original meat sauce. Add another layer of noodles, then half of the creamy meat sauce. Repeat once more, ending with a layer of overlapping noodles. There should be a total of 5 noodle layers and 4 sauce layers. Spread remaining tomato sauce over the top. Sprinkle with ¾ cup bread crumbs and 2 tsp nutritional yeast. Drizzle with 1 Tbsp extra virgin olive oil. Bake for 40-45 minutes. Serve hot and enjoy!

smash burgers
with onions + special sauce

WHAT, DANIELLE? ALL YOU NEED TO MAKE THE BEST BURGERS EVER IS SALT AND PEPPER? YES! THAT IS EXACTLY WHAT I AM SAYING! THESE BURGERS ARE ALL ABOUT THE TECHNIQUE. THE ONIONS AND SAUCE ARE JUST AN EASY BONUS. HOWEVER, AN EXTREMELY DELICIOUS BONUS! THE SAUCE IS COMPLETELY IRRESISTIBLE AND A HUUUUGE CROWD PLEASER.

SPECIAL SAUCE

3 Tbsp tomato paste
2 Tbsp honey
1 Tbsp apple cider vinegar
½ tsp granulated garlic
½ tsp granulated onion
⅛ tsp cayenne powder
½ tsp coarsely ground black pepper
2 tsp fish free Worcestershire sauce
¾ cup mayo
2 tsp yellow mustard
2 tsp pickle relish
½ tsp kosher salt
½ tsp balsamic vinegar

(Feel free to swap out the tomato paste, honey, and apple cider vinegar for **1 cup** ketchup.)

SMASH BURGERS

4 lb (1.8 kg) ground beef
4 Tbsp kosher salt
3 Tbsp coarsely ground black pepper
1 Tbsp canola oil

ONIONS

1 large or **2 small** yellow onion(s), halved, peeled, and super thinly sliced

FUN FACT

In a blind taste test between the special sauce made with traditional ketchup (-insert ew here-), everyone in my house, EVERYONE, chose the special sauce that was made completely from scratch. Just saying.

SPECIAL SAUCE

In a small nonstick pot or pan, combine tomato paste, honey, vinegar, granulated garlic, granulated onion, cayenne, pepper, and fish free Worcestershire sauce. Place over low heat.

Using a rubber spatula, continuously stir mixture for 5-6 minutes until the mixture has slightly darkened in color and is simmering.

Transfer mixture to a bowl.
Set aside to cool for at least 15 minutes up to overnight (in the fridge).

Once cooled, add remaining sauce ingredients.
Stir to combine.

Sauce will stay fresh in the fridge for up to 2 weeks.

Slather on everything and enjoy!

SMASH BURGERS

Preheat a cast iron skillet (or heavy bottomed pan) over medium high heat.

Combine salt and pepper in a small bowl.

Add meat to a large bowl.
Once pan is super hot, add 1 tablespoon canola oil.

Grab a palmful of beef (about ½ cup), give it a gentle squeeze, sprinkle a pinch of salt and pepper mixture on each side, then drop into the pan.
Using the bottom of a cup (I used a 1 cup measuring cup), press the burger to flatten.
Repeat until burgers fill the pan without crowding.

Cook for 2-3 minutes, then flip burgers and cook for another 2 minutes. Set aside.

ONIONS

After all the burgers are cooked, add onions to the pan.
Cook for 10-12 minutes, stirring often with a wooden spoon to scrape up bits from the bottom of the pan.
Cook until onions have softened and all those delicious bits at the bottom of the pan have been incorporated.

Top burger with special sauce, onions, and anything else you like on your burger, and enjoy!

moroccan stuffed artichokes

IF YOU'VE EVER WALKED INTO ANY SEPHARDIC RESTAURANT OR TAKEOUT PLACE, THEN YOU ALREADY KNOW EXACTLY WHAT THESE ARE. IF YOU HAVEN'T, THEN YOU NEED TO MAKE THEM, BECAUSE THEY ARE ABSOLUTELY DELICIOUS. THE BUTTERY ARTICHOKE, WITH THE HEARTY MEAT AND THE EARTHY TURMERIC AND BRIGHT LEMON, MAKE THE MOST WONDERFUL COMBINATION, RESULTING IN THE COMFORT FOOD YOU DIDN'T KNOW YOU WERE MISSING.

20 oz (600 g) frozen artichoke hearts (defrosted)

STUFFING

2.2 lb (1 kg) ground beef

½ cup chopped cilantro leaves

3 cloves garlic, minced

1 egg, lightly beaten

1 tsp kosher salt

½ tsp coarsely ground black pepper

1 tsp paprika

½ tsp ground cumin

¼ tsp coriander

⅛ tsp ground ginger

1 Tbsp white vinegar

DREDGING

4 eggs, well beaten

2 cups flour

TO COOK

2 Tbsp avocado oil

1 onion, diced

5 stalks celery, peeled, cut into 2-inch pieces

2 cloves garlic, minced

1 tsp turmeric

1 lemon, halved

3 cups chicken stock (additional **½-1 cup**, as needed)

½ cup cilantro leaves

Place artichoke hearts onto a sheet pan.

In a large bowl, combine all stuffing ingredients, mixing until incorporated. Fill artichoke hearts with stuffing mixture, filling fully and letting stuffing bulge out a bit.
Return to sheet pan.

In a large bowl, combine dredging ingredients.
Dip stuffed artichoke hearts into mixture, allowing excess to drip back into the bowl.

Return to sheet pan.

When all artichoke hearts are filled and coated, heat avocado oil in a high walled pan over medium high heat.

Add prepared artichoke hearts.
Sauté on both sides, using the backs of 2 spoons to gently turn them so they don't break.
You may need to do this in batches so as not to overcrowd the pan.

Transfer sautéed artichoke hearts to the sheet pan as they are done.

MAKE SAUCE

To the same pan, add onion, celery, and garlic.
Cook 4-5 minutes until onion and celery soften just a bit.
Add turmeric and cook for 1 minute.

Squeeze in lemon juice.
Add stock, using a wooden spoon to scrape up any bits accumulated on the bottom of the pan.

Add stuffed artichokes to the sauce. Add cilantro.

Reduce heat to low and cover the pan.
Simmer for 1½ hours, basting every 20 minutes.

Serve hot and enjoy!

NOTE

If you have any meat mixture left after stuffing all your artichokes, you are very lucky. Shape that extra meat into golf ball size balls and add them to the pan! Those are for you to snack on in the kitchen before you serve them. Which we all know is truly the best time and place to eat!

hamburger roll

I MEAN, WHAT CAN I REALLY SAY ABOUT THIS? IT'S A HAMBURGER WRAPPED UP IN PUFF PASTRY, TAKES 5 MINUTES OF ACTIVE WORK, AND NO MATTER WHAT ELSE YOU SERVE, IT'S ALWAYS THE FIRST THING THAT GETS FINISHED!

1 piece puff pastry, defrosted
(I used ¾ of a roll in Israel)

2 Tbsp brown deli mustard

1.1 lb (½ kg) chopped meat

1 tsp kosher salt

½ tsp coarsely ground black pepper

1 Tbsp garlic powder

5 Tbsp barbecue sauce
(I use a spicy one)

½ cup sautéed onions (page 22)

1 egg, lightly beaten

Preheat oven to 350°F / 180°C. Line a baking sheet with parchment paper.

On a floured surface, gently roll out puff pastry to thin it a little.
Use a pastry brush to spread a thin layer of mustard over the dough.

Break up meat over the dough; use your hands to spread the meat and create a flat, even layer over the mustard.
Sprinkle meat evenly with all three spices.
Drizzle with BBQ sauce; use a spoon to spread evenly over the meat.
Evenly spread sautéed onions over the BBQ sauce.

Roll dough, deli roll style. Transfer roll to prepared baking sheet.

Don't use a knife to lightly score the top (or it will crack open like mine did); just brush with beaten egg.

Bake for 40- 45 minutes until browned.

FREEZER TIP

This freezes very well. Cool for 10 minutes on pan. Then transfer to cooling rack to finish cooling completely. Once cooled, wrap in a few layers of foil. Freeze. When you want to serve it, make sure to unwrap it while it is still frozen. Then place on sheet pan and reheat, uncovered, for maximum crispiness!

maggie loves tacos

SHE DOES. BECAUSE TACOS ARE DELICIOUS. THEY'RE ALSO SUPER VERSATILE. YOU CAN USE GROUND BEEF, CHICKEN, OR TURKEY. YOU CAN USE SKIRT STEAK OR BONELESS CHICKEN BREAST. YOU CAN USE FISH OR EVEN GO FULL VEGETARIAN WITH TOFU OR VEGETABLES. ALL YOU REALLY NEED TO MAKE TACOS HAPPEN IS A TACO SHELL OR TORTILLA (DUH), SOMETHING TO FILL IT WITH (SEE PREVIOUS SENTENCES), AND A REALLY KILLER SPICE RUB THAT GIVES YOU ALL THE TACO FEELS. YOU'RE ON YOUR OWN WHEN IT COMES TO THE SHELLS; THE FILLINGS I'LL GIVE YOU IDEAS ABOUT AND, WELL, THAT KILLER SPICE RUB — THAT'S WHY WE'RE HERE. DOUBLE, TRIPLE, OR QUADRUPLE THE RECIPE AND TUCK IT AWAY IN YOUR SPICE CABINET SO THAT YOU HAVE SOME READY FOR ALL FUTURE TACO EMERGENCIES (IT'S A THING. JUST ASK MAGGIE)!

SPICE RUB

4 Tbsp chili powder

1 Tbsp cumin

1 Tbsp paprika

1 Tbsp kosher salt

2 tsp granulated garlic

2 tsp granulated onion

1 tsp coarsely ground black pepper

½ tsp oregano

2 Tbsp cornstarch

GROUND BEEF, LAMB, CHICKEN, OR TURKEY

2 lb (1 kg) ground meat or poultry

1 Tbsp canola oil

4 Tbsp spice rub mixture

¾ cup water, at room temperature

BONELESS CHICKEN OR STEAK

12 thin chicken cutlets OR **4** boneless skinless dark meat cutlets, halved OR **1 lb** skirt steak, cut into 2 inch pieces, soaked in water (mixed with **1 Tbsp** apple cider vinegar) for 30 minutes

3 Tbsp spice rub

2 Tbsp canola oil

juice of **1** lime

SPICE RUB

Place all spice rub ingredients into a jar.
Close jar tightly.

Shake to combine.

GROUND BEEF, LAMB, CHICKEN, OR TURKEY

In a large pan set over medium high heat, add oil and protein.
Use a wooden spoon to break up meat.

Once meat is cooked through and most of the liquid has evaporated, add 4 tablespoons spice rub.
Stir to distribute; add water.

Bring to a boil; allow mixture thicken for 2 minutes.
Remove from heat.

Serve with desired toppings!

BONELESS CHICKEN OR STEAK

In a large bowl, stir together all ingredients.

Set grill pan over medium high heat.
Lightly grease pan; add protein and cook on both sides till cooked through.

Chicken breast: 4 minutes on first side, 3 minutes on second side.

Dark meat cutlets: 7 minutes on first side, 5-6 minutes on second side.

Skirt steak: 5 minutes on first side, 4-5 minutes on second side.

NOTE

If using flour or corn tortillas, for best results, use tongs to circulate each tortilla on both sides over an open flame to lightly char. If you don't have an open flame or can't do that for kashrut reasons, heat a pan over high heat. Once hot, add dry tortilla to pan and toast for 1 minute on each side.

SERVE WITH

diced avocado • lime wedges • cilantro • shredded lettuce • shredded purple cabbage • corn • finely diced purple onion • lettuce • sliced radishes • black beans, rinsed and drained • soft corn tortillas • hard shell tacos • flour tortillas

moroccan keftas

THE MOROCCAN HAMBURGER. WHICH MEANS TONS OF FLAVOR, AND ALWAYS A CROWD PLEASER. SERVE THESE IN PITAS, OVER A SALAD, OR RUN A SKEWER THROUGH THEM TO MAKE KABOBS!

2 lb (1 kg) ground meat

2 tsp kosher salt

1 Tbsp paprika

¾ **tsp** coarsely ground black pepper

½ **tsp** coriander

½ **tsp** mustard powder

½ **tsp** cumin

1 onion, finely chopped

6-8 cloves garlic, chopped

1 cup parsley, finely chopped

½ **cup** cilantro, finely chopped

2 tsp rice vinegar

1 tsp oil, for frying

In a large bowl, mix together all ingredients until combined.

Remove 2-3 tablespoons of the meat mixture; form into an oval in the palm of your hand.

Gently press your fingers into the oval to create those iconic kefta ridges. Repeat with remaining meat mixture.

Preheat a frying pan over medium high heat.

Drizzle 1 teaspoon oil into the pan just to get started (the meat will release its own fat so you won't need to add more for other batches); add a few keftas at a time. Be sure not to overcrowd the pan.

Sear meat on each side for 1-2 minutes until you get a yummy crust on all sides.

If you like your keftas more well done, you can finish them in a 350°F / 180°C oven for around 10 minutes.

Serve hot and enjoy!

FREEZER TIP

Double or triple the recipe and freeze before frying. To freeze, cut parchment paper into 2x2 inch squares. Place a piece of parchment between each kefta; place into tightly covered freezer container. You can layer them by also adding a full piece of parchment between layers in a freezer container. Cover with plastic wrap directly on top layer; cover tightly. Freeze for up to 2 months. To defrost, pull out the amount you need 4 hours before you want to cook them. After they defrost, cook, following the recipe!

NOTE

You can make the mixture the night before or in the morning and just form and sear before serving!

sweet and sour meatballs

EVERY. SINGLE. SHABBOS. ON REPEAT.

AT THIS POINT, I'M AFRAID TO COME TO THE TABLE ON FRIDAY NIGHT WITHOUT THEM.

SWEET AND SOUR SAUCE

2 tsp canola oil

1 onion, diced

1 Tbsp kosher salt, divided

2 tsp coarsely ground black pepper, divided

1 can jellied cranberry sauce

¾ cups brown sugar

juice of **1 large** lemon

2 (15 oz/425 g) cans tomato sauce

15 oz (425 g) water (use a can to measure)

MEATBALLS

2.2 lbs (1 kg) ground beef

1 egg, beaten

1 cup panko breadcrumbs

1 Tbsp + 2 tsp granulated garlic

2 tsp paprika

2 tsp kosher salt

1 tsp coarsely ground black pepper

2 Tbsp sweet and sour sauce, above

SWEET AND SOUR SAUCE

In a large pot set over medium high heat, add oil, onions, 1 teaspoon salt, and 1 teaspoon pepper.
Cook for about 8 minutes, stirring often, until onions are translucent.
Add remaining sauce ingredients; stir to combine. Remove from heat.

MEATBALLS

To a large bowl, add all meatball ingredients.

Use your hands to gently mix the meat to incorporate ingredients.
Just remember to be gentle and not overwork the mixture! We want tender meatballs here, folks, and not overworking our meat will ensure that!

Return sweet and sour sauce to a boil.
Carefully add meatballs, one at a time.

Return to a boil again.
Reduce heat to low; cover the pot.

Simmer meatballs for 1 hour, gently stirring every 15 minutes or so.

FREEZER TIP

These freeze really, really well. Double the recipe and make portions to fit your needs. Refrigerate until completely cool. Once cooled, remove from fridge, place a layer of plastic wrap directly onto the meatballs, then cover freezer container with an airtight lid. If plastic wrap hangs out, that's fine. The lid should still fit tightly. Write the date on the container; use within 2 months.

NOTE

Feel free to add 3 cups shredded white cabbage in with the sauce and 1 cup raw rice instead of breadcrumbs into the meat mixture for a quick and easy version of unstuffed cabbage.

TIPS + TRICKS

To serve these meatballs on Shabbos day, follow these simple tips. Make the sauce in a crockpot set to high heat. Bring to a boil; then add in meatballs. Leave crockpot on high for 1 hour, then reduce heat to low. Serve Shabbos day. I recommend making these only 2 hours before Shabbos because I do find the meatballs can dry out if cooked for too long.

sloppy franks

ELI IS A FRANKS AND BEANS KIND OF GUY. MY KIDS ARE ALL ON BOARD WITH THE FRANKS, NOT SO MUCH THE BEANS. SO I CAME UP WITH THIS RECIPE AS A WAY TO GIVE EVERYONE WHAT THEY WANT. INCLUDING MYSELF, WHO NO LONGER HAS TO PICK BEANS OFF LITTLE PEOPLE'S PLATES! WOOHOO!

27 hot dogs, cut into ¼ inch rounds

1 Tbsp oil

1 onion, puréed or grated

1 thinly sliced chili pepper, optional

½ cup brown sugar

6 Tbsp apple cider vinegar

1 (15 oz/425 g) can tomato sauce

8 (12 inch) baguettes

To a wide pot or pan set over medium high heat, add hot dogs and oil. Cook for about 8-10 minutes until the hot dogs get just a bit crispy. Not crunchy. Just crisped up on the outside!

Add grated onion and chili pepper.
Stir to combine; cook for 1 minute.
Add sugar and vinegar. Stir.
Pour in tomato sauce. Stir to combine.

Bring to a boil, reduce heat to low, and simmer for 5-10 minutes.

Serve hot and enjoy!

TO SERVE

Slice baguettes crosswise to create 16 baguettes.
(Keep ends of baguettes intact!)

Use a fork to scoop out the center of the baguettes, being careful not break the crust.

Fill hollowed out baguettes with sloppy franks for mess free eating!

TIPS + TRICKS

Use scooped-out baguette serving method for so much more than sloppy franks. Think sloppy joes, tacos, chili, meatballs ....

I don't add salt because the hot dogs are plenty salty.

Taste to adjust to your liking!

If you have small children, for safety reasons cut your hot dogs into quarters the long way, and then cut into pieces.

sticky bbq deli and onion sandwich or salad

SOMETIMES, THE QUICKEST, CHEAPEST, EASIEST PREP DINNER IS JUST WHAT WE NEED. THAT'S WHAT THIS IS ALL ABOUT. THAT MEAL YOU CAN THROW TOGETHER OUT OF THE LEFTOVER DELI IN YOUR FRIDGE OR FREEZER TO SERVE YOUR FAMILY OR UNEXPECTED GUESTS, BUT YOU STILL WANT IT TO FEEL HOMEMADE AND SATISFYING.

1 lb (½ kg) assorted cold cuts (can be one type or a variety), chopped into ½ inch pieces

1 Tbsp canola oil

1 large yellow onion, diced

1 jalapeño pepper, thinly sliced (optional)

¼ cup favorite barbecue sauce

salad, optional, for serving

bread or rolls, optional, for serving

Place a large nonstick pan over medium high heat.
Add oil, onion, and jalapeño (if using).
Cook, stirring often, for 12-15 minutes.
Add cold cuts to the pan.

Cook for 6-8 minutes, until deli starts to crisp up.
Pour in barbecue sauce.
Stir to distribute sauce evenly throughout meat and onions.
Cook for 3-4 minutes, stirring constantly, to allow sauce to reduce and get sticky.
Remove pan from heat.

Serve sticky BBQ deli over a salad with Caesar dressing or stuffed into a delicious sandwich!

crispy braised meat ravioli

I MEAN, DOES THIS REALLY NEED AN EXPLANATION? I THINK NOT, BUT I'LL GIVE YOU ONE ANYWAY. CRISPY, CRUNCHY, SAVORY, ACIDIC, MEATY, HEARTY. DONE.

I LOVE THE IDEA OF THIS DISH FOR AN APPETIZER. TWO DELICIOUS RAVIOLI TO START OFF THE MEAL AND LEAVE YOUR GUESTS WONDERING WHAT COULD POSSIBLY BE COMING NEXT IF THIS WAS JUST THE APPETIZER!

MAKES ABOUT 25–30 RAVIOLI

3 lb (1½ kg) bone in beef spare ribs (about **6**)

2½ tsp kosher salt

2 tsp coarsely ground black pepper

1 Tbsp olive oil

4 cloves garlic, peeled and halved

1 tsp crushed red pepper flakes

½ cup dry red wine

2 cups tomato sauce (I like the crushed tomato sauce in the glass jars for this)

1 cup stock or water

1 bay leaf

1½ package wonton wrappers, defrosted

1 tsp kosher salt

oil, for frying

FREEZER TIP

Cook meat, fill and seal wontons, and freeze in layers with parchment between them. Boil and crisp ravioli before serving!

TIPS + TRICKS

To serve this on Shabbos, place crispy ravioli in a baking dish in a single layer. Place on plata or in warming drawer, uncovered, 1 hour before serving. Keep the sauce in a heatproof container; place on plata or in warming drawer, covered, until serving.

NOTE

You can easily shred the ribs and just serve over rice or pasta for a slightly easier but still delicious alternative.

Preheat oven to 250°F / 120°C.

Heat a heavy, ovenproof pot or pan (with a lid) over medium high heat.

Season ribs on both sides with salt and pepper.
Once the pan is hot, add oil and ribs.
Cook for 4 minutes on one side, then flip and cook for 3 minutes on the second side.
Once ribs are browned, remove them from the pan. Set aside.

Add garlic and pepper flakes to the pan. Cook, stirring with a wooden spoon to scrape up any bits from the pan, for 1 minute.
Add wine; scrape up any remaining bits that were stuck to the pan. Cook for 1 minute.

Add remaining ingredients, stir, and bring to a boil.
Return seared ribs to the pan.

Cover pan; bake for about 5 hours, turning ribs over after 2 hours and checking on them every 30 minutes after 4 hours.

Once ribs are soft and tender, remove pan from the oven. Set aside to cool for 1 hour.
Do not remove ribs from the sauce or the meat will dry out.
After 1 hour, use a fork to remove ribs from sauce and place on cutting board. Reserve sauce.

Use 2 forks to pull meat from the bones; place pulled beef into a bowl.

Lay out wonton wrappers.
Place 1 tablespoon pulled beef onto the center of a wrapper.
Wet the edges and cover with a second wrapper. Press firmly to seal the edges, forming a round ravioli. Repeat with remaining beef and wonton wrappers.

Once all the ravioli are made, fill a large, wide pan with water and 1 teaspoon salt. Bring to a boil over medium high heat.

When water is boiling, gently add a few ravioli at a time.
Cook for 2-3 minutes, until dough is tender.
Use a slotted spoon to transfer cooked ravioli to a paper towel lined bowl to drain.

To crisp ravioli, add 1½ inches oil to a pan set over medium high heat.
Once oil is hot, add a few cooked ravioli; fry for 1 minute on each side until they are slightly crispy and just golden.

Remove from pan and place on a cooling rack.

TO SERVE

Reheat reserved braising sauce in a small pan.
Spoon 2-3 tablespoons sauce into a plate.
Top with two crispy ravioli.

sticky asian beef + string beans

BY THE TIME THIS BOOK COMES OUT I WILL HAVE BEEN LIVING IN ISRAEL FOR 13 YEARS. I KNOW. IT IS SUCH A LONG TIME TO LIVE APART FROM SO MANY THINGS I LEFT BEHIND IN NEW YORK. LIKE FAMILY, FRIENDS, CUSTOMER SERVICE, CHEAP MANICURES, AND, MOSTLY, CHINESE FOOD. MY FIRST LOVE. AND SECOND. AND THIRD. JUST KIDDING. ELI, KIDS, I LOVE YOU MORE. SOMETIMES, THOUGH, I JUST NEED CHINESE FOOD, THE NEW YORK, JEWISH, TAKE OUT (BUT REALLY CHOSEN ISLAND WILL ALWAYS BE MY NUMBER 1) VERSION OF CHINESE FOOD THAT I LOVE SO DEEPLY!

1.5 lb (.6 kg) pepper steak, cut thin

2 Tbsp cornstarch

6 Tbsp soy sauce, divided

1 Tbsp canola oil

2 Tbsp chopped garlic

½ tsp minced ginger

½ cup scallions, white part only

1-2 thinly sliced Thai chilies (optional)

3 cups frozen, skinny string beans

2 Tbsp honey

¼ cup hot water

scallion greens, for garnish

In a large bowl, combine meat with cornstarch and 1 tablespoon soy sauce.

Heat a large pan or wok over high heat. Add oil.
Sear meat for a few minutes to begin cooking and so that a crunchy exterior can form.
Alternate between letting the meat sit for 1 minute and then stirring to prevent burning.

Add garlic, ginger, scallions, chilies (if using), string beans, 3 tablespoons soy sauce, and honey.
Cook for 2 minutes, stirring constantly.

Add hot water; stir, using a wooden spoon to scrape the bottom.
This may require a bit of elbow grease but the flavor that it adds is worth it!

Reduce heat to low; cover the pan and cook for 15 minutes.
Remove lid, raise heat to high, and add remaining 2 tablespoons soy sauce.

Stir for about 4 minutes, until string beans begin to blister slightly and meat re-crisps!

Top with scallion greens and serve over rice!

VARIATIONS

Do NOT feel limited by the string beans. Replace with or add frozen broccoli, baby corn, sliced peppers, sliced carrots ....

vietnamese beef bahn mi

THE STEAK SANDWICH DONE BETTER BY A FARAWAY CULTURE! A VACATION ON YOUR PLATE!

PICKLED VEGETABLES

4-5 large carrots, peeled

¼ lb radishes, washed and tops cut off

3 cups warm water

4 Tbsp rice vinegar

2-3 Tbsp sugar (depending on how sweet you like your pickles)

2 Tbsp kosher salt

SOY-LIME MAYONNAISE

1 egg

1 Tbsp Dijon mustard

juice of ½ lime

¼ tsp kosher salt

½ tsp coarsely ground black pepper

1 cup oil

1 Tbsp soy sauce

MEAT

1½ lb (600 g) very thinly sliced steak (think Philly style meat)

oil, for frying

MARINADE

3 cloves garlic, minced

2 tsp sugar

2 tsp coarsely ground black pepper

3 Tbsp soy sauce

1 tsp kosher salt

1½ tsp sesame oil

4 Tbsp canola oil

FOR SERVING

6 baguettes

cilantro leaves

Thai chilies, thinly sliced, to taste

NOTES

You can easily substitute the meat for chicken, scrambled eggs, tofu, even ground beef.

Also, it is very traditional to add a smear of liver pate. You can use any good quality pate! Definitely give it a try because it is absolutely delicious!

PICKLED VEGETABLES

In a food processor fitted with the grater with the largest holes, or using a knife, cut carrots into matchsticks.

Slice radishes very thinly.

Place carrots and radishes into jars.
(You can combine in one jar or jar separately.)

In a large bowl, combine remaining pickling ingredients.
Whisk until sugar and salt have dissolved.

Pour pickling liquid into the jars until the vegetables are covered.
Allow vegetables to sit in pickling liquid for 1 hour before using.

SOY LIME MAYONNAISE

Place egg, mustard, lime juice, salt, and pepper in a very tall, narrow 4 cup (1 liter) container.
Using an immersion blender, blend until well combined, 30-45 seconds.
(Alternatively, this can be done in a food processor).

Continue to blend while you begin streaming in the oil very slowly and evenly until the whole amount is incorporated.
Make sure the head of the blender is immersed toward the bottom of the cup, lifting upward periodically to draw down any oils on the surface.
The mixture should be thick and creamy.

Add soy sauce, gently folding in with a spatula.

Refrigerate mayo for at least 2 hours before serving.

MEAT

Add all marinade ingredients to a ziptop bag. Shake bag to combine.
Add meat; shake again to distribute the marinade all over the meat.
Marinate for 1 hour.

Preheat a skillet over high heat till it is very hot.
Add 1 teaspoon oil to the pan to prevent meat from sticking.
Working in small batches, add ¼ of the meat to the pan, stirring constantly to prevent sticking.
Since the meat is sliced very thinly it will only take 1-2 minutes to cook.
Once the meat is cooked, remove from the pan, set aside.

Continue to cook the rest of the meat in the same way.

TO ASSEMBLE

Slice baguettes in half lengthwise.
Spread bottom half with a nice amount of Soy Lime Mayonnaise.

Add a layer of meat; top with pickled vegetables.
Top vegetables with a few leaves of cilantro and some chili slices.

Eat right away and enjoy!

chipotle barbecue broiled skirt steak

#5IVEINGREDIENTFRIDAY. 'NUF SAID.

3 lb (1½ kg) skirt steak

1 Tbsp apple cider vinegar

1 cup fave BBQ sauce

2 chipotles in adobo, mashed with a fork

2 Tbsp adobo sauce

Cut skirt steak into 2-3 inch pieces.
Place in a bowl. Cover with cold water and vinegar.
Soak meat for 30 minutes, then rinse and pat dry.

In a bowl, combine remaining ingredients; add steak.
Marinate for 30 minutes or up to overnight in the fridge.

Set oven to broil. Line a baking sheet with parchment paper.

Place skirt steaks on prepared baking sheet. Reserve marinade.
Broil for 6 minutes on one side.
Remove from oven; brush with reserved marinade.
Flip steaks over, brush the second side with marinade.
Return baking sheet to oven. Broil for 4-5 minutes.

Remove from oven and enjoy.

(To cook more well done, after broiling, set oven to 350°F / 180°C, cover pan tightly with foil, and bake for 15 minutes.)

Slice meat AGAINST the grain and enjoy!

NOTE

We love this skirt steak on a Friday night and we love it even more on Shabbos day, sliced against the grain and added to a leafy green salad, topped with onions and whatever grilled veggies are left from Friday night, with either a balsamic vinaigrette, a creamy Asian vinaigrette, or a Caesar dressing!

french dip sandwiches

THIS IS REALLY A TWO-FOR-ONE RECIPE. YES, IT'S A SANDWICH RECIPE, AND IT'S ALSO THE WAY TO COOK THE MOST PERFECT, PINK IN THE MIDDLE, SOFT, MELT IN YOUR MOUTH, TRADITIONAL JEWISH ROAST BEEF. EVER.

2 (3 lb/1½ kg) boneless roasts

4 Tbsp extra virgin olive oil

2 Tbsp kosher salt

2 Tbsp coarsely ground black pepper

AU JUS

1 Tbsp extra virgin olive oil

3 yellow onions, halved, thinly sliced

4 cloves garlic, slightly smashed

1-2 Tbsp onion soup mix (depending how addicted to this stuff you are!)

1 cup sherry

1 cup red wine

6 cups beef broth

SERVE WITH

10-12 (6 inch) baguettes

horseradish mayo (page 28)

NOTES

You can make this dish in a crockpot. Cook roasts in crockpot on high heat until a thermometer inserted in the meat reads 120°F / 49°C. Transfer roasts to a platter; tent to keep warm. To the crockpot, add onions, garlic, and onion soup mix. Once onions have slightly browned, about 70 minutes, add remaining ingredients. After mixture boils, turn crockpot to simmer. Cook for 1 hour. After 1 hour add sliced meat to crockpot to keep warm.

TIPS & TRICKS

This is the perfect dish to add to any buffet because you can add the sliced meat to the au jus and let it sit for hours. The meat will lose its pinkness but it will be soft and delicious!

ROAST

Remove roast from fridge, rinse, pat dry, and allow to come to room temperature.

Preheat oven to 425°F / 220°C.
Place roasting rack into a roasting pan.
(If you don't have a roasting rack or pan, you can do this in a Dutch oven or any heavy-bottomed ovenproof pot.)

Drizzle 2 tablespoons olive oil over each roast.
Season each roast with 1 tablespoon each salt and pepper.
Be sure to rub oil and seasoning on all sides of the meat.

Place roasts onto roasting rack (you can cook both roasts in the same pan).
Roast for exactly 30 minutes.

After 30 minutes, lower oven temperature to 375°F / 190°C; roast for 33 minutes.

Transfer roasts to a platter.
Loosely tent the platter with foil; set aside.

AU JUS

Set the roasting pan or pot on the stove over medium high heat.
Add oil and onions; cook for about 8 minutes, stirring often, until onions wilt and brown slightly.
Add garlic and onion soup mix; cook for 1 minute.

Raise heat to high; add sherry and red wine.
Use a wooden spoon to scrape up any brown bits from the bottom of the pan.

Add beef broth.
Bring mixture to boil; reduce heat and allow to simmer for 5 minutes.
Taste to see if it needs more salt or pepper (this will vary based on the beef stock you use).

Remove onions with a slotted spoon into a bowl; set aside.

Add sliced meat to the au jus pot.

SLICE THE MEAT

Remove foil tent; add any juices that have accumulated on the platter into the au jus.

Place roasts on large cutting board.
Using your sharpest knife, very carefully slice the roast into the thinnest slices possible.
Don't worry if the slices are not perfect. It is more important for them to be thin.

Add sliced roast beef back to the au jus to keep warm.

TO ASSEMBLE SANDWICHES

Shmear horseradish mayo on one side of the bread.

Fill baguette with sliced roast beef and some of the reserved onions.

Dip the whole sandwich in the au jus and enjoy!

how to cook a steak
(+ red wine onion jus)

THERE ARE MANY DIFFERENT WAYS TO ACHIEVE WELL COOKED (NOT WELL DONE; HOWEVER, WITH THIS METHOD YOU CAN CHOOSE TO COOK YOUR STEAK TO YOUR LIKING) RIB EYE STEAK. YOU CAN SOUS–VIDE (IMMERSION CIRCULATE) YOUR STEAK TO TAKE ANY GUESSWORK OUT OF THE PROCESS. YOU CAN BROIL THE STEAK, REVERSE SEAR (BAKE FIRST, SEAR LATER), GRILL, OR EVEN START IN A FRYING PAN AND END IN THE OVEN. ALL THESE METHODS ARE PRACTICED AND ALL CAN YIELD A PERFECT STEAK WITH A LITTLE TECHNICAL KNOW–HOW. AT THE RISK OF NOT GIVING YOU ALL THE INFORMATION I POSSIBLY CAN, WHILE ALSO KEEPING IN MIND THAT WE NEED TO GET DINNER ON THE TABLE AND MAY NOT ALL HAVE A SOUS VIDE, I'M GOING TO ONLY GIVE YOU MY PAN FRY METHOD BECAUSE LIKE I SAID, IT'S MY FAVORITE AND ALL YOU NEED TO MAKE THIS HAPPEN IS JUST A GOOD HEAVY PAN. OH, AND A STEAK.

STEAK

1 (2 inch thick) bone-in rib eye steak

1½ tsp kosher salt

1½ tsp coarsely ground black pepper

2 tsp avocado oil

RED WINE ONION JUS

1 large purple onion, halved, thinly sliced

2 Tbsp honey

¾ cup dry red wine

1 cup beef stock

NOTE

For rare steak the temperature should be **125-130°F (51.6-54.4°C)**

For medium-rare steak the temperature should be **130-135°F (54.4-577.2°C)**

For medium steak the temperature should be **140-145°F (60-62.7°C)**

For medium well steak the temperature should be **145-150°F (62.7-65.5°C)**

For well-done steak the temperature should be **155-160°F (68.3-71.1°C)**

For Eli level doneness, which is highly discouraged, but what can you do, some people just like poorly cooked steak (coughelicough), the temperature should be 165°F and beyond.

Pat steak dry; season both sides with salt and pepper.
Allow steak to sit out for 1 hour to come to room temperature.

Once you are ready to cook, set large, heavy bottomed pan over medium high heat.
Add oil; place steak into the pan.

Gently use spatula or tongs (I prefer tongs), to press steak down so that all parts of the steak get a nice crust.
After 2-3 minutes, flip steak over; repeat with second side.

Use tongs to lift steak by the bone; sear the edges of the steak, allowing fat to render (about 1 minute).

If you want to be sure that your steak is cooked to the exact doneness you like, insert a meat thermometer into the center of the steak.
Be mindful that the steak temperature will continue to rise a few degrees while resting. (See Note for temperature guide.)

Remove steak from pan; set on a cutting board.
Loosely cover with foil; allow steak to rest for 10 minutes.

Slice and serve.

RED WINE ONION JUS

As soon as the steak comes out of the pan, whether you pan fried the whole time, or just seared after cooking sous-vide, add the onions.

Use a wooden spoon to stir onions around and scrape up any bits off the bottom of the pan.

Cook for about 8 minutes, stirring constantly.

Add honey; stir to coat.

Add wine; use a wooden spoon to scrape up any bits that were too stubborn until now.
Let the wine reduce down for about 1 minute; add beef stock.

Bring mixture to a boil; remove from heat, pour over steak or serve on the side, and … you guessed it, enjoy!

crockpot savory beef stew

I LOVE COMING HOME TO THIS ON A COLD WINTER DAY. IT'S DIFFICULT TO PICTURE YOURSELF WANTING TO EAT THIS FOR DINNER SO EARLY IN THE MORNING, BUT IF YOU JUST TRUST ME HERE AND PUT UP THE STEW ANYWAY, COME 4:30 P.M. WHEN YOUR ENERGY LEVEL STARTS TO DESCEND WITH THE SUN, AND PEOPLE COME POURING BACK INTO THE HOUSE, COLD, TIRED, AND MAYBE A LITTLE CRANKY, THE SMELL EMANATING FROM YOUR KITCHEN WILL MAKE YOU SO HAPPY YOU TOOK THE PLUNGE AND MADE THIS DISH!

2.2 lbs (1 kg) tender beef chuck stew meat

¼ cup flour

2 tsp kosher salt

1 tsp coarsely ground black pepper

3 carrots, peeled, cut into 1½ inch chunks

2 stalks celery, peeled, cut into 1½ inch chunks

1 onion, diced

3 cloves garlic, peeled, halved

4 small (or **2 large**) potatoes, peeled, cut into 2 inch chunks

2 bay leaves

2 cups beef broth

1 cup dry red wine

2 Tbsp fish free Worcestershire sauce

Coat the inside of a crockpot liberally with nonstick cooking spray.
Add meat.

Combine flour, salt, and pepper.
Pour over meat; toss to coat all the pieces.

Add carrots, celery, onion, garlic, and potatoes.
Toss again.
Add remaining ingredients.

Gently smush down to submerge meat.
It's OK if the meat pops back up; as it cooks it will go under the liquid.

Cook on high for 5-6 hours or on low for 8-10 hours.

Serve hot and enjoy.

easy peasy california roast

CUT FROM THE CENTER OF THE CHUCK, A CALIFORNIA ROAST IS EXTREMELY TENDER AND DELICIOUS. IT'S THE PERFECT ROAST TO MAKE AND SERVE FOR A SHABBOS LUNCH IF YOU'RE ALWAYS SEARCHING FOR THAT REALLY BEAUTIFUL PINK CENTER. COOK IT WHOLE, LET IT COME TO ROOM TEMPERATURE, THEN REHEAT COVERED, LOW AND SLOW. PULL THE MEAT OFF THE HEAT WHEN IT'S JUST WARM, SLICE, AND SERVE! IT'S TENDER, MELTS IN YOUR MOUTH, AND, THE BEST PART, LEFTOVERS MAKE THE MOST DELICIOUS STEAK SANDWICHES THE NEXT DAY!

1 California roast

2 Tbsp neutral oil

¼ cup garlic flakes

1 Tbsp paprika

2 Tbsp kosher salt

3 Tbsp cracked black pepper

Preheat oven to 450°F / 230°C. Coat a roasting pan lightly with nonstick cooking spray.
(If you have a roasting rack, great. If not, no worries!)

Place all the spices on a plate and mix well.

Drizzle oil over the roast, rubbing it in completely.
Roll oiled roast into the spices to create a crust.

Roast, uncovered, for 20 minutes.
Then lower temperature to 350°F / 180°C, cover, and bake.
See note for baking time.

NOTE

For any recipe using California roast, you can use this guide for baking in the oven on 350°F / 180°C after the initial 20 minute roasting on 450°F / 230°C.

For rare: 28 min/lb

For medium: 35 min/lb

For well done: 40-42 min/lb

no-boil, no-dishes corned beef

I KNOW WHAT YOU'RE THINKING. NO. NOT POSSIBLE. WELL, YES. TOTALLY POSSIBLE.

1 (3 lb/1½ kg) pickled corned beef (I use a pickled brisket)

⅔ cup brown sugar

1 Tbsp garlic powder

3 Tbsp dry mustard powder

3 Tbsp paprika

⅓ cup honey, for drizzling

Preheat oven to 300°F / 150°C.
Place two large pieces of foil (big enough to wrap around meat) one over the other.
Coat top piece of foil liberally with nonstick cooking spray.

Rinse off corned beef, pat dry, and place on foil.

In a bowl, combine sugar and spices.
Mix well; rub on both sides of the meat.
Drizzle honey over both sides.

Wrap meat tightly in both layers of foil.
Place foil packet into a 9x13 inch pan (or baking dish if you're not sick of doing dishes).
Cover pan with a layer of foil.

Bake for 3½ hours. Remove from oven and don't touch or uncover for 1 hour.
After 1 hour, carefully open foil, remove meat, slice against the grain, and return to the sauce that accumulated.

Serve hot and enjoy.

NOTE

I am of the belief that corned beef (and briskets) slice much more beautifully once they have cooled. If reheating this dish for Shabbos or after it's been frozen, I suggest slicing while it's cold!

mushroom smothered braised meat

THIS IS MY LOVE LETTER TO MUSHROOMS AND MY WAY OF CORRECTING EVERY SINGLE MUSHROOM DISH IN THE WORLD THAT DID NOT HAVE ENOUGH MUSHROOMS TO GET AT LEAST ONE ON EVERY FORKFUL OF FOOD YOU TOOK FROM YOUR PLATE. THE MEAT HERE IS JUST THE VEHICLE. A DELICIOUS, FLAVOR ENHANCING VEHICLE FOR SURE. BUT STILL. THIS IS ABOUT THE MUSHROOMS.

1 (4 lb/1.8 kg) boneless roast (silver tip, French roast, chuck roast, even brisket!)

3 Tbsp olive oil, divided

4 tsp kosher salt, divided

4 tsp coarsely ground black pepper, divided

1 large yellow onion, diced

2 lb (1 kg) assorted mushrooms, cleaned, stems removed, sliced

4 cloves garlic, minced

1½ cups dry red wine

2 cups beef or chicken stock

NOTE
The crockpot method is not my fave method because the meat may dry out from cooking too long and will not be sliceable.

Place a large roasting pan or pot (ideal if it has a lid!) over medium heat.
Drizzle 1 tablespoon olive oil over the meat.

Season with 2 teaspoons each salt and pepper.
Make sure to rub seasoning on all sides of meat.

Add remaining 2 tablespoons oil to the pan; add meat.
Sear meat on all sides for 4-5 minutes per side until nicely browned.
Transfer meat to a platter.

Add onion to the pan.
Cook, stirring often, scraping up whatever bits from the pan that you can, for 5-6 minutes.
Add mushrooms.

Cook, stirring every 3-4 minutes or so, until mushrooms cook down and all the liquid has evaporated.
Add garlic and remaining 2 teaspoons each salt and pepper; cook for 4 minutes.

Raise heat to medium high; add wine.
Immediately begin scraping the bottom of the pan to incorporate all those bits into the sauce.

Cook for 3 minutes; add stock.

Return meat to the pan; bring mixture to a boil.
Spoon mushrooms onto the meat; reduce heat to the lowest possible setting.
Cover pot tightly and allow to cook for 4-5 hours until meat is soft and tender.

Remove from heat; allow mixture to cool IN the sauce.
Once completely cooled, remove meat and slice.

Reheat in the sauce, serve hot, and enjoy.

TO ROAST IN THE OVEN

Preheat oven to 350°F / 180°C.

Follow the steps to sear meat, make sauce, and return the meat to the pot.
Cover tightly.

For medium rare, bake for 15 minutes per pound, medium for 18 minutes per pound, well done for 22 minutes per pound.

Continue the cooling/slicing process.

TO COOK IN CROCKPOT

Follow searing and sauce instructions. Transfer to crockpot 1-2 hours before Shabbos, not before. Cook on low.

pomegranate braised brisket

THIS HAS ROSH HASHANAH WRITTEN ALL OVER IT. I MEAN, BRISKET, POMEGRANATE, AND APPLES IN ONE DISH. IT'S BASICALLY THE GRAND SLAM MEAT FOR THE HIGH HOLIDAYS. ALTHOUGH POMEGRANATE IS THE STAR OF THIS DISH, IT'S REALLY THE HARD APPLE CIDER (WHICH IS ALCOHOLIC CARBONATED APPLE CIDER, NOT CIDER VINEGAR OR APPLE JUICE) THAT'S THE UNSUNG HERO, BRINGING JUST THE RIGHT AMOUNT OF SLIGHTLY SWEET ACIDITY TO BALANCE OUT THE TART POMEGRANATE.

1 (3-3.5 lb/1½ kg) 2nd cut brisket

RUB
3 Tbsp sugar
1 Tbsp kosher salt
1 Tbsp sumac
1 Tbsp ground mustard powder
1 Tbsp paprika
1 Tbsp garlic powder
1 tsp cracked black pepper
1 tsp cayenne pepper

MEAT
2 Tbsp canola oil
3 medium onions, halved and sliced
1 tsp kosher salt
1 tsp coarsely ground black pepper
3 cloves garlic, smashed
1 (11 oz/330 ml) bottle hard apple cider
½ cup tomato sauce (not marinara)
½ cup pomegranate molasses (syrup)
2 cups beef stock (or **1** beef bouillon cube dissolved in **2 cups** hot water)

TO GARNISH (OPTIONAL)
¼ cup pomegranate seeds

In a bowl, combine all rub ingredients.

Rinse brisket and pat dry very well.
Rub the spice mixture all over both sides of the brisket.
(The spice rub makes more than you will probably need. Freeze the rest for another brisket.)

Place spiced brisket into a ziptop bag; refrigerate overnight.
(If you're short on time, just let spiced meat come to room temp for 1 hour. Then continue with the recipe.)

Remove from the fridge; allow brisket to come to room temperature.

Preheat oven to 350°F / 180°C.

Heat a large Dutch oven or ovenproof pan over high heat.
Add oil and brisket.
Sear both sides of the meat for 4-5 minutes per side until nicely browned.
Remove from Dutch oven; set aside.

To the same pot, add onions, salt, and pepper.
Cook for 4 minutes until onions are soft and translucent.
Add garlic; cook for 1 minute.

Add hard cider, using a wooden spoon to stir it in and scrape up any browned bits from the bottom of the pan.

Add remaining ingredients.
Bring mixture to a boil; return brisket to the Dutch oven.
If you used a pan, pour the sauce and onions over the brisket.

Cover the pot tightly. Bake for about 1½ hours.

Remove from oven; turn brisket over. Return to oven.
At this point, cooking time will vary based on the size of your meat. I suggest giving it another 45 minutes, no matter the size, and after that checking it every 30 minutes until it is soft and tender.
Mine took 3 hours total for a 4 pound brisket.

Remove from the oven and allow brisket to cool completely in the sauce.
(Taking the brisket out of the sauce while it is hot will result in a dry brisket.)

If you want to shred the brisket, wait 45 minutes after you take it out of the oven and, while it is still warm, use 2 forks to shred it in the pot, where it can stay in the liquid.

To slice brisket, allow it to cool completely, then remove from sauce and slice against the grain. Garnish with pomegranate seeds, optional.

stovetop brisket

USUALLY SERVED ON PESACH BECAUSE IT'S COOKED ON THE STOVETOP THE WHOLE TIME, THIS BRISKET MAKES A SURPRISE APPEARANCE EVERY FEW MONTHS WHEN I NEED A MEAT THAT'S JUST SIMPLE, DELICIOUS, AND SAVORY. IT'S EASY TO PREPARE, CAN BE SERVED WITH ALMOST ANY STARCHY SIDE DISH BECAUSE OF ITS EASY FLAVORS, AND IS BASICALLY A CROWD PLEASER!

1 (3 lb/1½ kg) brisket

SPICE RUB

3 Tbsp kosher salt

2 Tbsp coarsely ground black pepper

2 Tbsp paprika

2 Tbsp garlic powder

3 Tbsp brown sugar

MEAT

1 Tbsp walnut oil

2 cups sautéed onions (page 22)

3 cloves garlic, sliced

3 cups red wine

2 cups chicken stock

2 bay leaves

1 tsp kosher salt

1 tsp coarsely ground black pepper

Heat a wide, heavy-bottomed pot over high heat.

In a small bowl, combine spices and brown sugar to form a rub.

Sprinkle spice rub liberally all over the brisket.

Add oil to the pot; add brisket.
Sear for 3-4 minutes on each side to seal in all that good flavor.
Set aside.

Add onions and garlic to the pot; cook for 3-4 minutes.
Add wine; bring to a boil.
Add stock, bay leaves, salt, and pepper.
Bring to a boil, then return brisket to the pot.

Lower heat to a very gentle simmer.
Cook for 2 hours, then flip meat over.
Continue cooking for 1-3 hours until meat is fork tender.

Make sure to cool meat in the pan sauce so that it doesn't dry out!

Store and reheat in the pan sauce!

Serve hot and enjoy.

slow roasted deckle

DECKLE IS JUST A BRISKET BY ANOTHER NAME. SORT OF. TECHNICALLY IT'S THE POINT OF THE BRISKET, THE PART THAT ATTACHES TO THE TOP OF THE RIB. IT IS MORE MUSCULAR, BUT ALSO FATTIER, MAKING IT AN EXCELLENT CONTENDER FOR THE LOW AND SLOW TYPE COOKING HERE. IT IS ALMOST IMPOSSIBLE TO SLICE BEAUTIFULLY BECAUSE OF HOW LUSCIOUSLY SOFT THE MEAT BECOMES, SO I PUT THE COOKED MEAT INTO A SLIGHTLY WALLED SERVING DISH, WITH A SERVING FORK AND SPOON, AND EVERYONE CAN SERVE THEMSELVES!

1 deckle roast
2 tsp kosher salt
2 tsp coarsely ground black pepper
3 carrots, peeled, cut into 2 inch pieces
2 onions, peeled and diced
2 stalks celery, peeled, cut into 2 inch pieces
3 cloves garlic
2 cups red wine
¾ cup balsamic vinegar
½ cup light soy sauce
1 (15 oz) can tomato sauce

Preheat oven to 300°F / 150°C.

Sprinkle meat generously with salt and pepper.
In a large, ovenproof pot over high heat, sear meat on both sides, 6-7 minutes per side.
Set aside.

Add vegetables to the pot; sauté for 8 minutes.
Add wine, using a wooden spoon to stir it in and scrape up any browned bits from the bottom of the pan.

Return meat to the pot.
Add remaining ingredients, bring to a boil.

Cover pot; bake 4½- 5½ hours, depending on the size of the deckle.
Check it every hour and baste with pan sauce.

Meat is ready when it is fork tender.

Serve hot and enjoy!

korean flanken roast

ABOUT EVERY 5-6 PAGES IN THIS BOOK, THERE IS A DISH WITH THIS FLAVOR PROFILE: SOY, GARLIC, CHILIES, AND LIMES. THEY ARE MY GO TO FLAVORS BECAUSE THEY ARE DELICIOUS, AND COMBINED, THEY ARE IRRESISTIBLE. I ALWAYS TELL ELI, IF I EVER AGREED TO DO A COOKING COMPETITION (WHICH, BY THE WAY, I WOULD NEVER), I WOULD DEFINITELY GO WITH THESE FLAVORS BECAUSE THEY ALWAYS WIN!

1 (6 bone) rack of ribs
1 tsp kosher salt
1 Tbsp coarsely ground black pepper
2 red Thai (or bird) chilies
6 cloves garlic
1 cup sambal olek
½ cup brown sugar
3 Tbsp low sodium soy sauce
juice of **2** limes

In a food processor fitted with the "S" blade, combine salt, pepper, chilies, garlic, sambal olek, brown sugar, soy sauce, and lime juice until a cohesive but still slightly chunky marinade forms.
Place marinade into a ziptop bag; add ribs.
Smush the bag so that the marinade is massaged into the ribs.
Refrigerate for 1 hour lying on its side.
Then place bag in the freezer so that the side that was on top in the fridge is now on the bottom in the freezer.

Freeze until the night before you serve.

Remove ribs from freezer to fridge to defrost the night before you want to cook.
The day you want to cook, remove ribs from fridge and allow to come to room temp.

Preheat oven to 425°F / 220°C.

Place ribs into a greased baking dish.
Spoon marinade over the ribs.
Roast, uncovered, for 30 minutes.

Remove from oven; reduce oven temp to 300°F / 150°C.
Spoon more marinade over the ribs.

Coat a large piece of foil with nonstick cooking spray; place sprayed side down over the ribs.
Seal tightly.
Make sure pan is tightly covered.

Return covered ribs to the oven; bake for 4-5 hours.
Check after 3 hours, to determine if they need more time.

You know ribs are done when they are fork tender.

bourbon braised short ribs

MY NUMBER ONE MOST POPULAR MEAT RECIPE. MOST LIKELY BECAUSE OF THE COPIOUS AMOUNT OF BOURBON REQUIRED TO MAKE IT, BUT NOT REALLY. IT'S BECAUSE IT'S DELICIOUS.

5 lb (2 kg) short ribs

kosher salt and coarsely ground black pepper, for seasoning ribs

canola oil, for searing

1 onion, diced

4 cloves garlic, peeled

1½ cups bourbon

¾ cup brown sugar

1 cup tomato sauce

⅓ cup cider vinegar

2 Tbsp fish free Worcestershire sauce

2 tsp kosher salt

1 tsp coarsely ground black pepper

Heat a heavy bottomed skillet over high heat.

Season ribs liberally on all sides with salt and pepper.
Drizzle a little canola oil into the pan; sear ribs on all sides till brown (about 4 minutes per side).
You may need to work in batches so as not to overcrowd the pan.
Remove ribs; set aside.

Add onion and garlic to the skillet. Cook for 2 minutes, till soft.
Carefully add bourbon; cook for 2 minutes.
Add remaining ingredients.

Bring mixture to a boil; return ribs to pot or pour sauce over ribs in a pan.

Seal tightly; bake at 350°F / 180°C for 1½ hours, then check on the ribs and turn them over.
Bake for 45 minutes; check to see if they are fork tender.
Depending on thickness of meat, they may need some extra time.

Once meat is tender, remove from oven and let cool completely in its own juices, if freezing, or serve fresh and hot.

TO FREEZE

Let ribs cool completely in the sauce. If you remove them from the sauce, they will dry out.

Wrap pan in a few layers of plastic wrap and then one layer of foil. Freeze for up to 6 months.

VARIATIONS

You can make these with so many cuts of meat. Think brisket, deckle, flanken ribs, spare ribs, etc.

horseradish crusted standing rib roast

HORSERADISH. AS IN THE LONG, WHITE, GINGER ROOT–LOOKING VEGETABLE WE GRIND FOR PESACH. NOT THE PRE-MADE, COMES IN A BOTTLE, SQUEEZABLE SAUCE STUFF WE BUY. SPREAD THAT ON A SANDWICH OR ADD TO A WRAP, YUM! FOR THIS MEAT, THOUGH, WE WANT THE GOOD STUFF. THE HORSERADISH IN ALL ITS BITTER GLORY THAT WILL CREATE THE PERFECT BALANCE TO OUR ROAST!

1 (6 lb/2¾ kg, 3 bone) standing rib roast

1 Tbsp neutral oil

1 Tbsp kosher salt

1 Tbsp coarsely ground black pepper

4 cloves garlic minced (optional)

HORSERADISH CRUST

¾ cup grated horseradish

6 Tbsp mayonnaise

¼ tsp kosher salt

Remove roast from fridge a full hour before cooking so that the meat can come to room temperature.

Preheat oven to 450°F / 230°C.

In a small bowl, combine oil, salt, pepper, and garlic.
Rub all over the roast.

Place rib roast in roasting dish (preferably over a rack, but if you don't have one, skip the rack!).
Roast, on the lower middle rack for 25 minutes.
Remove pan from the oven; reduce oven temperature to 325°F / 165°C.

In a small bowl, combine horseradish crust ingredients.
Use a spatula to spread all over the roast.

Return the roast to the oven; roast for 18 minutes per pound.
In this case, for a 6 pound roast, that would be 1 hour and 45-50 minutes.

Let the meat rest for a full 20-25 minutes to allow the juices inside to redistribute; then slice and serve!

TEMP TRICKS

If you want to be super awesome, you can take the internal temp of your roast by sticking a thermometer diagonally into the center of the roast. The temp you are aiming for is 125°F / 51.6°C (for medium rare) because the roast will continue to cook once it is out of the oven and resting.

However, if you are serving this on Shabbos and can't cook the roast fresh, I recommend cooking for 15 minutes less than you should to account for plata time!

NOTES

A few ounces over or under won't make a difference; however a pound or more difference will affect cooking time if you want a medium rare roast (which obviously you do, otherwise you'd be making brisket).

Please don't skip letting the roast come to room temperature before cooking! If the roast is cold all the way to its core, it will cook differently and the resulting roast will not look as perfect as in this photo!

sunday sauce

SUNDAY SAUCE IS THE ULTIMATE ITALIAN COMFORT FOOD. IT'S A FEW SIMPLE BUT HIGH QUALITY INGREDIENTS THAT ARE COOKED TOGETHER LOW AND SLOW SO THAT THE WHOLE FINISHED DISH IS EVEN BETTER THAN THE SUM OF ITS PARTS (WHICH IS REALLY SAYING SOMETHING BECAUSE THIS DISH HAS FACON, RIBS, AND MEATBALLS!). THOSE LONG, LAZY SUNDAYS, WHEN YOU HAVE AN HOUR OR TWO IN THE MORNING TO PUT THIS UP, THEN SOME TIME TO RUN ERRANDS, CARPOOL, MAYBE GROCERY SHOP FOR THE WEEK, ARE THE PERFECT DAYS FOR THIS. OR YOM TOV. BECAUSE IT'S BASICALLY THE GROWN UP VERSION OF MEAT SAUCE.

MEATBALLS

3 lb (1½ kg) ground beef

1 cup panko breadcrumbs

1 egg

1 tsp kosher salt

1 tsp coarsely ground black pepper

2 cloves garlic, minced

1 cup parsley leaves, finely minced

SUNDAY SAUCE

3 marrow bones

2 pkgs beef Facon, chopped

2 lb (1 kg) short ribs

2 lb (1 kg) 2nd cut brisket

1 piece flanken

2 lb (1 kg) thinly sliced pepper steak

2 Tbsp + 1 tsp kosher salt (divided)

2 Tbsp coarsely ground black pepper

8 cloves garlic, finely chopped

2 Tbsp tomato paste

¼ cup dry red wine

1 bay leaf

5 (17 oz/482 g) cans/jars/cartons tomato sauce

VARIATIONS

If you do not want to make meatballs, just use the 3 pounds of ground beef and disregard remaining meatball ingredients. Instead of forming and cooking meatballs, add ground beef after the pepper steak and use a wooden spoon to gently break it up (if you want big hunks of beef, don't over stir it!).

MEATBALLS

In a large bowl, combine the meatball ingredients; mix well.
Scoop out 3 tablespoons of the meat mixture at a time and form meatballs.
Place meatballs on a sheet pan; set aside.

SUNDAY SAUCE

Place meats (except Facon) out on a board.
Season both sides with 2 tablespoons salt and all the pepper.

Heat a very large pot over medium high heat.
Add marrow bones; sear for 4 minutes on each side.
Remove to a platter and set aside.

Add Facon, stirring continuously until all the fat has rendered and Facon is crispy.
Use a slotted spoon to remove Facon to a bowl; set aside.

Add meatballs, a few at a time so as not to overcrowd the pan.
Sear so that the outsides of the meatballs are nicely browned.
Remove to a platter and set aside.

Add short ribs, brisket, and flanken; sear for 3-4 minutes each side till browned. (You may need to do this in 1 or 2 batches so as not to overcrowd the pan.)
Remove to a platter and set aside.

Add pepper steak to the pot; stir till browned, about 5 minutes.
Remove to a platter and set aside.

Once the meat is cooked through, add garlic. Stir for 1 minute.
Add tomato paste; stir for 2 minutes.
Add wine, using a wooden spoon to stir it in and scrape up all the bits on the bottom of the pan.
Return all the meat and half the Facon to the pan.

Add all the tomato sauce, remaining teaspoon salt, and bay leaf. Stir to combine.

Raise heat to high; bring sauce to a boil.
Reduce heat to a very low simmer, cover the pot, and allow to simmer for 6-8 hours until meat is tender.

Serve hot, over a giant bowl of pasta, sprinkled with remaining crispy Facon!

NOTE

You can transfer to a crockpot before adding all the meat back into the sauce.

NOTE

Freezes excellently.

slow roasted veal pocket

VEAL, DUCK FAT, LOW AND SLOW. DOES IT GET MORE DECADENT? NO. IT DOES NOT. THIS IS THE ONCE IN A WHILE, SPECIAL OCCASION DISH YOU MAKE WHEN YOU REALLY WANT TO PULL OUT ALL THE STOPS. HOWEVER, NO ONE WILL EVER KNOW IT TAKES ONLY 5-10 MINUTES TO PUT TOGETHER. WELL, NOW THEY MIGHT.

1 breast of veal with pocket (you can ask your butcher to do this for you)

1 Tbsp kosher salt

2 tsp coarsely ground black pepper

2 Tbsp granulated garlic

2 Tbsp granulated onion

1 (4 oz/115 g) jar duck fat

Sprinkle both sides of the veal and the inside of the pocket with salt, pepper, garlic, and onion.

Using a spoon, place a tablespoon of duck fat in the pocket. Only use half the jar for the inside of the pocket.

Spoon remaining duck fat over the veal, gently pressing it down so it stays on top.

The fat will render and melt as it cooks, covering the whole breast of veal as it roasts.

Wrap breast of veal in 2 layers of plastic wrap and then 1 layer of foil.

Freeze until ready to use.

Defrost veal in the fridge the night before you want to cook it.
Remove from fridge in the morning to finish defrosting.

Preheat oven to 220°F / 105°C.
Place veal into a greased baking dish.
Bake breast of veal, covered, for 7 hours.

Serve hot and enjoy!

TIPS + TRICKS

Add 3 carrots, halved lengthwise, and 2 onions, quartered, to the pan to slowly roast in all those pan juices!

veal milanese

THE PREPARATION AND CONSUMPTION OF THIS RECIPE IS A FULL SENSORY EXPERIENCE. THE TOUCH REQUIRED TO BREAD THE VEAL, THE SIZZLING SOUND WHEN YOU COOK IT, AND THE CRUNCH WHEN YOU EAT, THE AROMA OF THE COLD SALAD HITTING THE CRISP VEAL, THE SIGHT OF THE VIBRANT PURPLE, RED, AND GREEN COLORS FROM THE SALAD, ALL CULMINATING IN THE FIRST BITE OF A PERFECTLY BALANCED DISH HITTING YOUR PALATE IS JUST ABSOLUTELY AMAZING! THERE'S A REASON THIS DISH IS A LONGTIME WORLD-FAVORITE AND THAT'S IT.

VEAL CUTLETS

12 pieces thin veal cutlets

1½ cups flour

6 large eggs, beaten

4 cups panko breadcrumbs

3 tsp kosher salt, divided

2 tsp coarsely ground black pepper, divided

oil, for frying

SALAD

2 cups quartered cherry tomatoes

1 bulb fennel, shaved thin, fronds discarded

1 purple onion, halved, thinly sliced

1 cup parsley leaves

1½ tsp kosher salt

1 tsp coarsely ground black pepper

¼ cup balsamic vinegar

2 Tbsp extra virgin olive oil

VEAL CUTLETS

Place veal between 2 pieces of parchment paper.
Using a meat mallet or rolling pin, pound veal till it's paper thin.

Place flour, eggs, and panko each in its own bowl or quarter size sheet pan with 1 teaspoon salt in each.
Add 1 teaspoons pepper to the flour and ½ teaspoon each to the eggs and panko. Stir to combine.

Dip each piece of veal into flour, then egg, and then panko to coat.

Heat a large pan over medium high heat. Add ¼ inch canola oil to the pan.

When oil is hot, fry cutlets in batches till crispy.

Transfer to a wire rack to cool.

SALAD

In a large bowl, toss together all salad ingredients. Salad is best made up to 1 hour in advance.

TO SERVE

Lay veal cutlets on a large platter and spoon salad over the top of each piece. Serve and enjoy!

NOTE

To serve on Shabbos, I reheat my veal cutlets by placing them in a SINGLE layer in a large pan on the plata two hours before the meal. After 1 hour, I flip them over. Top with salad only immediately before serving!

whole roasted lamb shoulder with crispy potatoes

THIS IS PROBABLY ONE OF MY GREATEST ACCOMPLISHMENTS. MOST OF US DO NOT HAVE ROTISSERIES. WHICH IS, IN FACT, THE BEST WAY TO COOK A LAMB ROAST, IN MY HUMBLE OPINION. SO I TRIED MANY TIMES ON A SHEET PAN OR ROASTING PAN, AND ALTHOUGH BOTH THOSE OPTIONS WERE DELICIOUS, THEY DID NOT YIELD THE RESULTS I WANTED. I WANT 360 DEGREES OF CRISPY LAMB OUTSIDE, WITH SOFT, TENDER MEAT INSIDE, AND I WANT ALL THE INSANELY FLAVORFUL LAMB FAT TO GO SOMEWHERE. NOT JUST SIT AND BURN ON A SHEET PAN. THAT IS WHAT THE TECHNIQUE BELOW ACCOMPLISHES. IF THE THOUGHT OF COOKING DIRECTLY ON YOUR OVEN RACK SCARES YOU, JUST KEEP IN MIND WHAT'S WAITING FOR YOU ON THE OTHER END: SUCCULENT, JUICY, AND AMAZING LAMB AND CRISPY POTATOES!

POTATOES

8-10 potatoes, peeled, cut into 2 inch cubes

1 Tbsp kosher salt

LAMB

1 whole lamb shoulder

4 cloves garlic, peeled

zest of **1** lemon

1 tsp kosher salt

1 tsp freshly cracked black pepper

3 sprigs fresh rosemary, leaves only

¼ cup olive oil

POTATOES

Place 1 oven rack on the lowest possible level and another rack in the middle. Preheat oven to 400°F / 200°C. Line a baking sheet with parchment paper.

While oven is preheating, place cubed potatoes into a large pot.
Add water to cover; add salt.
Bring to a boil; reduce heat and allow potatoes to simmer for only 5 minutes. (You don't want them cooked through, only par-boiled.)

Drain potatoes; return potatoes to hot pan to allow them to slightly dry.
Transfer potatoes to a prepared baking sheet.
Set aside to prepare lamb.

LAMB

If your lamb has a large fat cap on top, using a very sharp knife, score the fat on the top of the lamb shoulder in a crosshatched pattern.

Using a mortar and pestle (or food processor), combine garlic, lemon zest, salt, and pepper.
Crush them until they form a chunky paste.
Add rosemary; crush a little bit longer until the rosemary has slightly softened.

Drizzle olive oil all over the lamb.
Massage garlic and rosemary paste all over the lamb shoulder, being careful to get it into every nook and cranny.

Place pan of potatoes on the lowest oven rack.
Place the seasoned lamb shoulder directly on the middle oven rack.
There is no need to put it into a pan.
All the lamb drippings will fall directly onto the potatoes to season them.

Bake for 1½ to 2 hours, depending on how well done you like your meat!

Serve hot and enjoy!

NOTE

This is truly the best way I have ever cooked lamb! It gives it that super crispy outside but soft and tender inside that we love about lamb!

TIPS + TRICKS

If your lamb comes with netting or butchers twine, cook with twine on and remove before serving!

i have
so
mushroom
for you 
in my 
heart

sides

bar-b-cumin'd carrots

SWEET CARROTS, EARTHY CUMIN, ACIDIC LIME . . . YES, PLEASE!

20 carrots, peeled,
sliced in half lengthwise

2 Tbsp olive oil

zest of **1** lime

1 Tbsp cumin

1½ tsp kosher salt

1 tsp coarsely ground black pepper

DIP

1¼ cups vegan sour cream
(I used Tofutti)

zest and juice of **2** limes

2-4 tsp spicy chili powder

2 tsp kosher salt

CARROTS

Toss together all ingredients on a baking sheet.
Mix well to fully coat carrots.

Grill on a BBQ or grill pan for 4 minutes on the first side and 3 minutes on the second side.

Serve with dip.

DIP

Combine all dip ingredients in a bowl.

Refrigerate until serving.

VARIATION

If you don't want to grill the carrots, you can preheat a sheet pan in the oven for 15 minutes at 400°F / 200°C. Carefully remove pan from oven and drizzle with 3 Tbsp olive oil. Add coated carrots to the pan, flat side down. Roast for about 35 minutes until carrots are charred and just cooked through.

girls' favorite
moroccan stewed chickpeas

THIS DISH REALLY HAPPENED BECAUSE ELI AND MY BOYS DO NOT LIKE FISH BUT MOROCCAN FISH IS A FRIDAY NIGHT STAPLE. I DIDN'T WANT THEM TO MISS OUT ON MY FAVORITE PART OF THE FISH, THE SOFT, SAFFRON-Y, STEWED CHICKPEAS THAT YOU SMASH YOUR CHALLAH INTO. SO I SEPARATED OUT THE CHICKPEAS, STEWED THEM IN A SIMILAR PREPARATION TO THE FISH, AND LO AND BEHOLD — GUESS WHO CAN'T GO A FRIDAY NIGHT WITHOUT THEM NOW? MY GIRLS!!!

1-2 tsp saffron

3 cups boiling water

1 Tbsp olive oil

10 cilantro stems (without leaves)

6 cloves garlic, halved

1-2 jalapeño peppers, halved

1 Tbsp paprika

2 tsp kosher salt

1 tsp coarsely ground black pepper

1 (28 oz/800g) bag frozen chickpeas OR **3 (15 oz/425 g) cans,** drained and rinsed

1 cup tomato sauce

1 cup cilantro leaves

In a bowl, combine saffron and boiling water.
Use the back of a spoon to crush saffron against the wall of the bowl.
Cover with plastic wrap; set aside.

Heat a pot over medium heat. Add oil, cilantro stems, garlic, and jalapeño. Cook for 10 minutes, stirring often, until jalapeños blister and mixture is very fragrant.

Add paprika, salt, and pepper. Stir to combine.
Add chickpeas; stir to coat in spices.

Stir saffron mixture; add to the pot with tomato sauce and cilantro leaves. Stir.

Bring mixture to a boil. Reduce heat and cover loosely, leaving a tiny opening at the edge of the pot.
Simmer for 1 hour.

Serve hot and enjoy!

TIPS + TRICKS

Because the chickpeas are meant to be soft and live in a nice amount of sauce, they are very freezer friendly. You can double the recipe and freeze in portions so that you have some readily available every Shabbos! Just defrost a few hours before Shabbos and reheat in a covered ovenproof dish until serving.

NOTE

If you are using dried chickpeas, you will need to soak them in water overnight, drain them, add 1 additional cup water to the recipe, and simmer for 1 additional hour.

roasted vegetables

I'M REALLY NOT MUCH OF A KUGEL OR SIDE DISH PERSON. USUALLY FOR SHABBOS I MAKE A FEW DIFFERENT PROTEINS AND THEN SIMPLY ROAST UP WHATEVER VEGGIES ARE IN MY FRIDGE. THESE ARE TWO OF MY FAVORITE COMBINATIONS!

cayenne + maple roasted fennel and squash

2 fennel bulbs, quartered, fronds discarded

3 purple onions, cut into ½ inch rounds

1 kabocha or acorn squash, halved through the stem, deseeded, and cut into ¾ inch strips

2 Tbsp extra virgin olive oil

2 tsp kosher salt

½-1 tsp cayenne pepper (depending on how spicy you like things)

3 Tbsp pure maple syrup

I LOVE THESE VEGETABLES HOT OUT OF THE OVEN AS THE SIDE FOR A WEEKNIGHT DINNER, I LOVE THEM REHEATED FOR A FRIDAY NIGHT ROASTED VEGGIE PLATTER, AND MOSTLY, I LOVE THEM COLD ON SHABBOS DAY, WHEN I HAPHAZARDLY TOSS THEM ON TOP OF WHATEVER GREENS ARE IN MY FRIDGE AND DRIZZLE VINAIGRETTE ON TOP.

Preheat oven to 350°F / 180°C. Line 2 baking sheets with parchment paper.

Place all the vegetables into a large bowl.
Add oil, salt, cayenne, and maple syrup to the bowl; gently mix to combine, trying to avoid breaking up the onion rounds as much as possible.

Transfer vegetables to prepared baking sheets, making sure they are in a single layer.
Bake for 45-50 minutes until they are fully cooked, slightly charred, and the maple syrup has caramelized ever so slightly!

crispy roasted broccoli

SO BASIC, BUT COMPLETELY IRRESISTIBLE. DON'T BE TEMPTED TO ADD THE SOY SAUCE AT THE BEGINNING. LETTING THE BROCCOLI ROAST DRY FIRST MAKES ALL THE DIFFERENCE!

2 (24 oz) bags frozen broccoli (see Note)

2 Tbsp olive oil

¼ tsp kosher salt

1 tsp coarsely ground black pepper

2 tsp crushed red pepper flakes (optional)

6 cloves garlic

4 Tbsp low sodium soy sauce

Preheat oven to 350°F / 180°C. Line a baking sheet with parchment paper.

Place frozen broccoli on prepared baking sheet. (If frozen broccoli is clumped together, wait a little bit and then separate pieces, discarding any ice clumps that have accumulated.)
Drizzle oil over the broccoli.
Add salt, pepper, red pepper flakes (if using), and garlic. Toss to combine.

Roast for 45 minutes until the broccoli is cooked and the edges begin to char. Do NOT open the oven, mix the broccoli, or move around the pan AT ALL during those first 45 minutes.

Pull out oven rack and drizzle soy sauce over broccoli. Return to oven; roast for 5-6 minutes.

Remove from oven and serve hot!

NOTE
You can use either florets or cuts for this. I am personally partial to florets; however, the recipe works with either or both!

garlicky spinach
with lemon and facon (meat)

GIVE ME ALL THE WILTED GREENS. THEN ADD FACON. I'M DONE.

WAIT! SERVE ON THE SIDE OF CHICKEN OR MEAT. GET A LITTLE PROTEIN AND SOME OF THE FLAVORFUL FACON ON YOUR FORK FOR THE PERFECT BITE. 'K, NOW I'M DONE.

1 (4 oz/113 g) package beef Facon, cut into thin strips

9 oz (264 g) frozen spinach, defrosted, drained OR
10 cups fresh spinach

6 cloves garlic, minced

½ tsp kosher salt

1 tsp coarsely ground black pepper

juice of **1** lemon

1½ cups chicken or beef stock

Add Facon to a large sauté pan and place over medium high heat.
Cook for 6-8 minutes, stirring often, until Facon has rendered its fat and become crispy.
Use a slotted spoon to transfer Facon to a plate. Set aside.

Add spinach, garlic, salt, and pepper to the pan.
Cook, stirring often, for about 10 minutes, until most of the liquid has evaporated and spinach and garlic are totally heated through.

Raise the heat to high; add lemon juice and stock.
Use a wooden spoon to scrape up any bits from the bottom of the pan.

Cook for 3 minutes until liquid has slightly reduced.

Taste to adjust seasoning because, depending on the stock you use and the variety of Facon, you may need to add a pinch more salt.

Return crispy Facon bits to the spinach.
Serve hot and enjoy!

pesto salad sandwich

THE BETTER WAY TO MAKE A SALAD.
ALSO, 2 RECIPES IN 1, WOOHOO!

slices of good quality bread
(sourdough is my fave!)

PESTO

¾ **cup** salted, roasted cashews

2 cups fresh parsley

½ **cup** fresh mint

zest & juice of **1** lemon

2 tsp kosher salt

1 tsp coarsely ground black pepper

¾ **cup** olive oil

GRILLED VEGETABLES

1 zucchini, cut on a bias
into ¼ inch slices

1 red or orange pepper, quartered

1 purple onion,
sliced into ¼ inch thick rings

3 Tbsp olive oil

1 tsp kosher salt

1 tsp coarsely ground black pepper

1 clove garlic, minced

3 Tbsp balsamic vinegar

PESTO

In a food processor fitted with the "S" blade, process cashews until finely ground. Add parsley, mint, lemon zest and juice, salt, and pepper. Process till a paste forms.

While processor is running, drizzle in olive oil. (Taste to adjust seasoning if needed.)

GRILLED VEGETABLES

Combine all grilled vegetable ingredients in a ziptop bag or large bowl. Toss to coat.

Heat a grill pan over medium high heat.

Add vegetables in small batches so that you don't overcrowd the pan; grill until lightly charred on both sides (peppers and onions: about 5 minutes per side; zucchini: 3-4 minutes per side).

TO ASSEMBLE THE SANDWICH OF MY DREAMS

Smother one side of each bread slice with pesto.

Build sandwich by layering veggies. Top with a second bread slice.

Wrap tightly in parchment paper to hold it together and cut in half! #enjoy

**MORE OPTIONAL VEGETABLES
TO ADD TO YOUR SANDWICH**

lettuce • radishes • radicchio •
tomatoes • shredded carrots •
scallions • avocado • mango •
avocado • red Thai chilies

BONUS

For dairy meals, add a slice of cheese because cheese is delicious. OR, for meat meals, add a piece of grilled chicken. Because. Yum.

perfect potato latkes

SAY BYE BYE TO A HOUSE THAT SMELLS LIKE FRIED FOOD FOR DAYS AND OIL SPLATTERS ON YOUR CLOTHING! IT COMES DOWN TO TECHNIQUE. SIMPLE INGREDIENTS, TREATED PROPERLY TO MAXIMIZE WHAT THEY CAN DO FOR YOU IN TERMS OF FLAVOR AND TEXTURE. THAT'S WHAT THIS PAGE IS ABOUT. IF YOU WANT TO USE YOUR GRANDMOTHER'S RECIPE AND AMOUNTS, I SAY, GO FOR IT. JUST APPLY THE FEW SIMPLE BUT IMPORTANT TECHNIQUES HERE AND YOUR LATKES WILL BE CRISPY AND DELICIOUS EVERY TIME!

MAKES ABOUT 30 (2 INCH) LATKES

5½ lb/2.4 kg red waxy potatoes (a few ounces more or less will not make a difference), peeled

1 large onion, peeled

2 eggs, beaten

1 Tbsp + 1 tsp kosher salt

oil, for frying (I like avocado or canola)

1 carrot, washed, cut into 2 inch pieces

TIPS + TRICKS

Waxy potatoes make better latkes than Idaho potatoes.

Using 2 types of graters for the potatoes provides a soft creamy inside and a super crispy outside.

Do not form perfect round latkes and then put it in the pan. Plop a scoop in the pan and flatten with a spoon. All those "strands" that stick out will get super crispy and be the best part of the latke.

If you don't have a cooling rack, use a rack from your oven!

To keep warm or reheat, place entire cooling rack in a 200°F / 95°C oven, uncovered. Alternatively, place latkes in a single layer on a baking sheet, uncovered, at the same temperature. The rack method will yield a better result but a baking sheet will still work!

FUN FACT

There is no official name for that side of the box grater. I therefore dub that side of the box "The small prickly grater." Please inform Webster. Thank you.

Peel potatoes and place into a bowl of very cold water. (Peeled potatoes can stay in cold water in the fridge for a whole day before using.)

Set up 3 bowls. In one bowl place a colander or fine mesh strainer.

Using the "E" blade of your food processor or the small hole grater of your box grater (the one that looks like spiky circles), grate the onion.

Remove potatoes from water and dry them.

Grate half the potatoes in a food processor fitted with the "E" blade.

Next, switch the blade of the food processor to the fine shredder ("C" blade). Grate the remaining potatoes.

Add the contents of the food processor to the prepared colander.

Working quickly, remove a few handfuls of potato mixture and place onto the center of a tea towel.
Gather the four corners of the towel and, over the second bowl, twist and squeeze the towel tightly to extract as much liquid as possible from the potatoes. DO NOT DISCARD THE LIQUID YET.

Add the drained potato mixture, which should now be very dry, to the third bowl.

Continue this process until all the potato mixture has been squeezed and is now dry and in the third bowl.

Gently pour out all the liquid that was collected from the first two bowls until you reach the starchy layer that has accumulated on the bottom.
Use a spoon to scrape up the starch and add that to the potato mixture.

Add eggs and salt to potato and starch; mix to combine everything.
(I think it's easiest to mix this by hand, wearing a disposable glove.)

Place a frying pan over medium high heat.
Add ¼-½ cup oil (the amount will vary depending on how wide your pan is. You're looking for a little less than ¼ inch up the side of the pan.)
Add 1 carrot piece to the oil to absorb any unwanted "brown oil" that occurs from burned bits, and leave it there the whole time you are cooking. Replace carrot chunks as needed.

Set up a cooling rack over a piece of foil or parchment paper for the fried latkes.

Add 2 tablespoons potato mixture to the hot pan and use the back of a spoon to flatten the patty.
Cook for 2-3 minutes on the first side, until you see the edges darkening, and then flip and cook for 2 minutes on the second side.

Transfer latkes to a cooling rack to drain.

Serve hot and enjoy!

moroccan meat couscous with 7 vegetables

THIS IS PROBABLY THE MOST RECOGNIZABLE OF ALL THE MOROCCAN DISHES. MY MOTHER SERVES THIS AT EVERY HOLIDAY AND LARGE GATHERING. IT'S TRADITIONALLY BROUGHT TO SOMEONE WHO MOVES INTO A NEW HOME AS A SYMBOL OF WELCOMING, PROSPERITY, AND GOOD FORTUNE. IT IS A TRUE LABOR OF LOVE, ALTHOUGH YOU CAN USE INSTANT COUSCOUS TO EXPEDITE THE PROCESS, AND JUST MAKE THE VEGGIES.

YOU CAN MAKE THIS DISH DAIRY BY OMITTING THE BONES, REPLACING THE OIL WITH BUTTER (YUM!), AND USING PAREVE CHICKEN SOUP MIX TO FLAVOR THE VEGGIES. OR KEEP IT TOTALLY VEGAN USING OIL AND THE SOUP MIX!

COUSCOUS

2.2 lb (1 kg) couscous grains

4 cups warm water

2 tsp kosher salt

3 Tbsp olive oil

½ tsp coarsely ground black pepper

SEVEN VEGETABLES

4 marrow bones

2 tsp kosher salt

1 tsp coarsely ground black pepper

1 Tbsp canola oil

3 onions, peeled and diced

3 tomatoes, diced

1 tsp paprika in oil

4 prunes, halved lengthwise

4 turnips, peeled and quartered

2 zucchini, halved lengthwise, each halved crosswise

1 butternut squash, cubed OR **2 cups** cubed fresh pumpkin

1 head green cabbage, quartered

1 cup dried chickpeas, soaked in room temperature water overnight, then drained and rinsed

3 Tbsp honey

2 cups cilantro leaves

½ tsp saffron dissolved in **1 cup** boiling water

20 cups chicken stock (or **20 cups** water mixed with **½ cup** chicken soup mix)

1 bay leaf

COUSCOUS

In a large bowl, combine couscous grains, water, and salt. Work the grains between your palms to separate the grains as they absorb the water.
Once the grains begin to swell a little, let the mixture sit for 3 minutes to finish absorbing the water.

Add oil and pepper; work the grains between your palms until all the oil is absorbed. Now it's time to steam the couscous.
You can steam the couscous in a steamer placed over the stewed vegetables or you can simply steam the couscous separately; the technique is the same.

Fill a large pot half full of water. Bring to a boil; reduce heat to a gentle simmer. Place steamer basket over the simmering water, making sure the bottom of the basket does not touch the water. If the holes of your steamer basket are too large, place a sheet of cheesecloth over the holes.

Add prepared couscous grains. Cover tightly with a cover or a large piece of foil.

Cook for 30 minutes, stirring every 8-10 minutes so the grains can steam evenly and to prevent them from sticking together.

After 30 minutes, transfer couscous to a large platter, gently pushing down to spread out the grains. I like to finish mine with an extra drizzle of oil and a quick stir to make sure they don't become sticky after steaming.

For my favorite preparation, serve with the 7 vegetables!

SEVEN VEGETABLES

Season marrow bones on all sides with the salt and pepper.

Heat a large heavy pot over medium high heat.
Add canola oil and marrow bones; sear each side for about 4 minutes until browned. (Do this in batches if your pot is not big enough.) Set aside.

Turn heat to medium low. Add onions, tomatoes, and paprika; stir.
Add prune halves and turnips to the pot; stir.
Gather prunes and turnips into a corner of the pot.
Next add zucchini; give them a little stir around the onions and tomatoes and then move to a corner of the pot.
Repeat with butternut squash, cabbage, and chickpeas.

Return bones to the pot, nestling them between the vegetables.
(I keep the veggies separate and serve them in piles on the couscous, but you can stir them together!)

Drizzle honey over the the bones and veggies; add cilantro leaves.
Add saffron water and chicken stock; add bay leaf.

Raise heat to medium high; bring mixture to a boil.
Reduce heat to low; simmer for 2 hours, with the pot cover off center so that the steam can slowly escape and the liquid can reduce.
Every 20 minutes or so, alternate which part of the pot is being covered!
After 2 hours the vegetables should be tender and the liquid reduced by half.

Serve by ladling some of the liquid over couscous, then adding each vegetable over the couscous. Finish by pouring on 1 ladle of the succulent liquid.
Serve hot and enjoy!

sides

steakhouse style battered onions

THE EASIER AND FASTER BUT JUST AS DELICIOUS AND ACTUALLY MORE SATISFYING BECAUSE, SURFACE AREA, WAY TO MAKE A BLOOMING ONION.

Pour oil into a medium pot and set over medium high heat.

Cut onions into strips.

In a large bowl, combine flour, paprika, garlic powder, 2 teaspoons salt, and cayenne pepper (if using).

Add onion strips to the bowl; toss to coat all the onions strips with flour mixture.

In a second bowl, stir together cornstarch, flour, remaining 2 teaspoons salt, pepper, and beer to form a batter.

Dip a few floured onion strips into batter, then back into flour mixture, and then right into a pot of hot oil.

(To check if oil is hot enough, place a wooden spoon in the pot upside down. If it bubbles steadily around the handle, your oil should be good to go!)

When onion strips are golden brown, transfer to a wire rack to drain. Continue working in batches until you're all done. Serve with Honey Mustard Dip.

HONEY MUSTARD DIP

Stir together mustard, honey, and mayonnaise to combine. You can double the recipe, because even though it makes a big amount, it stays fresh in the fridge for a while!! Enjoy!!!

ONIONS

1 liter canola oil, for frying

1 large or **2 medium** Vidalia onions

2 cups flour

4 tsp paprika

2 tsp garlic powder

4 tsp kosher salt, divided

2 tsp cayenne pepper
(leave out if you want)

⅓ cup cornstarch

1½ cups flour

1 tsp coarsely ground black pepper

1 (24 oz) bottle beer

HONEY MUSTARD DIP

½ cup Dijon mustard

½ cup honey

¼ cup mayonnaise

spicy baked curly fries

4 large potatoes, peeled and spiralized

4 Tbsp canola oil

1 tsp kosher salt

½-1 tsp chili powder, to taste

1 tsp paprika

½ tsp granulated garlic

½ tsp granulated onion

½ tsp coarsely ground black pepper

NOTE

I switch off between using the fine spiral and the thicker one depending on what type of fry I'm in the mood for. If using the finest spiral, reduce cooking time to about 20 minutes so they don't burn!

SHOULD YOU GO OUT AND BUY A SPIRALIZER JUST TO BE ABLE TO MAKE CURLY FRIES? YES. YES, YOU SHOULD. IT'S INEXPENSIVE AND ALTHOUGH IT DOES REQUIRE EXPENSIVE REAL ESTATE IN YOUR CABINETS, IT MAKES THE PREP TIME SO MINIMAL. YOU CAN SPIRALIZE A WHOLE BAG OF POTATOES IN JUST A FEW MINUTES, AS OPPOSED TO CUTTING STICKS! BONUS, THE SPIRALIZED POTATO MAKES THE PERFECT SHAPE FOR BAKING YOUR FRIES INTO CRISPY PERFECTION!

Preheat oven to 400°F / 200°C. Line a baking sheet with parchment paper; coat liberally with nonstick cooking spray.

Add all spices to a bowl; stir to combine.

Lay potato curls on baking sheet.
Drizzle oil over potatoes; sprinkle with spice mixture.
Toss to fully coat.

Bake for about 40 minutes.
Check them after 30 minutes, to make sure they are not burning. (You may have to rotate the pan.)

Once crispy, remove from oven, serve hot and #enjoy!

ultimate french fries +
my favorite way to eat them

EVERY YEAR, ONE NIGHT OF CHANUKAH, USUALLY A NIGHT WITH A QUICKER CHALYMPICS GAME, WE SET OUT TO HAVE A FAMILY CHILI NIGHT. OUR ONLY FORM OF SUSTENANCE IS FRENCH FRIES. (OH, AND CHILI. BECAUSE WHAT'S PERFECTLY COOKED FRENCH FRIES WITHOUT 15 MINUTE CHILI TO SLATHER ON TOP?) THEY DO TAKE A CONSIDERABLE AMOUNT OF TECHNIQUE; HOWEVER, YOU CAN EASILY SEPARATE THE PROCESS OVER A DAY OR TWO TO MAKE THINGS EASIER. I CAN GUARANTEE, THOUGH, THAT IF YOU FOLLOW ALL THE STEPS, YOU WILL NEVER HAVE A BETTER FRENCH FRY IN YOUR LIFE!

potatoes, peeled and cut into thin strips

peanut oil, for frying (about 1½ liters)

table salt

Place cut potatoes into a bowl of ice water. You can do this step up to 48 hours in advance. If preparing in advance, refrigerate potatoes in the ice water.

Next, blanch the potatoes in oil. This step can be done up to 2 hours in advance. To blanch, place potato strips in a single layer on a kitchen towel; pat dry. Place a large pot of oil (leaving three inches from the top) on the stove over medium high heat; use a thermometer to determine when oil reaches 325°F / 163°C.
Add potatoes in small batches; blanch for 6-8 minutes until limp but slightly golden.
Remove fried potatoes to paper towels to drain; continue working in batches.

Once you are ready to serve, raise heat and bring oil to 350°F / 180°C.
In small batches, again fry potatoes for 1 minute, stirring to prevent sticking. Once golden and crispy, remove fries to a cooking rack; sprinkle generously with salt. Serve hot and enjoy!!

Also, for the love of everything good, please, at least attempt to dip your incredible French fries that you worked so hard to achieve in either good Dijon mustard or good mayonnaise. (Then, if you still want ketchup, fine. I give up.)

my favorite way to eat french fries ...
french fry salad!

THAT'S RIGHT. THROW THE HOT CRISPY GOLDEN STICKS OF GOODNESS ONTO A COLD CRUNCHY LEMONY SALAD AND I AM THE HAPPIEST PERSON EVER! DON'T BELIEVE ME? IT'S FINE. MORE FOR ME!

Add romaine and shallots to a large, wide bowl. Drizzle with ½ cup dressing. Toss to combine. Top salad with hot French fries. Serve immediately and enjoy!

3 cups fresh, crispy French fries

8 cups romaine hearts, roughly cut (not too small!)

2 shallots, thinly sliced

DRESSING OPTIONS

Meme's Vinaigrette (page 212)
Old School Balsamic (page 47)
Diner Style Vinaigrette (page 46)

ACCEPTABLE ADD INS TO MY FAVORITE SALAD:

FOR DAIRY MEALS

Parmesan cheese, sliced with a peeler to create shards

shredded sharp cheddar cheese

FOR MEAT MEALS

grilled chicken, thinly sliced

thin slices of hard salami or any good quality charcuterie

That's it. Enjoy!

sweet potato pie

WE'RE NOT HUGE KUGEL PEOPLE AROUND HERE; I MEAN, MAYBE SOME OF US ARE, BUT I DON'T REALLY MAKE KUGELS. OCCASIONALLY I'LL MAKE A POTATO KUGEL AND IF I HAVE SEMINARY GIRLS OVER FOR A MEAL, I'LL ALWAYS MAKE SOME SORT OF SWEET SIDE DISH BECAUSE FOR SOME REASON, SEMINARY + SWEET SIDE DISHES GO TOGETHER IN MY MIND. THIS IS MY GO–TO BECAUSE AFTER BOILING THE SWEET POTATOES, THE ENTIRE DISH COMES TOGETHER IN THE FOOD PROCESSOR IN NO TIME AT ALL!

2 large sweet potatoes, peeled & cubed

3 egg whites

½ cup sugar

½ cup nondairy whipped topping

1 tsp pure vanilla extract

½ tsp kosher salt

¼ tsp cinnamon

Preheat oven to 350°F / 180°C; lightly coat 1 (9 inch) baking dish or 2 loaf pans with nonstick cooking spray.

Place sweet potatoes into a pot and cover with cold water.
Bring to a boil; cook until potatoes are very soft (about 15 minutes).
Drain and return sweet potatoes to hot dry pot for 1 minute just to dry out.

Place cooked sweet potatoes into a food processor fitted with the "S" blade; process for 2 minutes, scraping down the sides every 30 seconds or so, until pureed.
Add egg whites, sugar, nondairy whipped topping, vanilla, and salt; blend until just combined.

Pour into prepared baking dish. Sprinkle with cinnamon.
Bake for 35-45 minutes (depending on size of baking dish).

The pie is done when it is still slightly jiggly in the center but just starting to crisp around the edges.

TIPS + TRICKS

This dish freezes beautifully. Double or triple the recipe and make a few at once so that you are ready for any last minute guest emergencies. Let the pie cool completely, then wrap in plastic wrap and finally foil. Freeze for up to 3 months. To reheat, defrost completely then place in a low temperature oven or on a plata for 1 hour before serving. Do not cover completely. Rather, lightly tent the dish so that the steam can escape while the pie remains moist!

NOTE

If you double or triple the recipe, boil all the sweet potatoes at once, but only place 1 batch into the food processor at a time. Most food processors can only hold 1 recipe at a time. Don't worry, though, there is no need to clean the food processor between batches!

meme's crack string beans

EVERY. SINGLE. SHABBOS. FROM THE TIME I WAS A LITTLE GIRL UNTIL NOW. AND BY "SHABBOS," I MEAN THE HOURS BEFORE SHABBOS ACTUALLY BEGINS. BECAUSE YOU KNOW THESE NEVER ACTUALLY MAKE IT TO THE TABLE, RIGHT?

3 Tbsp olive oil

6 cloves garlic, minced

1 (21 oz/600 g) bag frozen haricot vert (skinny string beans), mostly defrosted

¼ tsp kosher salt

¼ tsp coarsely ground black pepper

4 Tbsp soy sauce

Heat a large, wide pan over low heat.
Add oil and garlic; stir for 2-3 minutes until garlic is fragrant and no longer raw.

Raise heat to high; add string beans, salt, and pepper.
Very gently stir, being careful not to break up string beans (I like to use a rubber spatula for this) until garlic is incorporated.

Cook over high heat for around 20 minutes, stirring every 4-5 minutes until ⅓ of the string beans begin to look crispy.

Add soy sauce, stirring to coat string beans; cook 3-5 minutes until soy sauce has reduced completely and coats the string beans.

Remove from heat and try not to eat the whole thing yourself before you serve it!

TIPS + TRICKS

In all seriousness, double the recipe. If by some crazy chance you have leftovers, add them to every salad and sandwich you make while they last.

loubia
(moroccan stewed white beans)

I LOVE THE SAUCY BEANS OVER A HOT PLATE OF OILY WHITE RICE (ALTHOUGH MY GRANDMOTHER NEVER SERVED IT WITH RICE, ONLY COUSCOUS!) WITH A HUGE DOLLOP OF BRIGHT GREEN SCHUG AND A DRIZZLE OF TECHINA. WHAT I DID NOT KNOW WAS THAT MY ISRAELI CHILDREN HAD BEEN EATING LOUBIA OR, AS IT'S CALLED IN ISRAEL, SHI'UIT, IN SCHOOL ONCE OR TWICE A WEEK FOR LUNCH AND ALSO LOVE IT! WOOHOO!!! WE GREW UP WITH A SLIGHTLY MORE MOROCCAN VERSION, IN WHICH MY GRANDMOTHER WOULD ADD MARROW BONES AND SOMETIMES MEAT OR CHICKEN FOR AN INCREDIBLE VERSION OF THE SAME DISH, BUT I CHOSE TO KEEP THIS PAREVE BECAUSE AS A MOM MYSELF NOW, THAT IS HOW I SERVE IT IN MY HOUSE!!

2 cups dried cannellini beans, soaked overnight in room temperature water, uncovered

2 Tbsp canola oil

1 onion, diced

1 Tbsp kosher salt

2 tsp coarsely ground black pepper

¼ cup tomato paste

1 clove garlic, minced

1 Tbsp paprika (in oil is the best)

1 bay leaf

7 cups water

Drain the beans and discard the soaking water. Rinse beans in cold water; set aside.

Set a large pot over medium high heat.
Add oil, onion, salt, and pepper.
Cook, stirring often for about 8 minutes until onion becomes translucent.

Add beans, tomato paste, garlic, and paprika.
Stir for 4-5 minutes to allow tomato paste to slightly caramelize.

Add bay leaf and water.
Bring mixture to a boil, then cover the pot, and reduce heat to low.

Allow beans to simmer on low heat for 1½-2 hours until beans are soft.
Check pot every 20 minutes or so and if the beans seem dry or they have absorbed all the water, add more water, ½ cup at a time.

Serve hot over rice, with techina and spicy schug!

TIPS + TRICKS

If you have access to partially cooked frozen white beans you can absolutely use those. (Use an entire 28 oz/800 g bag.) You do not need to soak them overnight and you can reduce the cooking time to 1 hour!

VARIATION

If I ever have leftovers of my stewed beans, the next night I chop up whatever veggies I have in my house (carrot, celery, onion, zucchini, potatoes...). I sauté them in a bit of oil and add the leftover bean mixture and a little vegetable broth to repurpose it as a minestrone soup! Ten minutes before serving, I add tiny ditalini pasta to complete the dish!

NOTE

I do not recommend using canned beans here. If you did not soak your beans overnight, you can soak them all day as long as you have at least 8 hours of soaking time.

crispy baked falafel

I KNOW, IT'S SUPPOSED TO BE FRIED. AND I'M ALL FOR THAT. SO, YOU CAN DEFINITELY GO AHEAD AND FORM THE BASE MIXTURE INTO BALLS AND DEEP FRY. IT WILL WORK AND BE EXCELLENT. I WANTED TO TRY OUT BAKING THEM ONE DAY BECAUSE A FOOD THAT'S INHERENTLY HEALTHY SHOULD MAYBE STAY THAT WAY. SO, I DID IT, AND IT WAS DELICIOUS. CRISPY ON THE OUTSIDE, MOIST ON THE INSIDE, AND I GOT ALL THE FALAFEL FEELS I WAS LOOKING FOR. THE ONLY THING IS, IF I WAS BAKING THEM, I WANTED THEM TO BE AS PERFECT AS POSSIBLE. OF COURSE, THAT MEANT THE FLAVOR HAD TO BE ON POINT, BUT ALSO THE WHOLE EATING EXPERIENCE. SO, INSTEAD OF CREATING BALLS, I CREATED FLAT SEMICIRCULAR FALAFEL PATTIES, IF YOU WILL, THAT FIT IN PERFECTLY INTO HALF A PITA. THIS WAY, YOU GET CRISPY FALAFEL IN EVERY BITE!

8 cloves garlic

1 small onion

2 tsp fresh squeezed lemon juice

4 cups chickpeas soaked overnight in room temperature water, uncovered, drained (you'll need about **3 cups** dried chickpeas)

½ tsp cumin

1½ tsp paprika

2½ tsp kosher salt

1 tsp cracked black pepper

1 tsp baking powder

2 Tbsp olive oil

1 cup parsley leaves

½ cup cilantro leaves (optional)

¼ cup canola oil

THINGS TO SERVE WITH YOUR FALAFEL

Israeli salad

French fries

sumac pickled onions

fried eggplant

pickle salad

techina

amba

all the schugs

Preheat oven to 400°F / 200°C. Place a baking sheet into the oven to heat.

Meanwhile, add garlic, onion, and lemon juice to the bowl of a food processor fitted with the "S" blade.
Pulse, scraping down sides often until puréed and everything is evenly mixed.

Add chickpeas, spices, baking powder, olive oil, and herbs.
Pulse until mixture is finely blended, but still somewhat coarse, scraping down sides occasionally.

Remove baking sheet from oven; coat baking sheet with ¼ cup canola oil so that falafel patties don't stick!

Take a small fistful of mixture (about ⅓ cup); form it into a half circle directly on the baking sheet (about 8 "falafels" will fit on the sheet).
Drizzle a very small amount of oil over the patties. Bake for 35 minutes.

Use a spatula to gently remove them from the baking sheet.

Stuff into pitas with whatever you like and enjoy.

potato boreka flower

GIVE THE PARTAKER A FLAVOR COLLECTOR. A CENTER ACCEPTOR. A SANDWICH PRETENDER. A MOUTHFUL OF PLEASURE. A GASTRO ENDEAVOR. A CULINARY RECEPTOR. A STAPLE MADE BETTER. WHATEVER YOU DO, TAKE CARE OF YOUR FOOD.

6 potatoes, peeled and cut into 1 inch pieces

1 Tbsp kosher salt + **1½ tsp** salt, divided

¼ Tbsp canola oil

1 large or **2 medium** onions, diced

1½ tsp coarsely ground black pepper, divided

2 tsp paprika

2 egg yolks, lightly beaten

1 sheet puff pastry

1 egg, lightly beaten

paprika, for sprinkling

Wash potatoes and place into a large pot with water to cover.
Add 1 tablespoon salt; bring potatoes to a boil over medium high heat.
Simmer for about 15 minutes.

While potatoes are cooking, heat a medium pan over medium heat.
Add oil, onions, ½ teaspoon salt, and ½ teaspoon pepper.
Sauté for 25-30 minutes until onions are golden brown.

When potatoes are fork tender, drain well and return to the hot pot.

Add the oil from the sautéed onions, remaining teaspoon salt, remaining teaspoon pepper, and paprika. Mash very well.
Stir onions into mashed potatoes. Allow to cool slightly.

Mix in egg yolks, stirring vigorously so that the egg doesn't cook.
Set aside.

Preheat oven to 350°F / 180°C. Line 2 baking sheets with parchment paper; coat each with nonstick cooking spray.

On a well floured surface, roll out 1 sheet of puff pastry to form a long rectangle.
Spoon ½ the potato mixture along one of the long sides of the puff pastry.
Roll pastry from the edge of one side, leaving a 1 inch border on the edge of the second side.

Transfer log to 1 prepared baking sheet.
Gently shape the log into a circle. Attach the ends, overlapping the border from the second side of puff pastry over the side that was filled to the edge.
This will form a seal to the circle.

Using a sharp knife, cut ¾ of the way into the ring all around to create a slicing guide.
Using your hands, gently push the ring outward from the center to slightly separate the slices.

Brush the top with lightly beaten egg; sprinkle with paprika.
Repeat with remaining mashed potatoes and puff pastry.

Bake for 45 minutes, until pastry is golden brown.

Serve hot and enjoy!

TO SERVE

There are a few directions you can go with this. For meat meals, you can fill the center with anything from pulled beef to pulled chicken. Or you can go my favorite pareve route and fill it with all the elements of a traditional sabich. Pile in some fried eggplants, halved jammy eggs, pickled onions, freshly grated tomato, dollops of schug, and drizzle the whole center with some delicious techina. Everyone can grab a slice of the potato boreka flower and build the sabich of their dreams!

TO FREEZE

Once potato flower is completely cool, wrap gently in plastic wrap. Freeze overnight. Then remove, wrap in multiple layers of plastic wrap and 1 layer of foil. At this point it is already frozen and you can even stack things on top of it.

TO DEFROST

Remove from the freezer the night before serving, unwrap the flower, and place in fridge on baking sheet. If defrosting for same day, unwrap the flower and place on baking sheet. Leave it on the counter. Reheat in the oven or on a plata, uncovered.

moroccan nut crunch topping

IF YOU'VE EVER BEEN TO ANY SORT OF ISRAELI WEDDING OR BAR MITZVAH, YOU'LL RECOGNIZE SOME VERSION OF THIS DISH. THERE IS ALWAYS SOMETHING SWEET AND CRUNCHY SERVED ON THE PERFECTLY OILY WHITE RICE THAT GRACES THE CENTER OF EVERY TABLE. THIS IS THE MORE SOPHISTICATED, GROWN-UP VERSION THAT'S SO GOOD YOU'LL BE LOOKING FOR THINGS THAT YOU CAN TOP THIS WITH!

2 medium or **1 large** onion, halved and sliced

1 Tbsp canola oil

½ tsp salt

½ cup blanched, peeled, and halved almonds

½ cup slivered almonds

¾ cup halved (crosswise) and thinly sliced dried figs

3 dates, halved and chopped

½ cup hot water

3 Tbsp honey

2-3 tsp orange blossom water (optional but traditional and recommended)

To a medium saucepan, add oil, onions, and salt.
Sauté over high heat for about 8 minutes, stirring constantly, until onions become golden.
Transfer onions to a bowl; set aside.

Add both types of almonds to the pot, continuously swirling the pot so that the almonds do not burn.
Once almonds are lightly toasted and fragrant, lower heat; return onions to the pot.

Add remaining ingredients, stirring to combine.
Raise heat; bring mixture to a boil.
Lower heat; simmer until liquid has evaporated and mixture is sticky and delicious!

Serve over rice or roasted cauliflower.

fried rice my way, your way

I LOVE FRIED RICE. NOT JUST FOR ITS REPURPOSING LEFTOVER SHABBOS RICE IN THE MOST DELICIOUS WAY, BUT ALSO FOR ITS ABILITY TO GO FROM MEAT, TO DAIRY, TO TOTALLY VEGETARIAN, DEPENDING ON YOUR NEEDS, AND BEING JUST AS GOOD ALL THREE WAYS. REALLY, FRIED RICE IS A "WHATEVER IS IN YOUR FRIDGE" TYPE OF DISH. SO ADD OR SUBTRACT ANYTHING YOU HAVE LYING AROUND THAT YOU'RE LOOKING FOR SOMETHING TO DO WITH!

1 tsp sesame oil

2 Tbsp canola oil

1 large purple onion, halved and sliced

1 lb protein of choice (see below)

⅛ tsp kosher salt

2 cups chopped scallions (white & greens separated)

1 tsp minced ginger

5 cloves garlic, minced

1 Tbsp gochujang

2 cups purple cabbage

4 cups cold cooked rice

¼ cup soy sauce

1 egg, beaten well

sriracha, to taste

PROTEIN OPTIONS

DAIRY

haloumi cheese, cubed

MEAT

chicken cutlets, cut into ¼ inch strips

ground beef

chicken

turkey

VEGAN

cubed tofu

Heat a very large pan over high heat.
Add oils, onion, protein of choice, and salt.
Cook for about 5 minutes, stirring every 45 seconds or so to crisp up the protein.

Add scallion whites (or half the scallions), stirring to combine.
Add ginger, garlic, and gochujang; mix until fragrant.
Add cabbage. Stir well to make sure ingredients are evenly distributed.

Stir for 2-3 minutes until cabbage begins to cook down; add rice.
Stir to combine.
Add soy sauce, mixing very well. Cook for 5-6 minutes to make sure each grain of rice is coated and heated through.

Remove pan from heat; while mixing quickly, slowly drizzle in egg so that it coats everything.

Top with scallion greens and sriracha and enjoy!

sort of braised, definitely roasted cabbage

IF YOU'VE LEAFED THROUGH THIS COOKBOOK FOR EVEN A SECOND, THEN THIS RECIPE WILL COME AS NO SURPRISE. I AM A PURPLE CABBAGE LOVER. I OFTEN USE IT SHREDDED AS THE BASE OF MY SALADS, AND I MIX IT INTO THE LETTUCE TO ADD CRUNCH. I LOVE IT AS A WRAPPER TO HOLD FISH, CHICKEN, OR MEAT AND I ABSOLUTELY LOVE IT COOKED. IT WILTS EVER SO PERFECTLY, HOLDING JUST THE RIGHT AMOUNT OF CRUNCH AND IT'S JUST AS DELICIOUS THE NEXT DAY, COLD, AS IT WAS THE SECOND AFTER IT CAME OUT OF THE OVEN! THIS SPECIFIC RECIPE HAPPENS TO BE ONE OF MY FAVORITE ACCOMPANIMENTS TO THE ROAST CHICKEN DINNER, STEAK DINNER, AND EVEN COLD AS A SALAD COMPONENT!

3 Tbsp olive oil

1 tsp sesame oil

1 large or **2 small** heads purple cabbage

6 cloves garlic, peeled, minced

½ cup sherry

2 Tbsp soy sauce

1 Tbsp ume plum vinegar

1 Tbsp pure maple syrup

Preheat oven to 350°F / 180°C. Coat a baking sheet with olive oil and sesame oil.

Peel off and discard outer cabbage leaves.
Cut cabbage(s) in half right through the center of the core.
Cut each half into thirds directly through the core as well so that you have 6 wedges of cabbage from each head.

Rub minced garlic all over the wedges of the cabbage.

In a measuring cup or small bowl, stir together remaining ingredients until well combined.

Pour half the mixture onto the baking sheet; top with garlic rubbed cabbage wedges. Be sure to place the cabbage wedges flat side down.
Pour remaining mixture over the cabbage wedges.

Roast for 40 minutes.

Serve hot, room temperature, or cold and enjoy!

spicy sesame peanut zucchini noodle salad

I LOVE ME A NUTTY DRESSING. COMBINE WITH THE FRESHNESS FROM THE HERBS, THE CRUNCH FROM THE NUTS, THE HEAT FROM CHILIES, AND I AM ONE HAPPY CUSTOMER. MY FAVORITE PART OF THIS DISH IS THAT THE LONGER IT SITS, THE BETTER IT GETS. SO BE SURE TO SNEAK SOMEONE AWAY AND HIDE IT IN A SMALL CONTAINER IN YOUR FRIDGE SO THAT YOU HAVE A HIDDEN STASH FOR LUNCH THE NEXT DAY!

DRESSING

6 cloves garlic

1 large scallion (green + whites), roughly chopped

2 red Thai chili peppers (use **1** if you don't want the heat)

½ cup peanut butter

½ cup tahini paste

1 Tbsp sesame oil

1 Tbsp honey (if you like it sweeter add another Tbsp)

3 Tbsp soy sauce

2 Tbsp fresh lime juice (from **2-3** limes)

½ tsp kosher salt

⅔ cup cold water

SALAD

6 zucchini, spiralized (or peeled with a julienne peeler)

4 carrots, julienned

2 cups shredded purple cabbage

2 cups precooked edamame beans (optional)

1 cup chopped scallions

½ cup cilantro leaves

½ cup salted roasted peanuts, pink skins removed, lightly crushed

2 Tbsp sesame seeds, lightly toasted

1 red Thai chili pepper, thinly sliced on an angle

DRESSING

Place garlic, scallion, and chili peppers into a food processor fitted with the "S" blade.
Process until minced.

Add remaining dressing ingredients; process until well blended and all the ingredients come together.

Transfer to a jar or container; store in the fridge until 30 minutes before you're ready to use it.

SALAD

Lay zucchini spirals on a kitchen towel to dry out for 20-30 minutes.

Heat a large pan over medium high heat.
Add 1 teaspoon olive oil to the pan, a layer of zucchini, and a small pinch of kosher salt (you can fill the pan, but you only want 1 layer of zucchini so that you can toss it easily).
Constantly toss the zucchini for 1 minute.

Remove from the pan (even if they don't seem ready, they will continue to cook), and place into a bowl while you sauté remaining zucchini in batches.

Allow zucchini to cool for 15 minutes (or refrigerate until assembling), then toss together with carrots and cabbage.

Transfer mixture to a platter; top with dressing.
Spread edamame, scallions, cilantro, crushed peanuts, sesame seeds, and chili pepper, over the dish.

Serve family style and enjoy

VARIATION

Try swapping the zucchini for 1 pound of soba noodles, rice noodles, or spaghetti. Cook according to package directions and then just replace the cooked noodles for the spiralized zucchini in the recipe!

TIPS + TRICKS

To prep ahead: Dressing will remain fresh in the fridge for 10 days. Toasted sesame seeds can stay in the freezer for 1 month. Crushed peanuts will stay fresh for 2 weeks in an airtight container in a cool dark cabinet.

Spiralized and sautéed zucchini can be prepared 24 hours ahead. (I prefer them cold!).

TIPS + TRICKS

For a meat meal, marinate 6 thin chicken cutlets in 3 Tbsp soy sauce, 1 tsp sesame oil, 2 cloves minced garlic, and 1 tsp sriracha for 5 minutes. Heat grill or grill pan; grill cutlets for 2 minutes on each side. Then slice and add to salad! Discard any remaining marinade.

avocado egg rolls

AN ODE TO THE SUSHI RESTAURANT IN THE FIVE TOWNS THAT CAME AND WENT TOO QUICKLY BUT SERVED THE BEST AVOCADO EGG ROLLS EVER.

2 Tbsp chopped sun dried tomatoes

4 avocados, cubed (**2½ cups** cubed)

2 Tbsp chopped cilantro

½ jalapeño pepper, minced

1 tsp kosher salt

¼ tsp coarsely ground black pepper

1 lime, halved

1 (9 oz) package egg roll wrappers (each cut in half diagonally to create 2 triangles) OR square wonton wrappers

oil, for frying (I like avocado oil)

Add tomatoes, avocados, cilantro, jalapeño, salt, and pepper to a bowl.
Squeeze the juice of ½ lime over the avocados so they don't brown.
Gently mix to combine. Don't overmix or the avocado will turn into guacamole and we're not looking for that!

Place 1 heaping tablespoon of avocado mixture near the corner of an egg roll wrapper triangle, then brush the edges with a little water.
Roll over once, then fold the sides of the triangle over and continue to roll till closed. Do the same thing (if using) the square wonton wrappers.

Repeat with remaining avocado mixture and wrappers.

Heat 3-4 inches oil over medium high heat.
Once oil gets to 350°F / 180C° (the handle of a wooden spoon inserted into the oil will have bubbles form around it), fry 5-6 at a time for about 3 minutes.

Transfer to a cooling rack to drain.

Serve with chipotle mayo, spicy green sauce, or any dip you like!

To reheat, place in a foil pan in a single layer and reheat uncovered!

Enjoy!

NOTE

I would not freeze these. Something about defrosted avocado just doesn't do it for me.

a penne for your thoughts

dairy

haloumi + sweet potato salad with blueberry vinaigrette

IF YOU'VE EVER WALKED INTO ANY DAIRY CAFE IN ISRAEL, LIKE LITERALLY ANY, YOU KNOW EXACTLY WHAT THIS SALAD IS. CRUNCHY GREENS, CRISPY BAKED SWEET POTATO, HALOUMI GRILLED OR SAUTÉED TO CRUNCHY AND GOOEY CHEESY PERFECTION, DRIZZLED WITH A YUMMY DRESSING! IT'S THE CHEESY SALAD OF YOUR DREAMS AND THIS IS MY VERSION!

DRESSING

½ **cup** dried blueberries

¼ **cup** balsamic vinegar

¼ **cup** apple cider vinegar

1 shallot, finely diced

1 tsp Dijon mustard

1 tsp pure maple syrup

1 tsp kosher salt

1 tsp coarsely ground black pepper

¾ **cup** extra virgin olive oil

SALAD

2 large sweet potatoes (about **2.2 lb/1 kg** total), peeled and cut into ¼ inch thick sticks

1 tsp kosher salt

½ **tsp** coarsely ground black pepper

1 Tbsp + 1 tsp extra virgin olive oil, divided

3 cups baby spinach

3 cups arugula

1 purple onion, halved and thinly sliced

1 (1 lb/400 g) block haloumi cheese, cut into ½ inch cubes

DRESSING

Combine blueberries and vinegars in a bowl or jar.
Using a spoon, smush blueberries a bit to help them open up and release their flavor into the vinegars.

Add remaining dressing ingredients to the bowl or jar; whisk well or shake to combine.

Refrigerate until 15 minutes before you want to dress your salad!

SALAD

Preheat oven to 350°F / 180°C. Line a baking sheet with parchment paper.
Add sweet potato sticks, salt, pepper, and 1 tablespoon olive oil to prepared baking sheet; toss to combine.
Spread sweet potatoes so they do not overlap.

Bake for 45 minutes until sweet potato sticks are crispy.

While sweet potatoes are baking, arrange baby spinach, arugula, and onion on a large, rimmed serving platter; set aside.

Heat a dairy nonstick frying pan over medium high heat.
Add remaining 1 teaspoon olive oil and the cubed haloumi.
(You don't want to overcrowd the pan, so if your pan is on the smaller side, you may want to do this in batches.)

Cook haloumi for about 8 minutes, tossing cubes around every minute or so, so that all the sides can crisp up.
Once cubes are crispy and hot, remove from pan and place on prepared salad.

Add crispy sweet potatoes to the salad; drizzle blueberry vinaigrette all over!

Serve right away and enjoy!

NOTE

Not all haloumis are created equal. In the Middle East it's pretty easy to find good haloumi cheese. If you're not in the Middle East, however, I recommend you try a few different brands until you find one that you like!

TIPS + TRICKS

This dressing is delicious and completely irresistible. Try swapping out the haloumi cheese for a simple grilled chicken for a fun meat twist!

black bean crumble salad
with cilantro lime ranch

I LOVE A TEX-MEX STYLE BLACK BEAN BURGER —ALL THE FLAVORS IN THERE AND THE WAY THE BEANS GET CRISPY ON THE OUTSIDE. OOOOH, THAT CRISPY OUTSIDE. IT'S MY FAVORITE PART. AND IT'S WHAT LED ME TO THE CRUMBLE INSTEAD OF THE PATTY. SEE, THE PATTY GETS ONLY LIMITED CRISPY OUTSIDE BECAUSE OF ITS SHAPE. IF YOU PUT THE MIXTURE INTO A PAN, THOUGH, AND SLIGHTLY MASH THE BEANS AS THEY SAUTÉ, YOU CREATE WAY MORE SURFACE AREA AND THEREFORE EXTRA CRISPINESS. BONUS, YOU GET TO COOK EVERYTHING AT ONCE INSTEAD OF SITTING THERE SHAPING AND COOKING UP INDIVIDUAL PATTIES.

DRESSING

1 cup buttermilk
4 Tbsp mayonnaise
1 tsp kosher salt
½ tsp coarsely ground black pepper
½ tsp granulated onion
2½ tsp lime juice
1 clove garlic, minced
½ cup cilantro leaves

CRUMBLE

2 Tbsp extra virgin olive oil
3 shallots, minced
1 jalapeño peppers, ribs + seeds removed, minced (you can use less if you don't like it spicy)
2 (15 oz) cans black beans, rinsed, drained, set aside to dry
2 cloves garlic, minced
1 tsp tomato paste
1 tsp kosher salt
1 tsp smoked paprika
½ tsp cumin
1 lime, halved

SALAD

4 cups butter lettuce
3 cups shredded purple cabbage
1 tomato, diced
1 (15 oz) can corn, drained
2 cucumbers, halved, deseeded, sliced
1 avocado, cubed
1 purple onion, halved, thinly sliced
1 mango, diced
1 cup feta cheese, crumbled

DRESSING

Place all dressing ingredients into a blender, bullet, food processor, or mini processor.
Blend until fully combined and herbs are very finely chopped.

Transfer to an airtight container; store in the fridge for up to 5 days.

The dressing is actually better the next day, so I suggest prepping it a day in advance, or at least a few hours before serving!

CRUMBLE

Set a frying pan over medium high heat; add oil, shallots, and jalapeño.
Cook, stirring often, for about 3 minutes until shallots and jalapeño have just softened ever so slightly.

Add beans; stir to combine.
While stirring, use the back of a fork to gently press down on the beans to smush them.
You are looking to smush the beans just enough to crack them and expose the soft interior.
(We're not looking to create a mash here.)

Add garlic, tomato paste, salt, paprika, and cumin.
Stir to combine and distribute spices evenly.

Cook for about 4 minutes, stirring often; squeeze in the juice of the lime.
Cook for 1 minute. Remove from heat and add crumble to the salad!

SALAD

Layer all the ingredients in the order listed on a large rimmed platter.
Top with black bean crumble.

Drizzle dressing over the top.

VARIATION

Switch the whole thing and serve your black bean crumble in a wrap with tons of grilled (or not grilled) veggies for a fun lunch!

VARIATION

This dressing can be swapped a ton of different ways. Try changing up the cilantro for any herb you like and the lime for other forms of acidity, like lemon or vinegar!

NOTE

I want you to be able to use this book forever and as the kosher world is progressing by the day I want to let you know that if, one day maybe even by the time this goes to print, you find a good kosher Mexican cheese like cotija or manchego … use those instead of the feta!

TIPS + TRICKS

I like to make the black bean crumble at the beginning of the week and double the recipe so I have a quick protein to add to my lunch all week long!

french onion soup

THE ~~KING~~ QUEEN OF ALL SOUPS.

6½ lb (3 kg) yellow onions (about **14** medium onions)

2 Tbsp unsalted butter

1 Tbsp olive oil

1 Tbsp kosher salt

2 cups boiling water

16 grams dehydrated mushrooms (**½ cup**)

1 sprig thyme

3 Tbsp soy sauce

1 Tbsp Worcestershire sauce

⅓ cup red wine

12 cups vegetable stock

1 baguette, cut into ½ inch thick slices, very slightly toasted

6 slices gruyere cheese (or Swiss, or whatever cheese you like)

Add butter and olive oil to a large pot over low heat.
Add onions and a pinch of salt.

Cover the pot; cook onions over the lowest heat for about 15 minutes until they just begin to break down.
Remove the cover; stir.

Cook over low heat for 4-5 hours, stirring every 45 minutes.
Raise heat to medium; cook for 30-35 minutes, stirring frequently, until onions are deeply golden and "melty."

In a bowl, combine boiling water and dehydrated mushrooms; cover with plastic wrap and steep for 15 minutes.
Strain the liquid into a second bowl; discard mushrooms and reserve the liquid.

Raise heat to high; to the pot, add thyme, soy sauce, Worcestershire, and wine.
Cook for 2 minutes then add reserved mushroom liquid, stock, and salt.

Bring soup to a boil; lower heat to medium low, cover the pot, and simmer for 30 minutes.

During last 10 minutes of simmering, make your cheese "croutons."
Preheat oven to 400°F / 200°C; line a baking sheet with parchment paper.
Lay baguette slices on baking sheet; top each with a slice of cheese.

Bake for 4-6 minutes, until cheese is melty and golden.

Ladle soup into bowls and serve with cheese "croutons."

creamiest sweet potato soup

"ORANGE SOUP" IS A THING. BECAUSE IT'S DELICIOUS. AND IT'S A KID FAVORITE. THE ORANGE COLOR, THE SMOOTH TEXTURE, THE LACK OF ANYTHING GREEN AND POSSIBLY GOOD FOR YOU ... TOTAL KID APPEAL. THIS IS MY TAKE ON IT. THE ONLY DIFFERENCE BETWEEN MY RECIPE AND MOST OF THE OTHER ONES OUT THERE IS THAT MY ORANGE COLOR COMES FROM ONLY 1 VEGETABLE. THAT'S RIGHT. NO MATTER HOW MANY DIFFERENT WAYS I TRY IT, I ALWAYS COME BACK TO THE SWEET POTATO. IT PROVIDES THE CREAMIEST, VELVETIEST, COMFORTING VERSION OF THE ORANGE SOUP. TRY IT, YOU'LL SEE!!

1 Tbsp unsalted butter
1 Tbsp canola oil
1 large onion, diced
¾ tsp kosher salt, divided
½ tsp coarsely ground black pepper, divided
6 large sweet potatoes, cut into 1½-2 inch cubes
1½ cups dry white wine
water
½-¾ cup heavy cream

Heat a large pot over medium heat.
Add butter, oil, onion, ¼ teaspoon salt, and ¼ teaspoon pepper.
Cook for 12-15 minutes, stirring often, until onions are translucent and just beginning to brown on the edges.

Add sweet potatoes; stir to coat in the onions and butter mixture.
Increase heat to high; stir in wine. Cook for 4 minutes.
Add remaining ½ teaspoon salt, remaining ¼ teaspoon pepper, and enough water to cover the sweet potatoes by 1½-2 inches.

Bring the mixture to a boil, reduce heat to low.
Simmer for at least 1 hour and up to 3 hours.
Remove from heat; add ½ cup cream and use an immersion blender to puree.

Puree for 2 minutes more than you think it needs to get that extra-smooth consistency.
If you want the soup thinner, you can add a little more boiling water and if you want it a little creamier, you can add the remaining ¼ cup cream.

Taste and adjust seasoning!

cream of mushroom soup

IF YOU'RE A MUSHROOM LOVER LIKE ME, THIS SOUP IS FOR YOU. ALL THE MUSHROOM GLORY PACKED INTO ONE DELICIOUS BOWL OF STEAMING HOT SOUP. YOU'RE WELCOME!

2 Tbsp unsalted butter
1 Tbsp canola oil
1 onion, diced
1½ tsp kosher salt, divided
1 tsp coarsely ground black pepper
12 cups thinly sliced mushrooms (I like to use an assortment but use what you have!)
1 clove garlic, minced
½ cup sherry OR dry white wine
1 bay leaf
2 cups milk
1 cup heavy cream
4 cups water

Heat a large pot over medium high heat.
Add butter, oil, onion, ½ teaspoon salt, and pepper.
Cook, stirring often, until onions are translucent (6-8 minutes).

Add mushrooms.
Cook for about 25 minutes until all the water released from the mushrooms has cooked off.

Add garlic; stir for 1 minute.
Add sherry; cook for 2-3 minutes.

Add remaining ingredients.

Bring soup to a boil, cover the pot, and reduce heat to a simmer.
Simmer for 1 hour.

Remove and discard bay leaf.
Using an immersion blender, "juzz" soup until thick and creamy!

tomato soup with cheddar matzah balls

IN OUR HOUSE WE ARE EXTREMELY PICKY WHEN IT COMES TO TOMATO SOUP. WE WANT A HUGE BOWL OF A DELICIOUS TOMATO BROTH AND NOT A WARM MARINARA SAUCE. THAT'S WHERE THE IDEA OF KEEPING THE ONIONS AND GARLIC WHOLE CAME FROM. THEY CAN INFUSE THEIR FLAVORS DELICATELY INTO THE SOUP AND THEN BE REMOVED EASILY TO LEAVE A CLEAN, DELICIOUS, AND FLAVORFUL BROTH. THE CHEDDAR MATZAH BALLS — MAKE THEM. YOU'LL SEE.

MATZAH BALLS

1 cup matzah meal

1 tsp baking powder

1 tsp kosher salt

4 eggs

¼ cup oil

6 Tbsp shredded cheddar cheese

TOMATO SOUP

¼ cup unsalted butter

1 purple onion, peeled

5 whole cloves garlic

1½ tsp kosher salt

1 tsp coarsely ground black pepper

3 (15 oz) cans tomato sauce

MATZAH BALLS

In a medium bowl, combine matzah meal, baking powder, and salt.

In a large measuring cup, use a fork to beat together eggs and oil till combined.

Add egg mixture to dry ingredients; stir to combine.

Add cheese; mix until it is evenly incorporated.

Refrigerate for at least 45 minutes.

Remove from fridge, coat hands with a thin layer of oil, and form batter into ½ inch balls.
Drop into hot soup; cook for 15-20 minutes.

SOUP

To a large pot, over medium heat, add butter, onion, and garlic.
Stir until butter has melted and onion and garlic become fragrant.

Add all 3 cans of tomato sauce; refill each can with water.
Next, add all 3 cans of water to the pot as well.
Refill 1 can with water and add to pot for a total of 4 cans of water.

Cover the pot; bring mixture to a boil, then reduce heat, and simmer for 30 minutes.

Use a slotted spoon to remove and discard onion and garlic.

Remove matzah ball mixture from fridge, coat hands with a thin layer of oil, and form batter into ½ inch balls.
Drop into hot soup; cook for 20-25 minutes until matzah balls are cooked through.

Serve hot and enjoy!

TIPS + TRICKS

Think beyond the tomato soup. Matzah balls can be laced with all kinds of herbs and spices and cooked in a variety of flavorful broths and soups to make them fun and exciting.

spicy vegetable lentil soup

I LOVE THIS SOUP FOR ITS THICK, HEARTY VEGETABLE GOODNESS IN THE WINTER. IT HITS THE SPOT EVERY TIME. THE CHEESE, WHICH IN MY OPINION IS MERELY A BONUS AND IF YOU LEAVE IT OUT YOU WON'T MISS IT, IS JUST THE ICING ON THE CAKE. OR THE CROUTON IN THE SOUP. ER, OR THE CHEESE IN THE SOUP. YOU KNOW WHAT I MEAN. IT'S A BONUS AND IT'S AWESOME!

½ cup dried porcini mushrooms

4 cups boiling water

2 Tbsp extra virgin olive oil

1 onion, diced

1 leek, white and light green only, halved lengthwise, then chopped

3 carrots, peeled and diced

2 stalks celery, peeled and diced

1 jalapeño, minced
(If you're nervous about the heat, you can remove the seeds and ribs to take it down a notch!)

2 tsp kosher salt, divided

½ tsp coarsely ground black pepper

4 cloves garlic, minced

½ inch piece ginger, minced

1 tsp turmeric

2 Tbsp tomato paste

¾ cup red lentils

1 kohlrabi, peeled and diced

2 zucchini, diced

6 cups vegetable stock OR water

3-4 Tbsp shredded cheese per bowl, for serving

Combine mushrooms and boiling water in a bowl; set aside.

Heat a large pot over medium high heat.
Add oil, onion, leek, carrots, celery, and jalapeño to the pot, along with ½ teaspoon salt and the pepper.

Cook, stirring often, for about 12 minutes until the edges of some of the vegetables just start to brown a little.
Add garlic, ginger, and turmeric.
Stir to combine.

Add tomato paste; cook, stirring for 1-2 minutes, until tomato paste slightly darkens in color.
Add lentils; stir so that all the lentils are coated in the spices and tomato paste.

Strain mushroom liquid into a bowl, discarding mushrooms and reserving the liquid.

Add mushroom liquid, kohlrabi, zucchini, and stock to the pot.

Allow soup to come to a boil.
Reduce heat to low, cover the pot, and simmer for 45 minutes.

To serve, place 3-4 tablespoons of cheese into each bowl; ladle the hot soup right onto the cheese!

Serve hot and enjoy!

mac + cheese

THE ULTIMATE COMFORT FOOD. THE RECIPE HERE IS REALLY FOR THE CHEESE SAUCE, WHICH IS THE KEY ACTOR IN ANY MAC + CHEESE. PLAY AROUND WITH THE DISH BY USING DIFFERENT CHEESES, ADDING IN DIFFERENT ROASTED VEGGIES, OR EVEN USING THE CHEESE SAUCE TO TOP STUFFED SHELLS OR CANNELLONI!

¼ cup unsalted butter

⅓ cup flour

1 tsp kosher salt

1 tsp coarsely ground black pepper

1½ tsp mustard powder

1 tsp granulated garlic

¼ tsp ground nutmeg

1½ cups milk

¾ cup heavy cream

2 cups shredded cheese (see Tips+Tricks)

1 lb (500 g) pasta, cooked al dente

Melt butter in a pot over medium high heat.
Add flour.
Stir constantly for 2-3 minutes with a wooden spoon to cook out the raw flour taste.

Add salt, pepper, mustard, garlic, and nutmeg; stir with a wooden spoon for 1 minute to warm spices through.
Switch to a whisk; while whisking, slowly pour in the milk.
Keep whisking until mixture thickens.

Add heavy cream; whisk to incorporate.

After 3-4 minutes, switch back to the wooden spoon; stir in cheese.
Stir in a figure eight pattern until all the cheese is incorporated.

Add cooked pasta, stirring to coat with cheese sauce.
Serve right away and enjoy!

TIPS + TRICKS

Try switching out the types of shredded cheese. Different cheeses will add different flavors and a different type of unique cheesiness to the dish. I like to use a combination of cheddar, gruyere, and mozzarella for the ultimate cheesiness. Think different kinds of cheddar, mozzarella, gruyere, pepper jack, smoked Gouda, maybe even some feta!

VARIATION

Butter a baking dish and preheat oven to 350°F / 180°C. Combine cooked pasta and cheese sauce in the dish. Top with 1½ cups shredded cheese; dot the cheese with 1 tablespoon of butter that was cut into tiny pieces. Bake for 35-45 minutes until the top is golden and bubbly!

PHOTO ORDER
TOP TO BOTTOM
Baked Ziti
Rigatoni With Vodka Sauce
Mac + Cheese

dairy

the most perfect baked ziti

TUESDAY NIGHT. THE MOST ANTICIPATED NIGHT OF DINNER WHEN I WAS GROWING UP. MY MOTHER ALTERNATED BETWEEN DIFFERENT DAIRY DINNERS AND THIS ONE WAS OUR FAVORITE! SHE WOULD PUT OUT PEELED, DESEEDED, AND QUARTERED CUCUMBERS (YES, MY MOTHER UNDERSTOOD THE WAYS OF A CRUNCHY CUCUMBER), AND BRING OUT A PERFECTLY BROWN AND BUBBLY, PIPING HOT, OOEY-GOOEY, CHEESY BAKED ZITI TO THE TABLE! IT WAS EVERYONE'S FAVORITE NIGHT!

1 (1 lb/500 g) box penne pasta

2 Tbsp kosher salt, divided

2 (15 oz) cans tomato sauce

¼ cup ricotta cheese (not cottage cheese!)

3 Tbsp unsalted butter, cubed, divided

4 cups shredded mozzarella cheese, divided

1 tsp coarsely ground black pepper

½ tsp crushed red pepper flakes, optional

Preheat oven to 350°F / 180°C.

Bring a large pot of water to a boil.
Add 1 tablespoon salt and pasta.

Meanwhile, butter a 9x13 inch baking dish or aluminum pan.
Directly into the pan add tomato sauce, ricotta cheese, 2 tablespoons butter, 2 cups shredded cheese, remaining salt, pepper, and red pepper flakes (if using).
Before draining pasta, remove ½ cup pasta water and add to the pan, stirring to combine.

Drain pasta.
Add cooked pasta to the pan and stir to fully coat every single piece.

Top mixture with remaining 2 cups shredded cheese.

Dot remaining tablespoon of cubed butter over the top.
Bake for 40-45 minutes until the top is golden brown and bubbly.
Serve hot and enjoy!

FREEZER TIP

You can make the baked ziti up until the point you bake it. Add the shredded cheese, let the pasta cool completely, then wrap in a few layers of plastic wrap followed by a layer of foil. Freeze for up to 1 month. To reheat, defrost frozen baked ziti in the fridge overnight. Remove from the fridge 2 hours before reheating to come to room temperature. Place in a 350°F / 180°C oven; bake for 45 minutes until the top is golden and bubbly.

baked rigatoni with vodka sauce

REALLY, THIS IS ALL ABOUT THE VODKA SAUCE. BAKING IT WITH CHEESE ON TOP IS JUST MY EXTRA LITTLE TOUCH BECAUSE I CAN'T RESIST A GOLDEN CHEESY, CRUNCHY, GOOEY TOP! THE SAUCE, THOUGH, CAN TOTALLY HOLD ITS OWN AND SIMPLY POURING IT OVER ANY PASTA SHAPE YOU LIKE WILL BE EQUALLY DELICIOUS! IT IS A FAN FAVORITE IN MY HOUSE AND HAVING A CONTAINER OF THE SAUCE IN MY FRIDGE IS ACTUALLY GOLDEN, SO I ALWAYS DOUBLE THE RECIPE!

1 lb (500 g) any pasta,
cooked al dente
(I like to use a tubular pasta because
it catches the sauce)

2 cups shredded mozzarella cheese

¼ cup Parmesan cheese (optional
but highly recommended)

VODKA SAUCE

2 cloves garlic, minced

1 Tbsp unsalted butter

1 cup vodka

pinch (or 2) crushed red pepper
flakes

1 (15 oz) can tomato sauce

1 cup heavy cream

½ tsp kosher salt

1 Tbsp starchy pasta water

Preheat oven to 400°F / 200°C.
Butter a 9x13 inch baking dish or pan; set aside.

VODKA SAUCE

Add garlic and butter to a small pot over medium high heat.
Cook until garlic is fragrant but not browned.

Add vodka; stir until it reduces by half (3-4 minutes).
Add remaining sauce ingredients; stir.
Bring to a boil, then remove from heat.

Add pasta and vodka sauce to prepared baking dish; stir well.

Top with shredded mozzarella cheese and Parmesan, if using.

Bake until golden, bubbly, and slightly crunchy on top, about 40 minutes.

Serve hot and enjoy!

TIPS + TRICKS

If you double the recipe be sure
to use a big pot, because the
vodka will bubble quite a bit and
need extra time to cook down!

FREEZER TIP

If you need to make this ahead of
time, I suggest making only the
sauce, letting it cool completely,
and then freezing the sauce
alone. Simply defrost and add to
freshly cooked pasta to serve!

grandma lila & aunt janey's quiche

NO BREAKFAST IS COMPLETE IN THE GLEITMAN/GLODNEY HOUSEHOLD WITHOUT MY AUNT JANEY'S MOST DELICIOUS QUICHES. LITTLE DID I KNOW THAT AUNT JANEY'S QUICHE COMES STRAIGHT FROM THE ONE WOMAN IN MY LIFE WHOSE IMPACT ON ME WAS TREMENDOUS EVEN THOUGH MY TWO YEARS OF TIME WITH HER WAS SO SHORT — MY GRANDMOTHER, GRANDMA LILA. ONCE I HEARD THAT, I KNEW THIS RECIPE HAD TO GO IN THE BOOK. IT IS AN ODE TO EVERYTHING I BELIEVE IN. THE POWER OF FOOD TO CONNECT US TO GENERATIONS PAST. TO EAT SOMETHING THAT WAS FIRST MADE WITH LOVE FOR THE VERY SAME PEOPLE I LOVE WHO THEN MAKE ME THAT FOOD IS WHAT COOKING IS ALL ABOUT. CONNECTING US ALL.

BROCCOLI AND SPINACH ARE AUNT JANEY'S GO-TOS, SO I INCLUDED BOTH THOSE VARIATIONS IN THE RECIPE, BUT, LIKE AUNT JANEY SAYS, ANY COMBO OF VEGETABLES WILL BE DELICIOUS. THINK SAUTÉED LEEK + MUSHROOM, BRUSSELS SPROUTS + CRISPY POTATOES, KALE + ONION AND CAULIFLOWER . . . THE COMBINATIONS ARE ENDLESS!

ALSO, PLEASE NOTE, THE ORIGINAL RECIPE CALLS FOR A FROZEN, PRE-MADE PIE SHELL. I AM ALL FOR THAT. WE EAT THAT EVERY YEAR AND IT IS THE MOST DELICIOUS QUICHE EVER. FOR MY ISRAELI HOMIES, THOUGH, WHO CANNOT FIND A FROZEN, PRE-MADE PIE SHELL, I HAVE INCLUDED A SUPER SIMPLE AND FABULOUS HOMEMADE SAVORY PIE DOUGH!

PIE DOUGH

3 cups flour

¾ tsp kosher salt

¾ cup cold canola oil

4-6 Tbsp cold water

FILLING

4 Tbsp flour

1 lb (500 g) Swiss cheese, shredded

20 oz (567 g) frozen spinach, defrosted and drained

1 large bag frozen broccoli florets, defrosted and drained

2 cups milk, divided

6 eggs, divided

1 tsp kosher salt, divided

½ tsp nutmeg, divided

½ tsp coarsely ground black pepper, divided

VARIATION

If you would rather make 2 broccoli or 2 spinach quiches, simply double the amount of the vegetable you'd like to use.

TIPS + TRICKS

Refrigerating the canola oil till it's very cold will result in flakier pastry.

PIE DOUGH

Preheat oven to 350°F / 180°C. Coat 2 (9 inch) round pie pan with nonstick cooking spray.

In a large bowl, combine flour, salt, and canola oil with only 4 tablespoons water. Mix until dough comes together, adding more water only if necessary.

Divide the dough in half.
Roll out each half between two layers of parchment paper; place each round into a prepared pie pan.
Prick dough all over with a fork to prevent it from bubbling up.

Bake unfilled pie crusts in the oven for 12 minutes.
Remove from oven and allow to cool.

Meanwhile, prepare the filling.

FILLING

Preheat oven to 350°F / 180°C. Line a baking sheet with parchment paper.
Place baked pie crusts in the pie pans on the sheet pan (to keep your oven clean in case of overflow!)

In a small bowl, combine flour and cheese. Set aside.

Prepare two large bowls.
Add broccoli to one bowl and spinach to the second.

Cut off large broccoli stems; discard or reserve for another use.
Roughly chop florets.

INTO EACH BOWL: Add 1 cup milk, 3 eggs, well beaten, ¼ teaspoon nutmeg, ¼ teaspoon pepper, and ½ teaspoon salt.
Mix contents of each bowl well.

Add half the flour and cheese mixture to each bowl, stirring well to incorporate.

Pour the contents of each bowl into a baked pie shell.
Bake for 1 hour until the top of each quiche is a light golden brown.

Serve hot, or even at room temp, and enjoy!

sheet pan pizza

I LOVE A RECIPE THAT IS MADE TO FEED LOTS OF PEOPLE! ONE BATCH OF THIS DOUGH CAN FIT AN ENTIRE SHEET PAN WHICH, FOR ME, IS PERFECT. I CAN MAKE ONE HUGE REGULAR PIZZA, I CAN MAKE HALF CHEESE HALF CORN (NOT FOR ME, I PROMISE, FOR MY ISRAELI CHILDREN), OR I CAN DO A THIRD WITH SAUCE ONLY FOR DOVI (BLASPHEMY, I KNOW), A THIRD WITH CORN, FOR THE MOST ISRAELI AMONGST US, AND THE LAST THIRD, SAY, WITH OLIVES, FOR THOSE WHO KNOW. AND WHAT'S SO GREAT IS THAT BECAUSE THE BLANK SLATE I'M STARTING WITH IS SO BIG, THERE WILL BE ENOUGH FOR EVERYONE!

1 Tbsp + 1 tsp instant dry yeast

1 tsp sugar

2½ cups warm water, divided

2.2 lb (1 kg) white spelt flour OR white flour

1 Tbsp + 1 tsp kosher salt

¼ cup + ¼ tsp extra virgin olive oil, dividedl

1 Tbsp red wine vinegar

NOTE

You can absolutely go ahead and divide the dough into individual portions and make 4-5 smaller pizzas!

TOPPING COMBOS

Sauce + shredded cheese:

Add any or all: olives, corn, mushrooms, onions, jalapeño, peppers

Ricotta + defrosted, strained spinach + shredded cheese

Ricotta + shredded cheese (+ mushrooms/jalapeño/onion/ tomato)

Fresh tomato + fresh mozzarella + basil

Sour cream + sharp cheddar + apple slices

Labane + sumac + eggplant + onion + feta

Pesto + grilled veggies + smoked Gouda

In the bowl of a stand mixer fitted with the dough hook attachment, combine yeast, sugar, and 2 cups water.
Let stand for 3-4 minutes to activate yeast.

Add flour; turn mixer on at low speed.
Mix for 1 minute until a shaggy dough forms.
Add remaining water, ¼ cup oil, salt, and vinegar.

Once the liquid is absorbed, increase mixer speed to high; knead dough for 5 minutes.

Remove dough hook; drizzle remaining ¼ teaspoon olive oil over the dough.
Cover bowl with plastic wrap.
If you will use the dough in the next 1½-2 hours, leave the bowl on the counter so dough can rise.

If you want to make the dough in the morning and use it later that evening, immediately place covered bowl in the fridge to slow rise.
Remove bowl from fridge 45 minutes before you plan to shape the dough; let it come to room temperature.

Once the dough has doubled in size and you are ready to bake, preheat your oven to 350°F / 180°C and place a baking sheet (a real one, no disposables here!) into the oven to preheat.
While the oven and pan are getting hot, turn dough out on to the counter.

Gently the shape the dough into a large rectangle the size of the baking sheet by using your hands to gently push the dough outward, starting in the center and working your way toward the edges.
I have never found the need to flour the counter or to use a rolling pin in this recipe, however, if you'd like to use either, be gentle. Too much flour will dry out the dough!

When the dough is ready, remove hot baking sheet from the oven and coat liberally with oil or nonstick cooking spray.
Add dough to the baking sheet, gently pressing down to fit the dough to the size of the pan.
Bake for 10 minutes.

Remove from oven; add sauce and cheese and any other toppings you love (see Note)!
Increase oven temperate to 375°F / 190°C.
Bake for 12-14 minutes until the cheese is brown and bubbly and beautiful!

Serve hot and enjoy!

breakfast tacos

WE CALL THESE BREAKFAST TACOS AND THEY ARE MY GO-TO OH-NO-I-FORGOT-THESE-PEOPLE-NEED-TO-BE-FED-3-MEALS-A-DAY DINNER! IT REQUIRES ABOUT 25 MINUTES OF DEDICATED STOVETOP COOKING; HOWEVER THERE'S NO CHOPPING OR PRE PREP INVOLVED! I USE AMERICAN CHEESE FOR MINE BECAUSE NO MATTER WHAT I DO (OR HOW MUCH I BRIBE THEM), MY CHILDREN LOVE THE AMERICAN CHEESE. OH WELL.

MAKES 6 "TACOS"

3 fresh pitas halved into rounds (so that you end up with 6 rounds)

6 slices American cheese (or any variety of sliced cheese)

2 Tbsp unsalted butter, divided

6 eggs, each cracked into a small glass bowl or plastic cup

2 Tbsp extra virgin olive oil, divided

kosher salt, to taste

coarsely ground black pepper to taste

Place 1 slice of cheese onto the center of each pita round; set aside.

Place a small nonstick pan over medium high heat.
Add 1 teaspoon butter and 1 teaspoon oil to the pan.
Once butter has just melted, gently pour in one of the eggs, being careful not to break the yolk.
(I love to add ¼ teaspoon sumac or zaatar for a grownup version of a sunny side up egg.)

Cook for 2-3 minutes until the white is cooked through but the yolk is still runny.
(I sometimes like to cover the pan the last 45 seconds of cooking just to get the white on the top of the egg to cook through.)

Place egg on top of cheese, so that the cheese immediately starts to melt.

Fold pita in half to create a taco, popping the yolk and allowing it to flow over the pita.

Continue cooking eggs, 1 at a time, and adding to pita until everyone has been fed.

Congratulations, you are now a short order cook!

NOTE

Eggs and cheese (American cheese specifically) are staples in my house, to make sure I always have the ingredients for this dinner (because my "once in a while" emergency dinner definitely gets made more than I'd like to admit), and I always keep a package of pitas in my freezer. Simply defrost pitas a few hours before serving, wrap pile of pita completely in foil, and place sealed package in the oven on 350°F / 180°C for about 10 minutes to slightly reheat!

VARIATION

If you have pickled onions, some schug, and techina in your fridge, definitely consider adding them to your "taco" for my ultimate version!

corn fritters

THE CRUNCHINESS OF THE FRITTER, COMBINED WITH THE SWEET CORN, CREATES THE ULTIMATE BITE OF KID FRIENDLY FOOD! THIS MEAL IS A TOTAL WIN BECAUSE MY KIDS LOOOOVE THESE AND THEY ARE SO FAST TO MAKE! I ALWAYS DOUBLE THE RECIPE BECAUSE THEY EVEN LIKE TO TAKE THEM TO SCHOOL THE NEXT DAY!

1 cup flour (I used spelt)

1 tsp baking powder

½ tsp kosher salt + more for sprinkling

1 tsp sugar

1 Tbsp unsalted butter, melted

½ cup milk (1% or skim is fine)

1 egg, lightly beaten

1 (15 oz) can corn, drained

oil, for frying

In a medium bowl, combine flour, baking powder, salt, sugar, melted butter, milk, and egg.
Add corn and mix, but don't over mix.

Place a small pot filled with 4 inches of oil over medium heat.
Use two spoons to scoop up batter and drop into hot oil.

Fry, turning once, until fritters are golden brown (2-3 minutes). Transfer to a rack to cool and sprinkle with salt right away.

TIPS + TRICKS

You can test if the oil is hot enough by placing the handle of a wooden spoon into the pot; if the top of the oil gently bubbles around the handle of the spoon, you are ready to go! Alternatively, you can place 1 kernel of unpopped popcorn into the oil right when you place the pot on the stove. Once the kernel pops, you know your oil is at 350°F / 180°C.

NOTES

In our house we go a few different directions with how we serve this. Sometimes we keep it simple with a side of cottage cheese and a sprinkle of everything but the bagel spice; some people will only eat these dunked in ketchup (gasp); and if I have leftover homemade mayo (either garlic or horseradish) I add a dollop of adobo from a can of chipotles in adobo to add a smoky kick to the mayo and serve that alongside!

crispy baked cauliflower + broccoli hash browns

I LOVE A HASH BROWN. ESPECIALLY ONES THAT I CAN BAKE IN THE OVEN ALL AT ONCE INSTEAD OF STANDING OVER A STOVE AND FRYING. I LIKE TO MAKE A BIG BATCH OF THESE AT THE BEGINNING OF THE WEEK SO THAT I CAN PULL THEM OUT FOR A QUICK AND FILLING AFTERNOON SNACK FOR THE KIDS WHEN THEY GET HOME FROM SCHOOL!

3 cups riced cauliflower or broccoli (or a combo!)

½ cup grated Parmesan cheese

1 tsp kosher salt

¾ tsp coarsely ground black pepper

2 large eggs, beaten

2 tsp granulated garlic

2 tsp granulated onion

Preheat oven to 375°F / 190°C. Line a baking sheet with parchment paper; coat liberally with nonstick cooking spray.

In a large bowl, stir together all ingredients.

Wearing disposable gloves, scoop up about ½ cup of the mixture; place onto prepared baking sheet.
Use the palm of your hand to flatten the mound to be around ¼ inch thick.
Continue until all the mixture has been used, leaving ½ inch between individual patties.

Bake for 25-30 minutes until they are golden brown.
Remove baking sheet from oven.
Allow to cool for 4 minutes on the baking sheet and then transfer to a cooling rack to cool completely!

TIPS + TRICKS

Call these hash browns and kids will gobble them up. Call them cauliflower hash browns and no one will touch them. You choose.

FREEZER TIP

Cool hash browns completely, then wrap each one individually in plastic wrap before freezing. To reheat, remove from freezer about 20 minutes before serving then put in the toaster oven or oven at 350°F / 180°C to reheat!

NOTE

I sometimes like to serve these with a sunny side up or poached egg right on top for a quick breakfast or lunch!

shakshuka for a crowd

I THINK IT IS SAFE TO SAY THAT THE WORLD HAS ADVANCED ENOUGH TO ACCEPT SHAKSHUKA AS A CROWD PLEASING COMFORT FOOD. IT'S THE WARM HUG OF THE BREAKFAST FOODS AND IT'S COMPLETELY CUSTOMIZABLE TO YOUR LIKING, MAKING IT THE PERFECT DISH TO SERVE TO A CROWD. THE ONLY SNAFU WOULD POSSIBLY BE THE FACT THAT COOKING IT IN A PAN CANNOT FEED ENOUGH PEOPLE. SO I'VE SOLVED THAT ISSUE FOR YOU MAKING IT SUPER EASY TO FEED TONS OF PEOPLE SHAKSHUKA ALL AT ONCE!

1 Tbsp olive oil

1 onion, diced

3 cloves garlic, minced

2 jalapeño peppers, sliced into rings (optional)

55 oz (156 g) pure tomato sauce (not marinara) (I love the sauces that come in the glass bottles for this!)

2 tsp kosher salt

2 tsp coarsely ground black pepper

8-10 eggs (depending on how many people you want to feed), cracked into separate bowls or cups.

OPTIONAL TOPPINGS/GARNISHES

1 cup shredded cheese (any variety)

2 Tbsp chilies in adobo

1 cup parsley, loosely torn

½ cup chopped scallions

techina, for drizzling

lemon gremolata (page 30)

Preheat oven to 400°F / 200°C. Coat a baking sheet with nonstick cooking spray.

In a small pot, heat oil; add onion, garlic, and jalapeño.
Cook until fragrant (3-5 minutes).

Add sauce, salt, and pepper; bring to a boil.
Pour sauce into the sheet pan.

Use a spoon to make a little well in one corner of the sheet pan.
Slide 1 egg into the indentation.

Continue this process with remaining eggs, leaving a little space between each egg.

(If using) cheese, sprinkle over the sauce now.

Bake for 12-15 minutes until the egg whites are set but the yolks are still runny.

Remove from the oven, top with garnishes, and serve immediately!

VARIATION

For a really delicious, extra nutritious twist, add 3 cups of spiralized zucchini to the pot once the onion and garlic are fragrant. Allow zucchini to soften for 5-6 minutes before adding the sauce.

spinach dip

HOW I CONVINCE MY CHILDREN THEY LOVE SPINACH: ADD TONS OF CHEESE AND CREAM, SERVE IT HOT WITH CHIPS, TELL THEM IT'S SPINACH, TALK ABOUT HOW DELICIOUS THIS SPINACH IS, START CALLING IT "THEIR FAVORITE SPINACH THING," THEN GRADUALLY SERVE SPINACH IN OTHER DISHES AND REMIND THEM HOW MUCH THEY LOVE SPINACH.

1 large yellow onion, diced

¼ cup unsalted butter
(plus a little extra for greasing and dotting the top)

3¼ lb frozen spinach

1½ tsp kosher salt

1 tsp coarsely ground black pepper

1 cup cream cheese

1-3 Tbsp hot sauce (depending on how spicy you like it)

4 heaping cups shredded cheese (whatever kind you like), divided

½ cup heavy cream

Preheat oven to 350°F / 180°C. Butter 2 (9x13 inch) pans.

Place a large pot over medium high heat; add butter and onion.
Once onion becomes translucent, add frozen spinach, salt, and pepper.

Stir often for 12-15 minutes until spinach defrosts and the liquid evaporates from the pot.
Add cream cheese and hot sauce.
Stir to combine.

Add 1 cup shredded cheese and cream.
Stir to combine until heated through.

Transfer ½ the mixture to each prepared baking pans.
Top with remaining cheese.

Bake for 35-45 minutes until the top is golden and bubbly.

Serve with tortilla chips and enjoy!

leah baila's favorite parmesan crusted roasted broccoli

WARNING: NO MATTER HOW MUCH YOU MAKE OF THIS, IT WILL NEVER BE ENOUGH!

2 (24 oz) bags frozen broccoli florets

3 Tbsp olive oil, divided

½ tsp kosher salt

1 tsp coarsely ground black pepper

6 cloves garlic, minced

2 cups shredded Parmesan cheese, divided

Preheat oven to 350°F / 180°C. Line a baking sheet with parchment paper.

Place frozen broccoli on prepared baking sheet.
Drizzle with 2 tablespoons oil.
Add salt, pepper, and garlic; toss to coat.

Roast for 35 minutes.
Remove baking sheet from oven; drizzle with remaining olive oil.
Add HALF the Parmesan; mix very gently to coat broccoli.

Sprinkle with remaining cup Parmesan.
Roast for 15-20 minutes, until Parmesan crisps up.

Serve hot and enjoy!

TIPS + TRICKS

Double this recipe so that you have some to serve after you've singlehandedly polished off the entire first batch moments after it came out of the oven.

salted coffee chocolate chunk ice cream

SWEETENED CONDENSED MILK IS BASICALLY THE BEST THING THAT EVER HAPPENED TO THIS UNIVERSE. ALL I HAD TO DO WAS WHIP UP SOME HEAVY CREAM AND MIX IT WITH THE CREAMY JAR OF SWEETENED MILK. IT PRODUCED THE SOFTEST, MOST CREAMY ICE CREAM EVER. NO ICE CREAM MACHINE, FOOD PROCESSOR, OR BLENDING. AT ALL.

OBVIOUSLY, THE NEXT LOGICAL STEP WAS COFFEE ICE CREAM. BUT YOU CAN LITERALLY MAKE THIS ANY FLAVOR YOU WANT BY ADDING EXTRACTS OR INGREDIENTS TO THE MILK, SO GET CREATIVE AND DEFINITELY MAKE IT YOUR OWN. COFFEE ICE CREAM IS ONE OF MY FAVORITE FLAVORS (SHOUT OUT TO MY GRANDMOTHER, WHO ALWAYS HAD A STASH IN HER FREEZER) AND OF COURSE SALT AND CHOCOLATE MAKE EVERYTHING BETTER!

PHOTO ORDER
COUNTERCLOCKWISE FROM TOP LEFT
Sweetened Condensed Milk, Caramel, Ice Cream, Hot Fudge

1⅓ cups sweetened condensed milk (see recipe on page 358)

2 tsp coffee granules mixed with **1 Tbsp** hot water, cooled

1 tsp pure vanilla extract

1 tsp sea salt

2 cups heavy cream

1 cup chocolate chunks (I used a mix of dark and milk chocolate) (see page 359)

In a bowl, stir together condensed milk, coffee mixture, and vanilla. Stir in salt.

In the bowl of an electric mixer, whip heavy cream until soft peaks form. Fold 1 spoonful of whipped cream into the milk mixture. Then gently fold in remaining cream.

Layer ice cream mixture in a container with a tightly fitting lid, alternating with layers of chocolate chunks.

Cover and freeze until firm.

It is recommended to serve in bowls.

Once you take a spoon and eat directly from the container, it will be all over. You will not be able to stop at just one bite!

Serve with hot fudge and homemade caramel for extra yumminess.

VARIATIONS

This base can be changed to meet your likings.

Here is a list of variations:

Vanilla: Omit coffee mixture

Chocolate: replace coffee mixture with ¾ cups cocoa powder

Peanut butter: Replace the coffee mixture with ½ cup peanut butter.

Strawberry: Puree ½ cup fresh or frozen strawberries to replace coffee mixture.

Mint: Replace the coffee mixture with 1-2 tsp mint extract (depending on your taste) + 2 tsp green food coloring gel.

VARIATIONS

In addition to changing the ice cream flavors, you can also be creative and change up any of the toppings. Here are some fun suggestions and combos:

sprinkles

nuts

cookie dough

chocolate chips

caramel chips

peanut butter chips

white chocolate chips

cut up candy bars

crushed pretzels + salted caramel + milk chocolate chunks

cut up freeze dried raspberries + granola + milk chocolate chunks

cut up chocolate covered mints + crushed almonds + chocolate chips

cut up strawberries + cookie dough + salted caramel

roasted peaches + crushed oatmeal cookies + cinnamon

chocolate ice cream base + cookie dough + salted caramel

diy ice cream staples

homemade sweetened condensed milk

6 cups whole milk

2⅔ cups sugar

FOR THOSE WHO DON'T HAVE ACCESS TO STORE BOUGHT SWEETENED CONDENSED MILK, HERE'S A BONUS RECIPE FOR YA! IT TAKES A WHILE TO MAKE, BUT ONCE IT'S DONE THERE ARE SO MANY THINGS YOU CAN DO WITH IT! I HAVE A FEW IDEAS HERE FOR YOU, INCLUDING ICE CREAM, CARAMEL, AND EVEN A SLAMMING CUP OF COFFEE, BUT THERE ARE SO MANY MORE USES FOR THIS MAGICAL MILKY SYRUP THAT IT'S WORTH THE TIME IT TAKES!

Place a large heavy bottomed pot over medium high heat.
Add milk and sugar.
Stir continuously for about 10 minutes until the sugar is completely dissolved and steam begins rising from the milk.
(It is important to keep stirring and watching the pot to prevent the milk from coming to a boil.)

At this point, reduce the heat to the lowest possible heat setting.
Stir milk mixture every 15-20 minutes.
Allow milk to slowly and gently reduce by half.
This will take around 2 hours.
It will be thicker and syrupy at the end and slightly darker in color.

Allow to cool and then pour into jars or containers.
Refrigerate until using.

homemade hot fudge

THE CRAZIEST THING ABOUT THIS IS HOW EASY IT ACTUALLY IS TO MAKE. THE WHOLE THING COMES TOGETHER IN JUST MINUTES IN ONE POT! THAT'S RIGHT! OH, AND IT'S DELICIOUS!

In a nonstick small pot or medium pan, over medium heat, heat butter, cream, corn syrup, sugar, cocoa, and salt.
Using a spatula, stir constantly until the butter is melted and the cocoa powder has been incorporated into the mixture.
When the mixture is fully combined and shiny, remove from heat.

Immediately add remaining ingredients, stirring constantly for 2 minutes until the chocolate is fully melted and the mixture is smooth and shiny again.

The hot fudge will thicken as it cools.

¼ cup unsalted butter

1 cup heavy cream

⅔ cup corn syrup

⅓ cup sugar

¼ cup cocoa powder

¼ tsp kosher salt

1½ cups chocolate chips

1 tsp pure vanilla extract

1 tsp espresso powder dissolved in **1 tsp** boiling water

sweetened condensed milk
salted caramel

THE BEST VERSION OF CARAMEL EVER. IT IS CREAMY, THICK, MILKY, AND UTTERLY DELICIOUS! I KEPT THE SALT CONTENT ON THE LOWER SIDE BECAUSE YOU CAN ALWAYS ADD MORE BUT YOU CAN'T TAKE OUT. I PERSONALLY LIKE MINE A DROP SALTIER, SO PLAY AROUND AND TRY ADDING A BIT MORE SALT, 1/8 TEASPOON AT A TIME, UNTIL YOU GET THE EXACT AMOUNT YOU LIKE!

10½ oz/330 gr condensed milk

½ tsp Maldon salt or any coarse salt

Fill a small pot half full with water.
Place a medium heatproof glass bowl onto the pot, making sure that the water is not touching the bottom of the bowl.
(If it is, just pour out a little water.)

Remove bowl. Heat water in pot over medium low heat.
Pour the condensed milk into the bowl; cover with foil.

When the water begins to steam, replace the bowl on the pot.
Cook for 1-2 hours, whisking milk mixture every 30 minutes.
You will know it's ready when the condensed milk has darkened and looks like ... caramel!

Remove from heat and allow to cool for 15 minutes.
Stir in salt.

NOTE
As it cools it will thicken. If you want a thinner consistency, serve warm.

chocolate
chocolate chip cookie dough

1 cup flour

½ cup cocoa powder (if you don't want your cookie dough to be chocolate, replace the cocoa powder with **2-3 Tbsp** flour)

½ tsp baking soda

¾ tsp kosher salt

½ cup softened unsalted butter, at room temp

½ cup brown sugar

⅓ cup white sugar

1 tsp vanilla

3 Tbsp milk

1 cup mini chocolate chips (or white chocolate chips, caramel chips, peanut butter chips, sprinkles, assorted nuts...)

In a medium bowl, combine flour, cocoa powder, baking soda, and salt.
Set aside.
Prepare a sheet of parchment paper.

In the bowl of an electric mixer, cream the butter and both sugars for 4 minutes.
Scrape down the sides every minute or so, to ensure even mixing.
Add vanilla and milk. Scrape down the sides.

With mixer on low speed, gradually add flour mixture.
Add chocolate chips; stir until just combined.

Pour dough onto prepared parchment paper; form dough into a log.
Wrap log in parchment paper.
Twist both ends to create a "candy wrapper."

Freeze log.
It can be stored in the freezer for up to 1 month.

NOTES
This recipe is not meant to be baked. It is to be eaten as raw cookie dough.

You can use this cookie dough for so many things other than ice cream. Use the dough to make truffles by rolling pieces of dough into balls and freezing. Dip frozen balls into melted chocolate. Refreeze until serving. You can also put pieces of cookie dough in your cheesecake, or serve it as a topping option at an ice cream sundae bar.

Since cookie dough is my favorite ice cream add in, we've included a recipe for when you get creative!

cannoli cream trifles

MY FATHER INHERITED HIS LOVE OF CANNOLI FROM HIS MOTHER, MY GRANDMA LILA, AND LIKE ANY GOOD FATHER, HE KINDLY PASSED ON THIS LOVE TO ME. NOW REALLY, I LOVE NOTHING MORE THAN TO BE IN MY KITCHEN PATCHKING AWAY, MAKING THE WINE-INFUSED, LIGHT, CRISP, AIR-BUBBLE SPECKLED DOUGH THAT THE LUXURIOUS CREAM TRADITIONALLY SITS IN. BUT, LIFE. SO INSTEAD, I TOOK THE TRADITIONAL CREAM FILLING, WHICH IN MY OPINION IS THE BEST VERSION OF A CREAM EVER, AND TRIFLED IT WITH STORE BOUGHT COOKIES TO MAKE THINGS EASIER! FEEL FREE TO CHANGE UP THE COOKIE OR THE FRUIT ANY WAY YOU'D LIKE!

CRUMB LAYER

32 lotus cookies
(from **1 [250 g] package**)

¼ **cup** unsalted butter, melted

¼ **tsp** kosher salt

CANNOLI CREAM

2 cups heavy cream

¼ **tsp** kosher salt

1 tsp pure vanilla extract

1 cup ricotta cheese

½ **cup** powdered sugar

FOR ASSEMBLY

3 cups fresh blueberries
(or any fruit you like)

CRUMB LAYER

Place cookies into a food processor fitted with the "S" blade.
Pulse until cookies turn into very fine crumbs.
(They should not be coarse, but more like fine sand.)

Transfer crumbs to a bowl; add butter and salt.
Mix with a spoon to combine.

Add a layer of crumbs to 8 (6 oz) jars.
(Alternatively, you can use a big trifle bowl.)
Use a spoon or the top of a long-necked bottle to press down the crumbs.
Set aside.

CANNOLI CREAM

In the bowl of an electric mixer fitted with the whisk attachment, whip cream with salt and vanilla until stiff peaks form.
Add ricotta cheese and powdered sugar.
Mix again on low speed until just combined.
(Do not overmix or you will lose all the air you whipped into the cream!)

Use a large spatula to scoop cream mixture into a large piping bag or ziptop bag.
(This will just help make it easier to fill your jars more neatly.)

ASSEMBLE

Pipe the cream over the packed lotus crumb mixture until it reaches just under the halfway point of the jars or trifle bowl.
Add an equal layer of blueberries.
Top with a final layer of cannoli cream.

At this point you can close jars and refrigerate until serving or garnish and serve immediately.

I like to garnish each jar with two lotus cookies (because who needs spoons when you can have a cookie?) and a few blueberries.

Serve cold and enjoy!

strawberries & cream bread pudding

I LOVE TO SERVE THIS AT A BRUNCH OR DAIRY BUFFET INSTEAD OF INDIVIDUAL PANCAKES OR FRENCH TOAST. BREAD PUDDING FEELS OVERRATED. BECAUSE IT USUALLY IS. EITHER IT'S TOO MOIST AND TASTES RAW OR TOO DRY AND JUST NOT GOOD. KEY HERE ARE THE WHITE CHOCOLATE AND STRAWBERRIES, ADDING JUST THE RIGHT AMOUNT OF MOISTURE TO KEEP YOU COMING BACK BITE AFTER BITE.

8 cups (1 inch cubes) leftover challah (crust trimmed off)

7 oz (200 g) dairy white chocolate, broken into small pieces

1 (16 oz) bag frozen strawberries, defrosted, quartered

8 eggs, lightly beaten

2 cups heavy cream

2 tsp pure vanilla extract

½ tsp kosher salt

¼ cup unsalted butter, melted

1 cup sugar

Coat a 9x13 inch baking dish or pan with nonstick cooking spray or butter.

Place bread cubes into baking dish.
Add white chocolate pieces throughout all the cubes, tucking them into all the nooks and crannies!
Add strawberries, tucking them into the nooks and crannies!

In a large bowl, whisk together eggs, cream, vanilla, salt, butter, and sugar until well combined.
Ladle the mixture over the bread.

Wearing a disposable glove, use your hand to gently press the top of the bread down to ensure that all of it is moistened by the liquid mixture.
Set pan aside for 1 hour to absorb the liquid.

Preheat oven to 350°F / 180°C.
Bake for 45 minutes until the top is golden!

Serve hot and enjoy!

meir's popcorn granola

THIS IS A MAMAN (THAT'S ME) AND MEIR ORIGINAL. HE WAS STUCK AT HOME, SICK, AND I HAD A WHOLE BAG OF POPCORN FROM THE SHUK LEFT OVER FROM SHABBOS. OBVIOUSLY, WE COULDN'T LET IT GO TO WASTE. SO WE PLAYED AROUND AND CAME UP WITH THIS. THEN WE WENT OUT AND BOUGHT POPCORN EVERY DAY FOR WEEKS TO MAKE IT AGAIN. BECAUSE IT'S THAT GOOD!

8-10 cups popcorn

2 cups lightly crushed salted pretzels

2 cups chocolate (dark or milk. You choose!)

OPTIONAL ADD-INS

12-16 chocolate sandwich cookies, crushed

1 cup colored sprinkles

1 cup honey roasted peanuts

1 cup white chocolate, melted

2 cups lightly crushed potato chips

1 cup peanut butter chips

1 cup caramel chips

1 cup broken up chocolate bars

1 cup mini cookie dough balls (page 359)

1 cup granola (then it's realllllly breakfast)

Spread popcorn on a parchment paper lined baking sheet.
Add whatever addins you're using but just sprinkle them on top. Don't mix in. If you mix them in, they will just sink under the popcorn.

Melt chocolate in the microwave in 15 second increments or in a bowl placed over a pot of simmering water.
Use a spoon to drizzle the chocolate over the popcorn and again, don't stir!

Allow to cool until chocolate hardens!

Then serve and enjoy!

BONUS RECIPE: make your own popcorn

⅓ cup neutral oil (avocado or canola)

1½ cups popcorn kernels

1 tsp table salt + more to taste

Set a large pot (that comes with a lid) over medium heat.
Add oil and only 1 kernel to the pot.

Once the kernel pops, add the remaining kernels and 1 teaspoon salt.
Give the pot a gentle shake to coat all the kernels in the oil.

Cover the pot and DO NOT WALK AWAY!
Every 30 seconds give the pot another little gentle shake.
Within about 2 minutes, the kernels should start popping.
Let them pop, shaking the pot every 30 seconds so that any unpopped kernels can fall to the bottom.

Once the popping slows down to 1 pop every 2 seconds, immediately remove pot from heat and pour the popped popcorn into a large bowl.

Taste popcorn and sprinkle salt to your liking!

muffin man muffins

I'VE BEEN CHASING THE PERFECT MUFFIN EVER SINCE I LEARNED THE WORDS TO "DO YOU KNOW THE MUFFIN MAN." ABOUT 31 YEARS LATER, NOW I KNOW. I'M THE MUFFIN MAN. AND YOU CAN BE TOO. YOU'RE WELCOME.

1 cup room temp unsalted butter
3½ cups flour
2 tsp baking powder
1 tsp baking soda
¾ tsp kosher salt
1 cup white sugar
1 cup brown sugar
2 tsp vanilla extract
3 large eggs
1 cup yogurt
½ cup buttermilk

ADD INS:
3 cups fresh blueberries
3 cups chopped fresh strawberries
3 cups chocolate chips
4 cups mini chocolate chips
1½ tsp cinnamon + **3** apples, peeled, quartered, and thinly sliced

Preheat oven to 350°F / 180°C. Coat extra large or regular muffin tins with nonstick cooking spray or line with paper liners.

Melt butter; set aside for 5 minutes to cool.

In a medium bowl, combine flour, baking powder, baking soda, and salt. Set aside.

In the bowl of a stand mixer, combine both sugars and cooled but still melted butter, and vanilla.
Mix until just combined.

Add eggs, 1 at a time, mixing until each is just incorporated.

Add yogurt and about half the dry ingredients to the bowl; mix for 30 seconds.

Add buttermilk; mix until just incorporated.

Add remaining dry ingredients, using a spatula to fold in so as not to overwork the batter.
Stir in add ins of choice.

Spoon ⅔ cup batter into extra large muffin tins; bake for 22-25 minutes or until a toothpick inserted in the center of a muffin comes out clean.

For regular muffins, spoon ⅓ cup batter into lined or greased muffin tins and bake for 18-20 minutes.

TIPS + TRICKS

You can absolutely use frozen berries. Defrost them first by pouring the contents of a frozen fruit bag into a strainer set over a bowl or the sink so that they can thaw completely and extra liquid can drain off. Then proceed as above.

NOTE

If you added fruit to your muffin batter, add 2 minutes to the baking time!

lemon pound cake

THERE'S NOTHING QUITE LIKE A DAIRY CAKE. IT'S NOT THE TYPE OF THING I MAKE OFTEN BECAUSE I CAN'T SERVE IT ON SHABBOS AND WE'RE NOT BIG WEEKDAY CAKE EATERS, BUT IF I'M EVER IN THE MOOD FOR SOMETHING TRULY DELICIOUS, THIS IS THE ONLY CAKE I MAKE!

2 sticks unsalted butter, softened (not microwaved, softened by removing from the fridge and allowing to come to room temp naturally)

1¼ cups + 1 Tbsp sugar (I know it's strange but just go with it)

4 eggs

1 tsp pure vanilla extract

zest of **1 large** lemon (about **1 Tbsp**)

1 tsp fresh lemon juice (juice lemon into a bowl, then measure out **1 tsp**; reserve the rest for the glaze)

2 cups flour

1 tsp kosher salt

½ tsp baking powder

GLAZE

1½ cups powdered sugar

reserved lemon juice

water (if necessary)

Preheat oven to 350°F / 180°C.
Coat the bottom of an 8 inch loaf pan with nonstick cooking spray.
Place a piece of parchment into the pan, folding in the corners so that the parchment fits perfectly.
Coat the parchment paper with nonstick cooking spray; dust lightly with flour.

In the bowl of an electric mixer, cream butter until pale (about 2 minutes).
Add sugar; cream for 4 minutes until sugar begins to dissolve into the butter.
(Scrape down sides occasionally to ensure even mixing.)

In a second bowl, add eggs, vanilla, lemon juice, and lemon zest, but do not beat them together.

Once the butter and sugar have finished creaming, add eggs, 1 at a time.
(The vanilla and lemon will naturally pour in as you add in the eggs.)
Make sure to wait until each egg is incorporated before adding the next.

In a medium bowl mix together flour, salt, and baking powder.
With the mixer on low speed, slowly add flour mixture.
Once all the flour has been added, immediately shut down mixer.
(It is really important not to overmix this batter.)

Pour batter into prepared loaf pan.
Bake for 50-55 minutes until a toothpick comes out clean.

Cool cake in pan for 15 minutes; then use paper liner to help transfer it to a cooling rack.

Once cake is completely cooled, drizzle glaze on top.

GLAZE

Add powdered sugar to a medium bowl.
Add 1 teaspoon lemon juice at a time until the mixture is thin enough to create ribbons when you pour some out of a spoon.
(If you run out of lemon juice before you get to that point, you can use water.)

Use a spoon to drizzle over cake.

Drizzle glaze over cake after it has defrosted.

Enjoy!

FREEZER NOTE

If freezing, allow cake to cool completely. Do not glaze. Wrap the parchment paper it was baked in around the cake, then wrap tightly in plastic wrap. Freeze.

TO DEFROST

Remove from the freezer the night before or at least 4 hours before you intend to serve it.

vietnamese iced coffee

VIETNAM'S CUISINE HAS BEEN INFLUENCED FOR THE BETTER BECAUSE THE COUNTRY WAS GOVERNED BY THE FRENCH FOR A LONG TIME. WE HAVE THE BAGUETTE IN THE BAHN MI SANDWICHES AND, OF COURSE, THE INTRODUCTION OF SWEETENED CONDENSED MILK. IN VIETNAM THIS COFFEE IS SERVED HOT, WHICH BY THE WAY IS AN EXCELLENT IDEA. BECAUSE IT'S SO INDULGENT, THOUGH, AND MORE OF A TREAT IN MY HOUSE — OH, AND I LOVE ICED COFFEE — AT ANY TYPE OF DAIRY GET TOGETHER I LIKE TO SERVE IT IN A LARGE PITCHER SO EVERYONE CAN HELP THEMSELVES!

1 cup sweetened condensed milk

½ cup instant coffee granules + **4-5 cups** boiling water (depending how strong of a coffee flavor you want (OR 4-5 cups brewed coffee from your Keurig or Nespresso)

Place sweetened condensed milk into a large pitcher.
Add brewed coffee; stir to combine.
Cover pitcher; refrigerate until you're ready to serve.

Pour over ice and enjoy!

Alternatively, you can TOTALLY keep this coffee hot and make yourself a single-serve cup with 2 Tbsp condensed milk and 1 cup of hot coffee!

iced pecan mocha milkshake

THIS GOES OUT TO THE MOST WHIPPED CREAM LOVING PERSON I KNOW, WHO INTRODUCED ME TO ITS AMAZINGNESS! IT'S THE MILKSHAKE OTHER MILKSHAKES DREAM OF BECOMING. THE PECANS ADD JUST THE RIGHT AMOUNT OF BUTTERINESS TO THE ALREADY CREAMY CHOCOLATE MILKSHAKE AND, WELL, A SHOT OF COFFEE IN ANYTHING IS JUST NEVER A BAD IDEA!

MAKES 6 (8 OZ) CUPS

2 cups ice

1 pint chocolate ice cream

3 Tbsp instant espresso dissolved in **3 Tbsp** water

1½ cups pecans

chocolate syrup or homemade hot fudge (page 358), for drizzling

whipped cream, for serving

sugar coated pecans, for garnishing

Place ice, ice cream, and espresso mixture into a blender.
Blend to combine.
You may need to use the blender stick to help move it around.

When it's ¾ blended, add pecans; blend again.

Drizzle the inside of each cup with a little chocolate syrup or hot fudge.
Add milkshake.
Top with whipped cream and sugared pecans.

Serve with a straw and a spoon and enjoy!

TIPS + TRICKS

For homemade whipped cream, combine 1 cup heavy cream with ½ tsp salt, 1 tsp pure vanilla extract, and ½ cup powdered sugar. Whip until stiff peaks form.

NOTE

If you want it less coffee-ish, reduce the coffee and water combination to 2 Tbsp coffee and 2 Tbsp water.

and they lived apple-y ever after

sweets

dairy free frosting 3 ways

peanut butter

2 cups peanut butter (creamy or chunky)

½ cup powdered sugar

2 Tbsp pure vanilla extract

½ tsp kosher salt

1 cup nondairy whipping cream

4 Tbsp shortening OR nondairy butter substitute at room temperature

In the large bowl of a stand mixer (or in a large bowl with a handheld mixer), combine peanut butter, sugar, vanilla, and salt.

Mixing on low speed, slowly pour in whipping cream. Gradually increase speed to high; beat for 2 minutes.

Add shortening, 1 tablespoon at a time, beating until each tablespoon is fully incorporated before adding the next one. Once all the shortening has been added, beat on high speed for about 2 minutes, scraping down the sides once, until mixture is shiny, smooth, and creamy.

NOTE

If you are using these for a dairy meal, swapping butter for margarine and nondairy whipping cream for heavy cream is never a bad idea!

vanilla frosting

4 cups powdered sugar

½ tsp kosher salt

½ cup nondairy whipping cream

2 tsp pure vanilla extra extract

8 Tbsp nondairy butter substitute, at room temperature

In the large bowl of a stand mixer, combine powdered sugar, salt, and whipping cream. Mix on medium speed for 2 minutes, scraping down the sides once or twice.

Add vanilla; mix for 30 seconds.

With mixer on high speed, add butter substitute, 1 tablespoon at a time, beating until each tablespoon is fully incorporated before adding the next one. Once all the butter substitute has been added, let mixer run for a full 3 minutes, scraping down the side twice, until the frosting is nice and fluffy.

NOTE

I use regular brown vanilla extract and I find that it doesn't affect the overall whiteness of the frosting. In fact, I love to use homemade vanilla extract here so we get to see the speckles!

chocolate frosting

Place chocolate chips into a microwave-safe bowl; melt in the microwave in 15 second increments, mixing between each round of microwaving. Alternatively, place the bowl over a simmering pot of water and stir until chocolate has melted. Once shiny and smooth, set aside for 2 minutes.

To the bowl of a stand mixer, add powdered sugar, salt, vanilla, and whipping cream. Mix on medium speed for 2 minutes, scraping down the sides every 30 seconds.

With mixer turned to low speed, gently pour in melted chocolate. Once all the chocolate has been added, scrape down the sides again.

Turn mixer back to medium speed; add butter substitute 1 tablespoon at a time, beating until each tablespoon is fully incorporated before adding in the next one. Once all the butter substitute has been added, beat mixture on high speed for about 2 minutes, scraping down the sides once, until shiny, smooth, and creamy.

1 cup semisweet chocolate chips, melted

2 cups powdered sugar

½ tsp kosher salt

1 tsp pure vanilla extract

4 Tbsp nondairy whipping cream

6 Tbsp nondairy butter substitute at room temperature

VARIATION

For a mocha frosting, melt 1 Tbsp instant espresso powder or coffee with 1 tsp boiling water. Add mixture to the bowl with the vanilla.

NOTE

If using a microwave to melt chocolate, it is important to stir the chocolate every 15 seconds. It will feel unnecessary the first or second time; however, a microwave does not distribute heat evenly, so moving the chocolate around will ensure all the chocolate melts at the same rate.

NOTE

If using a bain marie (a heatproof bowl placed over a small pot filled with 1 inch of simmering water), be sure the bowl does not actually touch the water, only traps the steam in the pot and thus causes the bowl to heat in a very gentle manner so that the chocolate does not burn!

strawberry swirl cookie dough ice cream

IT WAS NOT EASY TO PICK ONLY ONE RECIPE USING THE BEST NONDAIRY ICE CREAM BASE EVER. TRUTH BE TOLD, I WAS REALLY TORN BECAUSE, WELL, MINT CHIP FOREVER (ONLY THE GREEN ONE. WHITE MINT CHIP ICE CREAM IS A CRIME). ANYWAY, BACK TO THIS ICE CREAM, I CHOSE THIS ONE BECAUSE IT IS THE ONLY ONE THAT I THINK LACKS ABSOLUTELY NOTHING BY BEING DAIRY FREE. ITS TASTE IS NOT SACRIFICED IN ANY WAY AND THAT, MY FRIENDS, IS SOMETHING TO BE CELEBRATED.

best dairy free diy ice cream base

I HAVE A THING ABOUT NONDAIRY ICE CREAMS. MOSTLY, I'M REALLY JUST NOT SO INTO THEM. THEY'RE USUALLY MADE WITH NONDAIRY WHIPPING CREAM AND HAVE A STRANGE, CHEMICALLY SWEET AFTERTASTE THAT I JUST CAN'T GET INTO. THIS RECIPE IS NOT THAT. IT ALSO REQUIRES MORE THAN DUMPING EVERYTHING IN A BOWL AND TURNING YOUR MIXER TO HIGH. HOWEVER, I GUARANTEE IT IS WORTH EVERY STEP. DOUBLE, TRIPLE, EVEN QUADRUPLE THE RECIPE. USE THE BASE TO STOCK YOUR FREEZER WITH ALL DIFFERENT KINDS OF ICE CREAM AND SAY GOOD BYE TO FLEISHAPHOBIA!

CUSTARD BASE

8 egg yolks

8 oz sugar

16.9 oz/500 ml unsweetened almond or rice milk

1 tsp pure vanilla extract OR
1 vanilla bean, scraped

ICE CREAM

2 cups/473 ml nondairy heavy cream, such as coconut cream

½ tsp kosher salt

FLAVORINGS
(I LIKE TO ADD THESE ALONG WITH THE VANILLA!)

1 tsp mint extract + a few drops of green food coloring (yes, the green is mandatory) + good quality dark chocolate cut into chunks

2 Tbsp instant coffee mixed with **2 tsp** boiling water

1 cup pureed berries (any kind you like)

NOTE
Remove from the freezer 15 minutes before serving to make scooping easier!

CUSTARD BASE

In the bowl of a stand mixer, whisk together egg yolks and sugar. Beat until thick and very pale.
With mixer on low speed, slowly pour in almond milk.

Once all the almond milk has been incorporated, transfer mixture to a small pot. (If using) real vanilla bean, add it to the pot now.

Place pot over medium heat; using a rubber spatula, stir continuously until mixture has thickened and coats the back of a spoon.

Pour custard base into a bowl. Place plastic wrap directly onto the surface to prevent a skin from forming.
Refrigerate until completely cooled. (This can be done up to two days in advance.)

ICE CREAM

Add heavy cream to the bowl of a stand mixer.
Turn mixer to high speed; add salt and desired extracts.
Whisk until stiff peaks form.

Strain custard base through a fine mesh strainer (to remove any clumps that may have formed); add to cream mixture.

Gently fold the custard into the cream to combine.
At this point you can add your topping of choice.
I actually prefer to layer the plain ice cream and add ins in a dish.

Freeze for at least 8 hours before serving.

strawberry swirl cookie dough ice cream

1 batch vanilla ice cream (page 376)

STRAWBERRY SAUCE

3 cups strawberries (I use frozen for this, and I do NOT even defrost!)

juice of **1** lemon

1 cup sugar

¼ tsp kosher salt

OATMEAL LACE COOKIES

½ cup nondairy butter substitute (e.g., Earth Balance)

1 cup sugar

1 Tbsp pure vanilla extract

¼ tsp kosher salt

¼ cup flour

1½ cup old fashioned oats (not quick cooking)

COOKIE DOUGH

½ cup nondairy butter substitute (e.g., Earth Balance)

½ cup packed dark brown sugar

⅓ cup white sugar

1 tsp vanilla extract

3-4 Tbsp unsweetened almond milk (depending on humidity)

1½ cups white flour

½ tsp baking soda

1 tsp kosher salt

1 cup mini (or standard) chocolate chips, optional

STRAWBERRY SAUCE

Add all sauce ingredients to a medium pot and place over medium high heat.
Cover; bring to a boil. Uncover; stir.
If strawberries are still frozen, replace cover and check back every few minutes or so.

Once strawberries are soft, uncover and reduce heat to low.
Allow mixture to simmer for 10 minutes.
After 10 minutes, use a masher or fork to break up the strawberries.

Keep strawberries over heat until most of the liquid has disappeared and the mixture has thickened. When you dip a metal spoon in, mixture should coat the back of the spoon.

Remove from heat; refrigerate until using.

OATMEAL LACE COOKIES

In the bowl of a stand mixer, beat together butter substitute and sugar until pale and fluffy.
Add vanilla and salt, beating to incorporate.

Add flour.
Add oats; mix until just combined.

Refrigerate dough for at least 1 hour.

Preheat oven to 350°F / 180°C. Line 2 baking sheets with parchment paper.

Use a 1½ inch cookie scooper (or just eyeball it) to make balls of dough.
Place balls on the baking sheets, leaving 3 inches of space between each. They will spread!

Bake for around 11 minutes until cookies are golden brown.
Remove from the oven; leave on the baking sheets for 2 minutes.
After 2 minutes, use a spatula to remove them to a cooling rack.

Once cooled, store cookies in an airtight container.

To use cookies for the ice cream: Freeze cookies; after they are frozen, gently crush them into big chucks.
Add to ice cream, reserving some crumbs for garnish!

COOKIE DOUGH

In the bowl of a stand mixer, cream together butter substitute and both sugars until light and fluffy (about 5 minutes).
Turn mixer speed to low; add vanilla and 3 tablespoons almond milk (reserve the last tablespoon to use only if dough is too dry), beating to incorporate.

Add flour, baking soda, and salt. Beat until combined.
(If using) chocolate chips (I omit for strawberry ice cream), fold them into dough.

Spoon dough onto parchment paper; form into a log.
Wrap tightly in the parchment paper and then wrap in plastic wrap.
Freeze until ready to use.

When ready to use, remove from freezer and cut into marble size pieces.
Work quickly; dough defrosts quickly and is easier to handle when frozen.

TO ASSEMBLE

Spoon ½ ice cream into a 2 quart (2 liter) dish or container with a tightly fitting lid.

Add ½ the strawberry sauce, using a knife to swirl it into the ice cream.

Crush the lace cookies into ½ inch pieces; add ½ the cookies to the first layer of ice cream, gently pressing them only slightly into the ice cream. Form ½-inch balls of cookie dough and place ½ of them over the first layer of cream.
Do not be stingy here, folks, too little cookie dough is the worst of crimes!

Repeat the process a second time: ice cream, strawberry sauce, lace cookies, cookie dough. Cover container tightly.

Freeze for at least 6 hours or until ready to use.
Remove from freezer 20 minutes before scooping.
Serve and enjoy!

NOTES

Here's the thing. There are lots of steps to this recipe. Do not go ahead and make them all in one day. Take 20 minutes of your time and make each component on a different day of the week. Then, on Thursday or Friday, all you have to do is assemble it. Also, double each component so that you make enough to have it again next week, because it is incredibly delicious.

inner child cookies

FOR THE INNER CHILD IN ALL OF US.

ALSO FOR THE MOTHER WHO NEEDS THE BEST BASE COOKIE RECIPE THAT SHE CAN DO WHATEVER SHE WANTS WITH AND THAT PRODUCES ENOUGH COOKIES TO ACTUALLY MAKE IT TO SHABBOS.

ALSO, THE MARSHMALLOWS CREATE THE MOST BEAUTIFUL STAINED GLASS EFFECT AROUND THE EDGES OF THE COOKIES AND I HIGHLY RECOMMEND INCLUDING THEM.

ONE LAST ALSO, JUMBO COOKIES > REGULAR SIZE COOKIES. SO I INCLUDED DIRECTIONS FOR BOTH. YOU KNOW, SO YOU COULD BE AWESOME, TOO.   YIELD ABOUT 48 (2 INCH) COOKIES.

2½ cups white flour

1 Tbsp cornstarch

¾ tsp baking powder

¼ tsp baking soda

¾ tsp kosher salt

1½ cups margarine, at room temperature

1 cup brown sugar

¾ cup white sugar

1 tsp pure vanilla extract

1 egg

ADD INS

¼ cup mini chocolate lentils

2 cups (110 g) lightly crushed potato chips

12 chocolate sandwich cookies, broken up

1 cup mini chocolate chips

1½ cups mini marshmallows

¼ cup colored sprinkles

1 cup cornflakes

In a small bowl, combine flour, cornstarch, baking powder, baking soda, and salt. Set aside.

Add margarine to the bowl of a stand mixer; beat on high speed for 1 minute. Scrape down sides; beat again for 1 minute.

Add sugars. Beat for 4 full minutes, scraping down the sides every minute.
Add vanilla. Mix until incorporated.
Add egg; beat until just combined.

Reduce mixer speed to low. Add flour mixture; beat until ¾ of the flour is combined.
Shut off mixer; incorporate remaining flour with a spatula.

Stir in desired add ins. I add the full amount of each; add what you like!

Transfer dough to a bowl. Place plastic wrap directly on dough surface.
I highly recommend refrigerating the dough for at least 2 hours or up to 3 days, but it's not absolutely essential.

TO BAKE

Preheat oven to 350°F / 180°C. Line a baking sheet with parchment paper.

FOR JUMBO COOKIES:

Scoop out 4 tablespoons of dough. Roll into a ball and place on baking sheet.
Repeat with remaining dough.
Leave 2 inches between each ball because they spread.

Bake for exactly 14 minutes (12 minutes if not refrigerated).
Remove from oven and allow cookies to cool on the pan for 10 minutes.
Transfer to a cooling rack to cool completely.

FOR REGULAR SIZE COOKIES

Scoop out 2 tablespoons of dough. Roll into a ball and place on baking sheet.
Repeat with remaining dough.
Leave 1 inch between each ball because they spread.

Bake for exactly 10 minutes (6 minutes if not refrigerated).
Remove from oven and allow cookies to cool on the pan for 10 minutes.

Transfer to a cooling rack to cool completely.
Store in an airtight container for up to 5 days, or in the freezer for 1 month.

raspberry oat bars

THE NUMBER ONE MOST POPULAR DESSERT ON THE BLOG. I'M PRETTY SURE IT'S BECAUSE THEY ARE MAGICAL. FINE, THEY DON'T HAVE ACTUAL MAGIC POWERS, BUT THEY DO CHECK OFF EVERY SINGLE DESSERT NECESSITY AND IF YOU'RE THE ONE MAKING THESE, YOU KNOW THAT'S ITS OWN KIND OF MAGIC. ONE BOWL — CHECK. PANTRY STAPLE INGREDIENTS — CHECK. MAKES A BATCH BIG ENOUGH FOR A CROWD — CHECK. FREEZER FRIENDLY SO THAT IF YOU DON'T HAVE A HUGE CROWD YOU CAN POP SOME IN THE FREEZER FOR NEXT WEEK — CHECK. CUSTOMIZABLE — CHECK.

4 cups flour

2 cups instant oats

1½ tsp baking soda

1 tsp kosher salt

1 cup oil

2 eggs, lightly beaten

1 cup dark brown sugar + **1 cup** light brown sugar (OR **1½ cups** dark brown + **½ cup** white)

24 oz (**680 g**) raspberry jam

Preheat oven to 350°F / 180°C. Coat a baking sheet liberally with nonstick cooking spray.

Put first 8 ingredients into a bowl; mix to combine into crumbs.
Remove 2½ cups of the crumb mixture; reserve for the top.

Press remaining mixture into the sheet pan.
You will be nervous that there won't be enough, but there will be.
Just be patient and keep nudging it toward the edges, flattening as you go.

Once crumb layer is spread out, use a spoon to gently spread jam over the entire top.
Sprinkle the reserved crumb mixture over the top.

Bake for about 40 minutes until the top is golden and the jam is bubbling on the sides.
Remove from oven, cool for 15 minutes, then use a sharp knife to cut into bars.

Cool on baking pan until completely cooled!

Serve any way you like (we like them straight from the freezer!) and enjoy!

VARIATIONS

Try switching up the filling. Here are a few of my favorites: peanut butter and jelly swirl, raspberry and apricot jam swirl, chocolate hazelnut spread, lotus spread, fig jam and almond butter swirl ....The options are endless.

NOTE

Because the recipe makes so many, you can even make two types of bars at once. Spread one filling over half or a third of the sheet pan and a second and/or third over the rest. One dessert to make all the picky people in our house happy!

chocolate covered peanut butter pretzel bites

THE PERFECT BITE. CRUNCHY, SALTY, SWEET, AND UTTERLY ADDICTIVE. THIS ALSO HAPPENS TO BE A VERY, VERY KID FRIENDLY ACTIVITY. I LIKE TO TAKE AN AFTERNOON, ELUL TIME, AND GET THE KIDS TO WORK MAKING THE PEANUT BUTTER SANDWICHES AND STOCK MY FREEZER WITH 100'S OF THEM TO HAVE ALL YOM TOV SEASON.

1 (about 14 oz/400 g) bag salted mini pretzel shaped pretzels

1 cup peanut butter

⅔ cup powdered sugar

1 tsp pure vanilla extract

½ tsp kosher salt

1 (about 9 oz/255 g) bag semisweet chocolate chips

In the large bowl of a stand mixer, beat together peanut butter, powdered sugar, vanilla, and salt.
Mixture should reach a dough like consistency; if necessary, add more powdered sugar.

Using 1 pretzel as a scoop, scoop up about 1 teaspoon of the peanut butter mixture; cover with another pretzel to make a "pretzel sandwich."
Continue until you have used all the peanut butter mixture.

Place peanut butter sandwiches on cookie sheets; refrigerate or freeze till firm.

Meanwhile, place chocolate chips into a heatproof bowl over boiling water in a double boiler, or heat in 30 second increments in a microwave safe bowl in the microwave until chocolate is smooth and shiny.

Line a baking sheet with parchment paper.

Take frozen sandwiches out of freezer; dip ¾ of each pretzel sandwich into the melted chocolate. Allow excess chocolate to drip back into the bowl. Place dipped sandwiches onto prepared baking sheet.

Once all sandwiches are dipped, freeze them for 1 hour.
After 1 hour, transfer to a container with a tightly fitting lid; store in freezer.

These are best when eaten frozen!

BONUS

Make a batch of vanilla ice cream, (page 376) or buy some, soften it very slightly, and add 1 spoonful of ice cream to the center of each sandwich after spreading with the peanut butter mixture. You'll have to work quickly to get the sandwiches into the freezer and then again when you're dipping in the melted chocolate, but I guarantee you will never have a dessert or snack that gets eaten as quickly!

eli's favorite strawberry shortcake

THIS CAKE EVOLVED FROM A BOXED CAKE MIX, TO USING THE BEST ALL PURPOSE RECIPE, COURTESY OF ETA STAHLER, TO BEING MADE WITH THE BEST HOMEMADE STRAWBERRY JAM. EVERY STEP OF THE WAY ITS BEEN ELI'S FAVORITE DESSERT AND THEREFORE ONE OF MY FAVORITES TO MAKE!

POUND CAKE

2 cups flour

1 (3½ oz/99 g) package instant vanilla pudding mix

2 tsp baking powder

1 tsp kosher salt

¾ cup orange juice

½ tsp pure vanilla extract

2 cups sugar

¾ cup oil

4 eggs

STRAWBERRY JAM

3 cups strawberries, roughly chopped (**1 bag** frozen strawberries)

juice of **1** lemon

¾ cup sugar

pinch kosher salt

WHIPPED CREAM

2 cups nondairy whipping cream

¼ tsp kosher salt

½ cup powdered sugar

1 tsp pure vanilla extract

TO ASSEMBLE

1 cake, sliced through the middle to create two thinner layers (unless you used the 2 (8 inch) round pans then leave as is!)

1 batch strawberry jam

1 batch whipped cream

2 cups sliced strawberries

PRO TIP

When you take the whisk out of the bowl, the cream should form a peak that is bent over slightly. This is called a soft peak and it's exactly what you're looking for.

POUND CAKE

Preheat oven to 350°F / 180°C. Coat a 9x13 inch baking pan or 2 (8 inch) round pans with nonstick cooking spray.

In a bowl, combine flour, pudding mix, baking powder, and salt. Set aside.

In a second bowl, combine orange juice and vanilla. Set aside.

To the bowl of a stand mixer, add sugar and oil. Combine at medium speed. While mixing, slowly add eggs, one at a time.
Once the eggs are incorporated, add ½ the flour mixture, then the orange juice mixture, then the rest of the flour mixture.

Pour into prepared baking pan(s); bake in 9x13 inch pan for about 45 minutes.*

Once cake has cooled for 10 minutes, remove it from the pan and set on a cooling rack to cool completely before assembling.

*For the strawberry shortcake, I like to bake the cake in 2 (8 inch) round pans for about 35 minutes or until a toothpick inserted in the center comes out clean. The second the cakes come out of the oven, I poke holes in them and spoon over some of the strawberry jam so it seeps down into the cake.

STRAWBERRY JAM

Put all jam ingredients into a pot; bring to a boil. Reduce heat, cover pot, and simmer for 20 minutes. Uncover pot. Mash strawberries with a fork.

Allow mixture to cook, uncovered, until the mixture has reduced and ... looks like jam!

You should have some leftover strawberry jam. That extra jam is magical and Eli's favorite part! Spoon a little bit of it over every slice you serve!

WHIPPED CREAM

Place all whipped cream ingredients into the bowl of a stand mixer. Beat on medium low speed for 1 minute.

Once mixture has thickened slightly, turn speed to high; beat for 1-2 minutes until mixture is thick and creamy.

TO ASSEMBLE

Place 1 layer of cake on a cake stand or tray.
Spoon strawberry jam over the cake, leaving a 1 inch (2 cm) border around the edges to allow jam room to spread when you add the second layer.

Layer ½ the strawberries over the jam.
Spread 1 cup of whipped cream over the strawberries.

Top with second cake layer.
Again, spoon jam over the top, this time being sure to go all the way to the edges.
Add remaining whipped cream.
Decorate the top with remaining sliced strawberries.

Refrigerate until serving.

salted dark chocolate almond joy truffles

I LOVE ANYTHING COCONUT. AND THEN ADD IN DARK CHOCOLATE. YUM. BONUS, THAT THEY'RE EASY TO MAKE, GLUTEN FREE, AND CUSTOMIZABLE!

2 cups shredded coconut, sweetened or unsweetened

½ cup powdered sugar (if your coconut is sweetened already, leave out the sugar)

¼ cup almond butter

7 oz (200 g) good quality dark chocolate (I like 70% cocoa for this)

1 tsp coconut oil

Maldon salt

Line a baking sheet with parchment paper.

In a bowl, combine coconut, sugar (if using), and almond butter.
Mix well to fully distribute the almond butter throughout the coconut.
(I like to put on disposable gloves and do this by hand.)

Remove a heaping tablespoon of coconut mixture and form into a ball.
Place ball on prepared baking sheet. Repeat with remaining coconut mixture.

Freeze for at least 1 hour.

Meanwhile, combine dark chocolate with coconut oil.
Melt until it is smooth and shiny.
(You can do this step in the microwave, melting in 15 second increments and stirring each time, or by placing chocolate and oil into a heatproof bowl set over a pot of simmering water and stirring until melted.)
Once chocolate is melted and shiny, dip frozen coconut balls into chocolate, gently shaking off any excess chocolate.

Place on prepared baking sheet; sprinkle with salt.
Refrigerate until chocolate has hardened.

VARIATIONS

I gave you the basic form of this recipe to leave room for you to experiment and customize to your liking. Go ahead and replace the almond butter with any nut butter you like. Some of my favorites are peanut, hazelnut, and sun!

TIPS + TRICKS

If you want to add a crunch factor to these truffles (which I highly recommend) think about adding chopped nuts to the coconut mixture, and then sprinkling them onto the chocolate with the salt so that everyone knows what's in them!

NOTE

If you're not into the whole dipping chocolate thing, feel free to place melted chocolate in a ziptop bag, snip off a tiny piece of one corner, and simply drizzle over the coconut balls.

perfect meringues

THIS RECIPE WILL ALWAYS BE DEDICATED TO MY SON, WHO NEVER GOT TO EAT THEM. IT IS THE LAST RECIPE I POSTED ON MY BLOG BEFORE HE LEFT THIS WORLD, AND EVERY TIME I SEE OR THINK OF MERINGUES, I THINK OF HIM. AND I THINK OF ME. THE RECIPE EXISTS IN A SMALL, UNSEEABLE TO ANYONE ELSE, SPACE OF TIME THAT I GO BACK TO IN MY MIND OFTEN. THE TIME WHEN I ENTERED MY OWN PERSONAL GALUS AND MY LIFE BECAME A BEFORE AND AFTER. THE ME BEFORE I EXPERIENCED LOSS AND THE ME AFTER. THE MERINGUES, A RECIPE THAT TOOK ME OVER 5 YEARS TO PERFECT AND THEN 2 WHOLE PESACH HOLIDAYS TO ACTUALLY PHOTOGRAPH AND POST, ARE FOR ME THE BEST REPRESENTATION OF WHAT OUR ROLE IN THIS WORLD IS. IT IS TO WORK ON OURSELVES INTERNALLY, QUIETLY, LITTLE BY LITTLE. ACCUMULATING GROWTH DAY BY DAY UNTIL IT TURNS INTO YEAR BY YEAR LIKE WATER DRIPPING ON A ROCK. IF WE ALL LOOK INWARD ENOUGH, AND ALLOW OURSELVES TO BE TRANSFORMED BY GROWTH EVEN THE TINIEST, MOST UNSEEABLE BIT, DAY BY DAY, EVENTUALLY, AS A NATION, WE WILL TRANSFORM TO BEING THE PEOPLE WHO WILL GREET MASHIACH. AND WHEN HE COMES, I WILL MAKE MERINGUES.

a very clean bowl and whisk (yes, it's an ingredient because it's important)

8 egg whites

2 cups sugar

¼ tsp kosher salt

1 tsp white vinegar

Preheat oven to 250°F / 121°C. Line 2 baking sheets with parchment paper.

In the very clean, large bowl of a stand mixer, use the whisk attachment to beat egg whites, starting on low speed and gradually increasing to high.
Once egg whites form stiff peaks, start adding in sugar, 1-2 tablespoons at a time, until each addition has been incorporated.

Once all the sugar has been added and the mixture is glossy and beautiful, add salt and vinegar. Beat for 30 more seconds to incorporate.

Place meringue mixture into a ziptop bag or piping bag (or do what I usually do and just spoon them on in dollops) and pipe onto prepared baking sheet.

Lower oven temperature to 200°F / 93°C.
Bake for 1½ hours. After 1½ hours, do NOT open oven door.

Turn off the oven and leave meringues inside to dry out for at least 3 hours or overnight!

Store in an airtight container!

moroccan style orange blossom shortbreadish cookies

THESE ARE THE COOKIES I IMAGINED MY GRANDMOTHER WOULD HAVE MADE HAD SHE BEEN EXPOSED TO GINGERBREAD MEN AND SHORTBREAD COOKIES. REALLY, I DON'T KNOW ANY MOROCCAN WHO MADE THESE. THE FLAVOR PROFILE JUST BRINGS ME BACK TO THE TANGERINE GARDENS OF THE LE MAMOUNIA HOTEL IN MARRAKECH WHERE I WAS LUCKY ENOUGH TO SHARE A ROOM WITH MY GRANDMOTHER. THE COMBINATION OF THE TANGERINE ZEST, THE ORANGE BLOSSOM WATER THAT WEAVES IN AND OUT OF SO MANY MOROCCAN DISHES, AND THE SPICES ARE ALL TANGLED TOGETHER IN THE MEMORIES THESE AROMAS BRING UP.

1½ cups +2 Tbsp flour

½ tsp baking powder

¼ tsp kosher salt

1 tsp ground ginger

¾ tsp cinnamon

½ tsp cardamom

½ cup nondairy butter substitute, at room temperature

¾ cup sugar

3 Tbsp extra virgin olive oil

1 tsp orange blossom water

1 tsp pure vanilla extract

1 egg, lightly beaten

OPTIONAL FOR TOPPING COOKIES

½ cup chocolate chips, melted

crushed pistachios, for sprinkling over chocolate

Line a baking sheet with parchment paper.

In a bowl, combine flour, baking powder, salt, ginger, cinnamon, and cardamom. Stir to combine; set aside.

In the bowl of a stand mixer, cream butter substitute and sugar on high speed for 3 minutes, scraping down the sides of the bowl every 35 seconds or so.

With mixer on medium low speed, drizzle in olive oil. Add orange blossom water and then vanilla.
Scrape down the sides of the bowl.

Turn mixer back to medium low speed; add egg.
Once the egg is mostly incorporated, shut mixer off and mix with a spatula if necessary.

Turn dough out of bowl onto the center of the prepared baking sheet.
Wearing disposable gloves, gently pat the dough down to create a large, flat rectangle that is approximately ¼ inch thick.
To smooth out the top of the dough, lay a second piece of parchment paper over the top and very, very gently go over it with a rolling pin once or twice.
Leave top layer of paper on dough; refrigerate for 3 hours.

Preheat oven to 350°F / 180°C. Line a baking sheet with parchment paper.

Using a scalloped edge pastry dough cutter (or just a knife, that's fine too), cut dough into 2 inch squares.
Places squares on prepared baking sheet, leaving ½ inch between cookies.

Bake for 12-15 minutes, until the edges of the cookies just begin to turn a light golden brown.

Allow cookies to cool on the pan for 4 minutes, then gently transfer to a cooling rack to finish cooling completely.

If dipping in chocolate, do so once they are completely cooled.
Dip in melted chocolate and sprinkle with chopped pistachios.

Serve with good Moroccan tea and enjoy!

strawberry rhubarb blood orange crisp

THERE IS A SMALL WINDOW OF TIME IN ISRAEL WHEN ALL THREE OF THESE ARE IN SEASON. IT'S USUALLY AROUND DECEMBER/JANUARY AND IT IS MY FAVORITE PRODUCE SEASON OF ALL. OUR LEAFY GREENS ARE VIBRANT AND DELICIOUS, THE FRUIT IS JUICY AND SWEET, AND THE CITRUS, OH THE CITRUS, IS SO DELICIOUS! YOU CAN EASILY MAKE THIS ALL YEAR, THOUGH, BY SWITCHING OUT ANY OF THE COMPONENTS FOR WHATEVER OTHER FRUITS ARE IN SEASON AT THAT TIME!

4 cups diced strawberries
(about **1 lb/½ kg**)

4 cups chopped rhubarb (**7-8 stalks**)

zest of **1** blood orange

1½ cups sugar

¼ tsp salt (kosher or Maldon)

½ cup blood orange juice
(from about **2**)

1 Tbsp cornstarch

TOPPING

2 cups flour

2 cups old fashioned oats

½ cup brown sugar

½ cup white sugar

½ tsp salt (kosher or Maldon)

1 cup oil

Preheat oven to 350°F / 180°C.

Coat a baking dish with nonstick cooking spray. Add strawberries, rhubarb, zest, sugar, and salt.

Mix together juice and cornstarch till there are no more lumps; add to baking dish.
Stir to combine.

In a second bowl, combine all topping ingredients, mixing well.
Crumble over fruit mixture.

Place baking dish on a baking sheet to catch any leaks.
Bake for 45 minutes–1 hour until the top is golden, the juices are bubbly, and your house smells insanely amazing!

Remove from oven and allow to cool for at least 10 minutes before serving.

Best served warm with a heaping serving of whipped cream!

healthy-ish cookies

BASICALLY THERE'S JUST A TON OF BRAN, WHICH MAKES THESE COOKIES SIGNIFICANTLY MORE HEALTHY THAN COOKIES THAT DON'T CONTAIN ANY BRAN; HOWEVER THERE IS SUGAR. AND NOT A LITTLE BIT OF IT. HENCE THE "ISH." THEY ARE ELI'S FAVORITE COOKIES' THOUGH, AND WE CALL THEM HEALTHY COOKIES IN THIS HOUSE. AS IN "DANIELLE, CAN YOU MAKE HEALTHY COOKIES FOR SHABBOS? AGAIN?" "YES, YES, I CAN." BECAUSE THEY REQUIRE NO MIXER, TAKE 2 MINUTES TO THROW TOGETHER, AND I FEEL BETTER ABOUT EATING AND SERVING THEM BECAUSE OF ALL THAT BRAN!

2 cups oat bran (or wheat bran)

1 cup whole wheat or spelt flour

1 cup old fashioned or quick cooking oats

½ tsp baking soda

½ tsp kosher salt

4 egg whites, lightly beaten

1 cup canola oil

1 tsp pure vanilla extract

1½ cups light brown sugar

¾ cup dried cranberries

1 cup white chocolate chips

Preheat oven to 350°F / 180°C. Line a baking sheet with parchment paper.

In a large bowl, combine oat bran, flour, oats, baking soda, and salt.
Stir to combine.

In a second bowl, combine egg whites, oil, vanilla, and sugar.

Make a well in the center of the flour in the bowl.
Add egg mixture and remaining ingredients to the well; stir to combine.
The batter will be very loose but will hold together once baked.

Form into balls (I like to use an ice cream scoop for this) and place 1 inch apart on prepared baking sheet.
Bake for 10-15 minutes, depending on how chewy or crunchy you like your cookies.

Remove from oven and allow to cool on the baking sheet.

Store in an airtight container for up to 1 week.

FREEZER TIP

These cookies freeze really well. Once cooled, store them in an airtight container with a piece of parchment between the layers and freeze. Remove from freezer 30 minutes before serving.

peppermint marshmallows

HOMEMADE MARSHMALLOWS ARE NOTHING LIKE THEIR STORE BOUGHT MASS PRODUCED TWINS. THEY ARE CREAMIER, FLUFFIER, AND ACTUALLY TASTE LIKE MARSHMALLOWS. DON'T LIKE PEPPERMINT? NO PROBLEM, CUSTOMIZE THE FLAVOR ANY WAY YOU WANT. JUST TO BE SURE TO GIVE THIS RECIPE A TRY. THEN TOP YOUR HOT COCOA WITH THEM, AND THEN WRITE ME AN EMAIL TELLING ME HOW ENLIGHTENED YOU HAVE BECOME!

1 cup powdered sugar + more to coat the pan

2 oz unflavored vegetable gelatin

1 cup cold water, divided

2 cups sugar

⅔ cup light corn syrup

¼ tsp kosher salt

1 tsp mint extract or flavoring of choice

1 vanilla bean, scraped OR **1 tsp** pure vanilla extract

red food coloring

Coat 1 (8 inch) square baking pan with nonstick cooking spray; sprinkle with a very liberal amount of powdered sugar, making sure the whole pan and all sides are sufficiently coated.

To the bowl of a stand mixer fitted with the whisk attachment, add gelatin and ½ cup cold water. Set aside.

Combine remaining ½ cup water, remaining 1 cup powdered sugar, corn syrup, and salt in a medium pot over medium heat. Stir until sugar has dissolved. Once it has dissolved, stop mixing.

Place candy thermometer into sugar mixture and wait for it to come to temp.

Once it reaches 240°F / 115°C, turn mixer to medium low speed. Remove sugar mixture from heat; very slowly, with mixer running on medium low speed, drizzle into gelatin mixture. Be very careful not to let hot sugar mixture hit the whisk or it will splatter.

Once all the sugar mixture has been added, gradually increase mixer speed to high. Whip until the mixture is white and thick like fluff, about 12 minutes.

Turn off mixer, add extract, and whip on medium high for 3 minutes.

Use a greased spatula to help transfer marshmallow mixture to the prepared pan.

Add red food coloring to the top of the marshmallow mixture and use a toothpick to swirl through the mixture to create a marbled effect.

Sprinkle more powdered sugar over the top of the marshmallows and allow to sit, uncovered, at room temp overnight.

Cut into squares with a knife dipped into powdered sugar and serve!

VARIATIONS

Replace the mint extract with any extract you like and the food coloring with any color, or no color! Really, one of my favorite versions is made with a real vanilla bean that is split open lengthwise and the beans inside scraped out and added to the marshmallow batter. Those little specks of vanilla are beautiful and so satisfying to see!

inside out apple crumble

I LOVE THIS RECIPE FOR HOW EASY IT IS TO PUT TOGETHER, HOW LIGHT IT IS, AND HOW COMFORTING IT CAN BE ON A LONG WINTER NIGHT!

6 apples, washed and cored (any variety apple will do)

¾ cup brown sugar, divided

1 Tbsp pure vanilla extract

1 Tbsp bourbon (or whiskey, amaretto ...)

¾ cup quick cooking oats

½ cup flour

½ tsp kosher salt

¼ cup canola oil

Preheat oven to 350°F / 180°C. Coat 1 (9 inch) round or rectangular oven to table baking dish with nonstick cooking spray (just make sure the apples will fit in it!).

Sprinkle ¼ cup sugar into the pan.
Drizzle vanilla and bourbon over the sugar.
Add cored apples.

In a bowl, combine remaining ingredients, mixing until well blended into a crumble.
Stuff about 2 tablespoons crumble into the cavity of each apple.
Sprinkle any remaining crumble into the nooks and crannies between the apples.

Liberally coat a large piece of foil with nonstick cooking spray; cover the baking dish tightly. Bake for 45 minutes.

Remove foil; bake 10 minutes.

Serve hot and enjoy!

raspberry rice krispy treats

REALLY I NEEDED THE WHOLE WORLD TO KNOW THE RIGHT WAY TO MAKE RICE KRISPY TREATS. AND THAT IS WITH MARSHMALLOW CREME. NOT MARSHMALLOWS. AND I STAND BY THAT. FOREVER. ADD ANY PULVERIZED FREEZE DRIED FRUIT TO ADD FUN COLOR AND FLAVOR, OR LEAVE THEM PLAIN. IN MY OPINION, THEY ARE THE UNIVERSAL DESSERT. GLUTEN FREE, SWEET, CRUNCHY, AND CUSTOMIZABLE. AN ABSOLUTE CROWD PLEASER!

16 cups (400 g) Rice Krispie cereal

2 (1.2 oz/34 g) bags freeze dried raspberries (or any freeze dried berry you like!)

3 (7.5 oz/213 g) jars marshmallow creme

2 Tbsp canola oil

¼ tsp kosher salt

Prepare all your ingredients before you start because once you begin it goes fast!

Use your hands to crush and crumble one bag of the berries. Set aside.

Open jars of fluff and, if you have a microwave, zap for 15-30 seconds to loosen the creme.

Meanwhile, place a pot over medium heat.

Once the pot is hot, remove pot from heat and liberally spray the pot and your spatula with nonstick cooking spray, then return pot to the stove.
(This is crucial to the cleaning process later!)
Add oil, salt, and loosened creme to the pot.
Stir to combine.

Add crushed berries and Rice Krispies.
Mix well until every single Rice Krispie is covered in creme.

Pour mixture into a greased baking dish or muffin pans with paper liners.

Open second bag of berries, grab a handful, and lightly crush while sprinkling over the top for extra berry flavor and because it looks super awesome!

Seal tightly with foil or plastic wrap and serve any way you like!

TIPS + TRICKS

Since this dessert comes together in just a few minutes, on a Yom Tov when you leave your stove on, I like to have all the components in my house and while the table is being cleared, I sneak away into the kitchen and make a fresh batch of Rice Krispy Treats and bring the whole pot filled with hot gooey marshmallowy goodness right to the table, and serve it warm, straight out of the pot. It's such a fun dessert surprise!

VARIATION

You can absolutely leave out the raspberries to make the best Rice Krispy Treats ever or you can even go wild and change up or swap the raspberries for freeze dried blueberries or strawberries!

FREEZER TIP

To make them the only way Eli will eat them, press mixture into greased muffin tins and pop them into the freezer. Store in a container or ziptop bag and serve them for a fun frozen treat!

fat free biscotti

ARE THEY HEALTHY? EH. BUT THERE'S NO OIL. SO I FEEL BETTER ABOUT EATING THE ENTIRE BATCH.
ALSO, I HAVE LITERALLY NEVER MET A PERSON WHO DID NOT LIKE BISCOTTI, SO IN MY MIND, THEY'RE THE PERFECT
THING TO FILL YOUR COOKIE JAR WITH FOR SHABBOS. I LIKE TO DOUBLE THE RECIPE, THEN DIVIDE THE DOUGH IN
FOUR, AND ADD DIFFERENT NUTS, DRIED FRUITS (NOT RAISINS. NEVER RAISINS.), SPRINKLES, AND CHOCOLATE CHIPS
OR CHUNKS TO EACH LOG SO THAT I END UP WITH A VARIETY OF BISCOTTI TO PLEASE ANYONE WHO WALKS IN.

1 cup sugar

2 eggs + **1** egg yolk

1 Tbsp lemon juice

1 tsp pure vanilla extract

1½ tsp baking powder

¼ tsp kosher salt

2¼ cups flour (I use **2 cups** spelt & **¼ cup** white. Use any flour or any combo you like)

ADD INS

1 cup dried cranberries + **1 cup** chopped pecans + **½ cup** slivered almonds + **½ cup** pistachios)

1 cup mini choc chips + **1 cup** slivered almonds + **1 tsp** cinnamon & replace lemon juice with vanilla and/or almond extract

OPTIONAL TOPPING

cinnamon sugar

Preheat oven to 350°F / 180°C. Line a baking sheet with parchment paper.

In the bowl of electric mixer, on medium speed, beat together sugar, eggs, and egg yolk.
Add remaining ingredients except add ins.
Mix until combined. (Batter will be very thick.)

Pour in add-ins you're using.
Mix until just incorporated.

Divide batter into 2 portions.
Place each portion on one end of the baking sheet.

Wet hands slightly and mold each portion into a 2½ inch wide log.
(Sprinkle sugar or cinnamon sugar on top if desired.)

Bake for 30 minutes.
Remove from oven and lower oven temperature to 325°F / 165°C. Return pan to oven and bake for 10 minutes.

Using a large serrated knife, slice logs into ¼ inch slices (the thinner the better, I think!).

Lay slices on their sides on baking sheet.

Return to oven, bake for 6-8 minutes.

Remove from oven and cool biscotti on a rack.

Serve with tea and enjoy!

2 ingredient chocolate mousse

THIS RECIPE COMES FROM MY FRIEND WHO GOT THE RECIPE FROM HER FRIEND. THE TECHNIQUE IS STRANGE, BUT IT PRODUCES THE ABSOLUTELY BEST CHOCOLATE MOUSSE IN THE WORLD. IT MAY TAKE YOU ONE OR TWO TRIES TO GET IT RIGHT, BUT STICK WITH IT. IT'S WORTH IT.

14 oz (400 g) dark chocolate (bars, discs, semi-sweet, bitter, or a combo)

8 eggs, separated

Bring a medium pot of water to a boil.

Meanwhile, break up chocolate into as similar size pieces as possible and place into a nonstick pan.
Place pan as close to the sink as possible.

Once water is boiling, pour just enough water over the chocolate so that all the chocolate is submerged.
Do not move, swirl, or mix the pan or the chocolate once the water is added.
Allow mixture to sit for around 10 minutes.

While chocolate is resting, separate eggs.

Add egg whites to the bowl of an electric mixer fitted with the whisk attachment.
Beat until egg whites form stiff peaks.

Turn mixer to the lowest setting. Add egg yolks, one at a time, beating well after each addition.
As soon as all the yolks are in, stop mixing.
You want to be careful not to overmix because we want to keep in as much air as possible.

Gently tip pan with chocolate on its side so that the water can stream out and spill into the sink.
You will want to use the lid of a pan at the end to get out the last of the water without the chocolate slipping out.
Be sure not to mix melted chocolate at all.

A little water will remain in the pan and that is fine! Immediately turn mixer to low and tip pan toward the eggs so chocolate can stream in.
Once all the chocolate has been added, use a spatula just to scrape any remaining chocolate in the pan into the mixer bowl.

Shut off mixer right away and use spatula to gently fold mixture until egg and chocolate are combined.

Pour mousse into cups or a dish and refrigerate until serving!

big batch granola
+ theory of a fruit salad

THIS IS SUPER BASIC, SO PAY ATTENTION: WHEN MAKING A FRUIT SALAD, IF SOME OF YOUR FRUIT IS NOT RIPE OR NOT FULLY IN SEASON (COUGH, DON'T USE THEM, COUGH, BUT IF YOU DO ANYWAY...), SPRINKLE 1 TBSP SUGAR OVER THE ROW OF THAT SPECIFIC FRUIT BEFORE JUICING THE LIME OVER THE TOP. THAT WILL MACERATE THE FRUIT AND BRING OUT ITS OWN NATURAL JUICES.

GRANOLA

3 cups canola oil

2 cups silan (organic date syrup)

2½ cups brown sugar

5 Tbsp pure vanilla extract

2 Tbsp kosher salt

20 cups oats (I mix quick cooking & rolled, makes better clumps!)

6 cups chopped, roasted, salted almonds

4 cups dried cranberries

FRUIT SALAD

2 cups strawberries

3 persimmons or **3** nectarines

1 small pineapple

4 kiwis

3 pears

1 papaya or **2** mangos (never both; together they will ruin the texture!)

2 limes, for juicing

VARIATION

For the quickest, least amount of shopping fruit option to pair with granola, try cutting up 4 cups of strawberries, sprinkling ½ cup of sugar over the top and add ¼ cup of balsamic vinegar. Allow strawberries to macerate for 20 minutes, then spoon into small cups and top with whipped cream and granola!

GRANOLA

Line 2 baking sheets with parchment paper. Preheat 2 ovens to 325°F / 165°C (or use 1 oven, but only bake 1 sheet at a time).

In a large bowl, combine oil, silan, brown sugar, vanilla, and salt. Mix well to combine into a syrup.

Place 10 cups of oats and 3 cups nuts on each baking sheet, mixing to combine.
Pour about 2 cups of the syrup mixture over the oats.
Using your hands, work the syrup into the oat mixture until all are coated.
(To do this, I like to wear disposable gloves that I spray lightly with nonstick spray.)

Bake 1 baking sheet for 15 minutes.
Open oven door and gently stir the oat mixture around so that it bakes evenly.
Close oven door; bake for 15 minutes.
Remove baking sheet from oven. Pour ¼ of remaining syrup over oat mixture.
Mix gently and return to oven for 15 minutes.

Take out of the oven, add ½ the almonds and ½ the cranberries; stir to combine.
Pour ¼ of remaining syrup over the oat mixture, only this time, DO NOT MIX.
Just put back in the oven for 15 minutes.
Take out of oven and allow to cool for 1 hour without touching or mixing at all.

Repeat with remaining baking sheet.

Pour into container, gently breaking into clumps.
(Don't overdo it, because they naturally break on their own!)

Keep in an airtight container for up to 2 weeks.

NOTE

You can halve or even quarter the granola recipe to make smaller batches, although I must warn you, you will be sorry you did!

FRUIT SALAD

A few hours or the night before serving, cut up whatever fruit is in season into tiny little ¼ inch cubes. Why? So that all the varieties of the fruit can fit on the fork or spoon at the same time. You can keep fruit in the same dish; however, do not mix them together until right before serving. I keep mine in a glass dish or baking dish, and make neat rows of each fruit. Last, cut up a lime or two (depending how much fruit you have), and squeeze the fresh limes (yes, only real lime juice here, folks) over the fruit. Wrap bowl with plastic wrap and refrigerate until serving. To serve, toss, spoon into bowls or cups, and for an extra bonus, top with Big Batch (raisin free!) Granola.

VARIATIONS

Here are a few of my favorite ways to customize the granola:

2 tsp cinnamon + 1½ tsp cardamom + 1 tsp ginger; combine to form a syrup

Replace 1 cup silan with 1½ cups maple syrup (+ 2 tsp cinnamon)

Replace half the cranberries with shredded coconut

Add 1½ cups mini chocolate chips per baking sheet of granola once cooled

Use any nuts you'd like

Swap out 1 cup of oil for 1½ cups butter for the best dairy granola ever!

mufletta

AS I SIT HERE TYPING THE BLURB FOR THIS RECIPE I HAVE TEARS IN MY EYES. FROM THE TIME I WAS OLD ENOUGH TO REMEMBER THIS WAS MY ABSOLUTE MOST FAVORITE FOOD ON THE PLANET. IT WAS THE FIRST AND LAST DISH I REQUESTED FROM MY GRANDMOTHER AT EACH VISIT. WHEN I WAS A TEENAGER, SHE SPENT MANY HOURS TEACHING ME THE EXACT RIGHT WAY TO STRETCH OUT THE DOUGH TO MAKE THE MUFLETTA PAPER THIN AND AS LIGHT AS POSSIBLE. THESE "PANCAKES," WHICH ARE REALLY CLOSER TO CREPES, ARE PERFECTLY LIGHT, CRISPY, CHEWY, AND SATISFYING ALL AT THE SAME TIME. ASIDE FROM BEING DELICIOUS ALL YEAR LONG, MUFLETTA IS TRADITIONALLY SERVED AT A HENNA (A PRE-WEDDING MOROCCAN PARTY) AND ALWAYS RIGHT AFTER PESACH. HOURS AFTER PESACH HAS ENDED, THERE IS THE TRADITIONAL MIMOUNA PARTY, WHERE PEOPLE OPEN THEIR HOMES AND EVERYONE GOES FROM HOUSE TO HOUSE TASTING ALL THE NEW DELICIOUS CHAMETZ TREATS THAT EACH HOME HAS TO OFFER.

MUFLETTA

2.2 lb (1 kg) white flour, sifted

3 Tbsp sugar

1 Tbsp kosher salt

2½ cups warm water

3 Tbsp + 3 cups canola oil (or any neutral oil), divided

TIPS+TRICKS

To make this possible hours after Pesach, here's what I do .... Right after Havdalah, assign everyone in the house a job in the kitchen to help turn back over to chametz. Meanwhile, sneak outside your house, onto the driveway, porch, balcony, or hallway, and get busy making the dough (which takes less than 10 minutes). Once dough is prepared, go back inside and wash your hands in the bathroom sink. While dough is resting for that first hour, get to the kitchen and help everyone finish turning over. Once the kitchen is done, take dough into the kitchen and move on to forming the balls. Within 2 hours after Pesach, you will have warm, fresh mufletta!

orange blossom syrup

1½ cups sugar

¼ cup orange blossom water

½ cup water

Place all syrup ingredients into a small nonstick pot; place over medium high heat.
Stir constantly to dissolve sugar.

Once sugar has dissolved, cook mixture for 1 minute to slightly thicken.

Remove from heat; drizzle over mufletta.

MUFLETTA

Add flour to a large bowl; make a deep, large well in the center.
Add sugar to the center of the well.

Pour 1 cup warm water into the well.
Using a wooden spoon, gradually start stirring from the center of the well, slowly pulling in flour as you stir.

Once half the flour is incorporated, add 1½ cups warm water.
Start mixing with your hands to combine.
Knead for 3 minutes. The dough should come together but still be sticky.

Pour 3 tablespoons of oil over the dough. Cover bowl with plastic wrap and cover bowl with a kitchen towel. Allow dough to rest for 2 hours.

After 2 hours, place 2 baking sheets on a work surface. Spread ¼ cup oil onto each sheet pan.

Add 2 cups of oil to a bowl; set aside.

Add a little oil to the palms of your hands and rub your hands together to create a nonstick coating.
Place one hand over the rested dough with your palm directly on the dough. Create a circle with your thumb and forefinger.
Using your pinky and ring finger, gently push about 2 tablespoons of dough through the center of the circle created by your thumb and forefinger.
Pinch your thumb and forefinger together to close the circle and release a smooth ball of dough.

Place dough ball on oiled sheet pan. Using a pastry brush or spoon, spread a little of the reserved oil in the bowl over the top of the dough ball.

Continue until all the balls of dough have been formed and oiled.

Place a layer of plastic wrap loosely over the sheet pans. Allow dough to rest for 45 minutes – 1 hour.

TO COOK MUFLETTA

Clear and clean a work space right next to your stove.
(The best way to do this next step is directly on your countertop.)

Preheat a pan over medium heat.

Drizzle ½ teaspoon of oil over the countertop; spread over the area.
Remove one ball of dough from the sheet pan and place directly on the countertop.
Dip both your forefingers into the remaining oil.

Using oiled fingers, gently press down on the center of the dough.

Working carefully but quickly, keep pressing down on the dough with your forefingers while gently pressing your forefingers from the center of the dough outward.
The dough should be slippery from the oil, preventing it from tearing while stretching.
If it doesn't feel slippery, dip your fingers into oil again.

Continue stretching the ball of dough this way until the dough is so thin that it is see-through.

Place 1 teaspoon oil into the preheated pan; carefully lift the stretched dough and place into the pan.

Working quickly, stretch another ball of dough.
Flip the mostly cooked dough in the pan; place newly stretched dough directly on the one in the pan.

Remove another ball of dough and stretch it.
Again flip "pile" of muflettas in the pan so that the one you put on before can cook and the newly stretched dough is on the top.

Continue working in this manner (stretching, flipping pile, adding new dough...) until your pile contains about 15 sheets of mufletta.

Remove pile from the pan, immediately roll entire pile, jelly roll style, place on a plate, and cover with a kitchen towel to keep warm.

Start a cooking a new pile the same way as the first pile.
Continue until all balls of dough are cooked.

TO SERVE

Gently peel one mufletta at a time from the roll.
Drizzle a little syrup over the flat circle.

Roll up like a wrap, eat, and enjoy!!!

VARIATION

Another very traditional way to eat the mufletta is by spreading butter over the warm sheet of mufletta, drizzling with a little honey, rolling it up, and digging in!

sweets

apple blueberry turnovers

THESE ARE JUST DELICIOUS. FRESH, DEFROSTED, WITH PIE DOUGH OR PUFF PASTRY. IT'S LIKE THE COMFORT FOOD OF DESSERTS.

1 pkg (2 rolls) sweet pie dough OR **4-5** sweet pie shells, defrosted and rolled out

4 Granny Smith apples, peeled, thinly sliced

¼ tsp kosher salt

1 tsp pure vanilla extract

¼ cup bourbon

¼ cup brown sugar

2 tsp cornstarch

1 cup fresh blueberries

1 egg, lightly beaten

white sugar, for sprinkling

Place peeled apples into a medium nonstick pot set over medium high heat.
Add salt; carefully stir until all the liquid has evaporated.
(Alternatively, you can allow the mixture to cook for 1 minute so the salt can draw out any liquid from the apples, and then drain out water.)

Once there is no liquid in the pot, carefully add vanilla and bourbon; stir to coat.
Cook for 3 minutes until bourbon has reduced by half.

Add brown sugar to the pot; stir and cook for 2 minutes.

Sprinkle in cornstarch; stir immediately to combine.
Cook for 2 minutes.

Turn off heat; immediately add blueberries.
Gently stir to combine.

Set aside to allow mixture to cool completely.

Preheat oven to 350°F / 180°C. Line a baking sheet with parchment paper.

Cut pie dough into 6x3 inch rectangles.

Using a pastry brush, brush a very small amount of egg on the borders of 2 sides of each rectangle.

Place 1 heaping tablespoon of apple mixture on the first ⅓ of each rectangle.
Fold rectangles in half diagonally so that the apple mixture is completely covered.
Use a fork to press the edges of the dough together.
Brush the tops with beaten egg and a very light sprinkling of sugar.

Place on prepared baking sheet. Bake for 14-18 minutes until baked through and golden.
Cool on baking sheet for 2 minutes, then transfer to a cooling rack to cool completely.

VARIATION

You can use any pie dough or puff pastry you like to make these. Even store bought crescent dough or a homemade pâte brisée (page 136) would be great!

FREEZER TIP

Once completely cool, lay in a single layer, wrap gently in plastic wrap and freeze overnight. Once frozen, store in a ziptop bag. Remove from freezer 2 hours before serving!

VARIATION

You can absolutely trade the puff pastry for store bought sweet pie dough. In Hebrew it is called *batzek parish matock*, and it is delicious!

sfinge (moroccan donuts)

I AM WRITING THIS BLURB LITERALLY DAYS AFTER CHANUKAH. THIS YEAR, IT TOOK ME UNTIL THE VERY LAST DAY TO MAKE THEM, BUT AS THEY WERE FRYING UP I CLOSED MY EYES AND WAS TRANSPORTED TO THE VAN IN MOROCCO, WITH MY PARENTS, BROTHERS, AND GRANDMOTHER, DRIVING THROUGH THE WINDY MOUNTAIN ROADS AND SEEING TINY LITTLE STORES SPECKLED ALONG THE SIDE WITH MEN AND WOMEN SITTING AT LITTLE ROUND TABLES DRINKING TEA AND SNACKING ON FRESH, HOT OUT OF THE OIL SFINGE. AS THEY COME OUT OF THE POT, THEY ARE IMMEDIATELY DUNKED INTO A PLATE OF BEAUTIFUL WHITE SUGAR AND THEN HUNG ON STRING SO THAT THEY DON'T GET SOGGY. IT IS ONE OF MY MOST MOUTHWATERING MEMORIES AND I HOPE IT BECOMES ONE OF YOURS, TOO!

2.2 lb (1 kg) flour
2 heaping Tbsp dry yeast
1 scant Tbsp kosher salt
2-3 cups warm water
oil, for frying
3 cups sugar on a plate

Place flour into a large bowl.
Make a well in the center; add yeast.

Make an indentation into the flour around the edge of the bowl so that the salt can be sprinkled around the outer edge of the flour.

Slowly add 1 cup water to the well.
Let it sit for 2 minutes.

Use your hands to work the flour into the yeast in the water, slowly pulling in more flour. Gradually add more water till all the flour is incorporated.
Add in ¼ cup water at a time. (You can always add more but you can't take out!)
You will need to add at least 2 cups water but maybe more depending how dry your kitchen is.
You are looking to create a very sticky but not liquidy dough.

Knead dough with your hands for 3 minutes until dough is only slightly less sticky.
Cover with a kitchen towel and allow to rest for 1-1½ hours until doubled in size.

In a large pot, heat 4 inches of oil to 350°F / 180°C.

Place a bowl of water next to you on the countertop.
Dip your hands into the water (to prevent dough from sticking) and pull a handful of dough from the bowl.
Make a hole in the center; use your hands to slightly stretch out dough.

Place in oil and fry on both sides till golden brown.
Remove dough from oil and immediately roll in sugar, covering completely. Set aside.

Repeat with remaining dough. Serve with tea and enjoy!

NOTE

The first two doughnuts never come out good. (I don't know why, it's just how it is.)

churro muddy buddies

FOR THE NON-CHOCOLATE LOVERS AND PEANUT BUTTER ALLERGIC PEOPLE IN MY LIFE. A SALTY AND SWEET VARIATION TO THE ORIGINAL AND BELOVED CHOCOLATE AND PEANUT BUTTER COMBO THAT DOESN'T FEEL LIKE A COMPROMISE AT ALL, BECAUSE THEY ARE AMAZING. IT'S WHAT I MAKE WHEN I KNOW I'LL NEED TO HAVE SOMETHING AROUND FOR PEOPLE TO SNACK ON. IT ALSO MAKES THE PERFECT SNACK TO PUT IN A HUGE JAR, TIE A RIBBON ON, AND SEND TO SOMEONE AS A GIFT!

1 box Corn Chex cereal

⅔ cup sugar

2 tsp cinnamon

1½ tsp kosher salt

½ cup nondairy butter substitute (or butter, for dairy treats)

1 cup brown sugar

¼ cup light corn syrup

¼ tsp baking soda

Preheat oven to 350°F / 180°C. Line a large baking sheet with foil. Coat well with nonstick cooking spray.

Pour the cereal into a large bowl; set aside.

In a small bowl, combine sugar, cinnamon, and salt; set aside.

To a heavy saucepan, add butter substitute, brown sugar, and corn syrup. Stir over medium high heat until mixture comes to a boil. Immediately add baking soda, stir, and remove from heat.

Working quickly, pour mixture over cereal; mix well until cereal is well coated. Pour cereal onto prepared baking sheet; sprinkle with sugar mixture.

Bake for about 5 minutes until cereal is golden brown. Allow to cool completely.

Transfer to an airtight container and enjoy!!

how to hack a napoleon

AN ODE TO MY PARENTS, WHO CANNOT RESIST A REAL FRENCH NAPOLEON WHEN THEY SEE ONE. THEY PASSED ON THEIR LOVE OF THIS PASTRY TO US AND ALTHOUGH THIS ONE IS A BIT OF A SHORTCUT NAPOLEON, USING STORE BOUGHT PUFF PASTRY INSTEAD OF MAKING OUR OWN, IT IS DELICIOUS AND MAKES FOR A BEAUTIFUL PRESENTATION!

SHEETS

3 (14x8 inch) puff pastry sheets

3 Tbsp canola oil, divided

6 Tbsp sugar, divided

CREAM

1 (16 oz/453 g) container nondairy sour cream

1 (3½ oz/99 g) package vanilla instant pudding mix

3 Tbsp bourbon

1 tsp pure vanilla extract

2 Tbsp cornstarch

2 cups nondairy whipped topping

½ tsp kosher salt

GANACHE

1 cup semisweet chocolate chips

3 Tbsp nondairy whipped topping

3 Tbsp canola oil

VARIATION

I love how easily this dish can be transformed to fit a theme. On Chanukah I cut the puff pastry sheets to be a dreidel, on someone's birthday I make a balloon or cut out the letters of their name, on Shavuos I make a Torah …. The shape can be adjusted to fit any theme you like!

SHEETS

Preheat oven to 350°F / 180°C. Line a baking sheet with parchment paper and have a second baking sheet ready.

Lay one sheet of puff pastry on prepared baking sheet.
Use a fork and dock the dough all over — don't be stingy with the docking. (Docking the dough means pricking the dough with a fork to create small holes all over so that the dough does not puff up while baking.)

Use a pastry brush to brush the top of the dough with 1 tablespoon oil.
Sprinkle 2 tablespoons sugar all over the dough from high up to evenly distribute.

Place a second piece of parchment paper directly on the sugared dough.
Cover paper topped dough with the second baking sheet.

Bake, covered for 50 minutes. After 50 minutes, remove top baking sheet.
If dough doesn't seem browned enough, bake, uncovered, for 10 minutes.
(I don't always need that step. It depends on the brand of pastry dough you use and, of course, your oven.)

Allow pastry to cool for 10 minutes in the pan.
Gently transfer the baked puff pastry sheet to a cooling rack to cool completely.

Repeat with remaining pastry sheets, oil, and sugar.

Once cooled, sheets can be stored in an airtight container for up to 4-5 days.

CREAM

Place nondairy sour cream, vanilla pudding mix, bourbon, vanilla extract, and cornstarch into the large bowl of a stand mixer.
Whip on high for 3 minutes until mixture is blended, light, and fluffy.
Transfer mixture to a large bowl.

To the bowl of the stand mixer (no need to wash it first), add whipped topping and salt. Beat on high for 4 minutes until stiff peaks form.

Using a soft rubber spatula, gently fold whipped cream into the sour cream mixture until just combined.

(This mixture will stay fresh for a few days in an airtight container in the fridge if you want to do this step a day or two in advance.)

TO ASSEMBLE

Lay one sheet of baked pastry on the platter you want to serve the napoleon on.
Spread ½ the cream over the pastry.

Add second sheet of baked pastry.
Spread remaining cream over the top.
Top cream with remaining layer of baked pastry.

Place the napoleon in the refrigerator for at least 2 hours.

Once napoleon has set, you can top with powdered sugar or make the ganache and spread on top.

TO MAKE GANACHE

Place all ganache ingredients into a heatproof bowl.

Place bowl over a simmering pot filled with 1 inch of water, making sure the bottom of the bowl does not touch water. Stir the mixture continuously until the chocolate has melted and the ganache is glossy.

Alternatively, you can place all ganache ingredients into a microwave safe bowl and pop in the microwave for 15 second increments, stirring between each 15 seconds.

Pour ganache onto the center of the chilled napoleon; use an offset spatula or the back of a spoon to nudge it gently toward the edges.
Return napoleon to fridge to set.

TO SERVE

Remove from fridge 30 minutes before serving.
Cut, serve, and enjoy!

moroccan mint tea

THIS RECIPE IS MORE OF A TECHNIQUE THEN A RECIPE. ACTUALLY, EVEN THE TECHNIQUE IS PRETTY SIMPLE. PUT EVERYTHING IN A POT, LET IT SIT. POUR, STRAIN, POUR BACK IN POT, SERVE, AND ENJOY. THE BOOK JUST DID NOT FEEL COMPLETE TO ME WITHOUT A RECIPE FOR THE UBER SWEET, DELICIOUS, STEAMING HOT POT OF TEA THAT IS SO CENTRAL TO A MOROCCAN HOME. FOR THE FULL EFFECT, YOU NEED A REAL MOROCCAN TEA GLASS THAT'S SHORT AND THIN, WITH NO HANDLE. YOU HOLD THE CUP BY PUTTING YOUR THUMB AND FOREFINGER AROUND THE EDGE OF THE GLASS AND YOUR PINKY ON THE BOTTOM TO STABILIZE IT. THEN YOU TAKE A BITE OF WHATEVER PASTRY OR FRUIT IS ON THE TABLE AND WHILE THE FOOD IS STILL IN YOUR MOUTH, YOU SLOWLY SIP THE VERY HOT TEA (BE CAREFUL!) TO WASH IT DOWN. MMMMMM. THERE IS LITERALLY NOTHING BETTER!

3 bags green tea (no flavor)
(OR **1 Tbsp** loose good quality dried green tea leaves)

1 packed cup fresh mint leaves

5 cups boiling water

⅓ cup sugar

Place all ingredients in the teapot; stir.
Cover teapot with lid and allow tea to steep for 4 minutes.

Pour 1 cup of tea through a small strainer into a glass.
Then pour that cup back into the pot.
(That's right. The first cup always gets poured back in the pot. Don't ask questions, just do it. It's the Moroccan way.)

Now, using the strainer, pour everyone a cup of tea.

Serve with any sort of delicious pastry, fresh or dried fruit, and nuts, and enjoy!

NOTE

The best variety of great tea leaves to make authentic Moroccan tea is the "gunpowder" green tea leaves that get their name because as they dry, the leaves roll up into themselves and resemble gun powder. Most spice shops around Israel carry this variety, so stock up on your next visit!

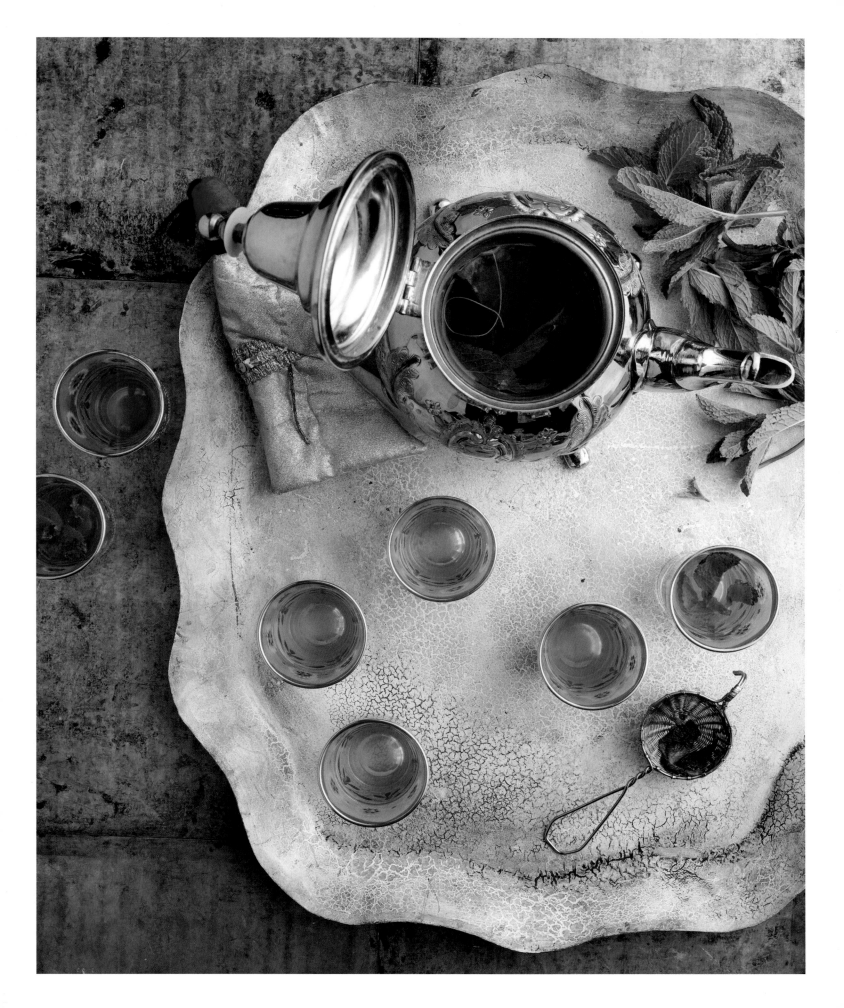

index

a

Almond Joy Truffles, Salted Dark Chocolate, *388*

ALMONDS
Almond "Techina" (Sesame Free), *36*
Big Batch Granola + Theory of a Fruit Salad, *408*
Gremolata, *51*
Moroccan Nut Crunch Topping, *314*
Quinoa, Sweet Potato, Cranberry & Almond Salad, *62*
Savory Granola, *82*
Spiced Nuts, *82*

APPLES
Apple Blueberry Turnovers, *412*
Apples & Honey Mustard Chicken, *204*
Inside Out Apple Crumble, *400*
Muffin Man Muffins, *366*
Roasted Sweet Potato, Apple, and Leek Soup, *90*

APRICOTS
Apricot Soy Chicken, *159*
Miso + Apricot Roasted Turkey Breast, *216*
Moroccan Chicken Tagine, *198*

ARTICHOKES
Artichoke and Arugula Salad, *58*
Artichoke Chicken, *172*
Moroccan Stuffed Artichokes, *230*
Spinach Artichoke Chicken Burger, *160*

ARUGULA
Artichoke and Arugula Salad, *58*
BBQ Chicken Rice Salad, *70*
Brick Roast Salad with Creamy Scallion Dressing, *72*
Haloumi + Sweet Potato Salad with Blueberry Vinaigrette, *326*
Sumac Scented Fennel & Tangerine Salad, *66*

AVOCADOS
Avocado Crema, *168*
Avocado Egg Rolls, *322*
Black Bean Crumble Salad with Cilantro Lime Ranch, *328–29*
Modernized Taco Salad with Grilled Skirt Steak, *76*
Shaved Fennel & Avocado Salad, *50*

b

Babaganoush, Fire Roasted, *38*

Barley Vegetable Soup, Meaty, *98*

BASIL
Abby's Pesto, *38*

BEANS. *See also* **CHICKPEAS; STRING BEANS**
Black Bean Crumble Salad with Cilantro Lime Ranch, *328–29*
15 Minute Prep Chili, *224*
Layered Grain Salad with Orange Juice Dressing, *64*
Loubia (Moroccan Stewed White Beans), *308*
Mexican Chicken and Rice, *164*
Mexican Chicken Soup, *110*
No Cream Cream of Broccoli, *96*

BEEF. *See also* **FACON; VEAL**
Beef/Veal Stock, *86*
Bourbon Braised Short Ribs, *272*
Brick Roast Salad with Creamy Scallion Dressing, *72*
Chipotle Barbecue Broiled Skirt Steak, *250*
Crispy Braised Meat Ravioli, *244*
Crockpot Savory Beef Stew, *256*
Easy Peasy California Roast, *258*
15 Minute Prep Chili, *224*
French Dip Sandwiches, *252*
Fried Rice My Way, Your Way, *316*
Grilled Chicken Panzanella Salad, *74*
Hamburger Roll, *232*
Hawaij Beef Soup, *108*
Horseradish Crusted Standing Rib Roast, *274*
How to Cook a Steak (+ Red Wine Onion Jus), *254*
Italian Wedding Soup, *102*
Korean Flanken Roast, *270*
Maggie Loves Tacos, *234*
Meat Borekas + Mushroom Sauce, *222*
Meat Sauce, *226*
Meaty Vegetable Barley Soup, *98*
Meme's Chicken Fricassee, *212*
Modernized Taco Salad with Grilled Skirt Steak, *76*
Moroccan Harira Soup, *104*
Moroccan Keftas, *236*

Moroccan Meat Couscous with 7 Vegetables, *298–99*
Moroccan Stuffed Artichokes, *230*
Mushroom Smothered Braised Meat, *262*
No-Boil, No-Dishes Corned Beef, *260*
Pastella (Moroccan Shepherd's Pie), *220*
Pomegranate Braised Brisket, *264*
Slow Roasted Deckle, *268*
Smash Burgers with Onions + Special Sauce, *228*
Spicy Meat Soup, *112*
Sticky Asian Beef + String Beans, *246*
Stovetop Brisket, *266*
Sunday Sauce, *276*
Sweet and Sour Meatballs, *238*
Vietnamese Beef Bahn Mi, *248*

Beer Battered Chicken Nuggets, *170*

BEETS
Roasted Beet Salad, *50*
Spiralized Beet Radish and Carrot Salad, *56*

Biscotti, Fat Free, *404*

BLUEBERRIES
Apple Blueberry Turnovers, *412*
Cannoli Cream Trifles, *360*
Haloumi + Sweet Potato Salad with Blueberry Vinaigrette, *326*
Muffin Man Muffins, *366*

BOK CHOY
Asian Chicken Crumble Salad, *80*
Asian Style Halibut en Papillote, *140*

BOREKAS
Meat Borekas + Mushroom Sauce, *222*
Moroccan Tuna Borekas, *136*

Bourbon Braised Short Ribs, *272*

BRAN
Healthy-ish Cookies, *396*

BREAD-BASED DISHES
Grilled Chicken Panzanella Salad, *74*
Strawberries & Cream Bread Pudding, *362*

BREADS. *SEE* **CHALLAH; SANDWICHES**

BROCCOLI
Asian Style Halibut en Papillote, *140*
Crispy Baked Cauliflower + Broccoli Hash Browns, *348*
Crispy Roasted Broccoli, *290*
Grandma Lila & Aunt Janey's Quiche, *342*

family faves

boys   eli   girls

menu suggestions

conversion charts

A NOTE ON SPICES AND HERBS

Many recipes in this book call for fresh herbs. If you want to replace fresh herbs with dried spices, please be mindful to adjust the amounts. 1 tablespoon of freshly chopped cilantro does NOT equal 1 tablespoon of dried cilantro. I prefer fresh herbs; however, sometimes dried herbs must happen. When using them, measure out what you need, then place them in the palms of your hands and gently rub the dried herbs to help release their flavors before adding to the dish.

1 tsp dried herbs = 1 tbsp fresh herbs

In addition, it is important to remember that spices dull in flavor and potency as they sit. It is ideal to buy spices in smaller amounts and replenish your stash often.

I like to keep my spices in glass jars with tightly fitting lids. The spices I use most often are in bigger jars as I finish them more quickly!

MEASUREMENT CONVERSIONS

1 tsp = 5 ml

3 tsp = 1 Tbsp = 15 ml

4 Tbsp = ¼ cup = 60 ml

5 Tbsp + 1 tsp = ⅓ cup = 80 ml

8 Tbsp = ½ cup 120 ml

10 Tbsp + 2 tsp = ⅔ cup = 160 ml

12 Tbsp = ¾ cup = 180 ml

16 Tbsp = 1 cup = 240 ml

2 cups = 1 pint = 475 ml

4 cups = 1 quart = 0.95 L

4 quarts = 1 gallon = 3.8 L

QUANTITY CONVERSIONS

1 oz = 28 g

4 oz or ¼ lb = 113 g

⅓ lb = 150 g

8 oz or ½ lb = 230 g

⅔ lb = 300 g

12 oz or ¾ lb = 340 g

1 lb or 16 oz = 450 g

2 lbs = 900 g

TEMPERATURE CONVERSIONS

FAHRENHEIT (°F)	CELSIUS (°C)	GAS NUMBER
225°	110°C	¼
250°	130°C	½
275°	140°C	1
300°	150°	2
325°	165°	3
350°	177° (I use 180 because my oven only increases by 5's.)	4
375°	190°	5
400°	200°	6
425°	220°	7
450°	230°	8
475°	245°	9
500°	260°	10
550°	290°	10